Transnationalism and American Literature

Routledge Transnational Perspectives on American Literature

EDITED BY SUSAN CASTILLO, *University of Glasgow*

1. New Woman Hybridities
Femininity, Feminism, and International Consumer Culture, 1880-1930
Edited by Ann Heilmann and Margaret Beetham

2. Don DeLillo
The Possibility of Fiction
Peter Boxall

3. Toni Morrison's Beloved
Possible Worlds
Justine Tally

4. Fictions of the Black Atlantic in American Foundational Literature
Gesa Mackenthun

5. Mexican American Literature
Elizabeth Jacobs

6. Native American Literature
Towards a Spatialized Reading
Helen May Dennis

7. Transnationalism and American Literature
Literary Translation 1773-1892
Colleen Glenney Boggs

Transnationalism and American Literature

Literary Translation 1773-1892

Colleen Glenney Boggs

Routledge
Taylor & Francis Group
NEW YORK AND LONDON

First published 2007 by Routledge

First published in paperback 2009 by Routledge
605 Third Avenue, New York, NY 10017
4 Park Square, Milton Park, Abingdon, Oxon OX14 4RN

Routledge is an imprint of the Taylor & Francis Group, an informa business

© 2007, 2009 Taylor & Francis

All rights reserved. No part of this book may be reprinted or reproduced or utilised in any form or by any electronic, mechanical, or other means, now known or hereafter invented, including photocopying and recording, or in any information storage or retrieval system, without permission in writing from the publishers.

Notice:
Product or corporate names may be trademarks or registered trademarks, and are used only for identification and explanation without intent to infringe.

British Library Cataloguing in Publication Data
A catalogue record for this book is available from the British Library

Library of Congress Cataloging in Publication Data
  Boggs, Colleen Glenney.
  Transnationalism and American literature : literary translation 1773-1892 / Colleen Glenney Boggs.
      p. cm. – (Routledge transnational perspectives on American literature ; 7)
  Includes bibliographical references and index.
  I1. American literature–19th century–History and criticism. 2. American literature–1783-1850–History and criticism. 3. Multilingualism and literature–United States. 4. Nationalism and literature–United States–History. 5. Literature publishing–United States–History. 6. Translations–Publishing–United States–History. 7. Transnationalism. 8. Translating and interpreting. I. Title.
  PS217.M85B64 2007
  810.9'358–dc22   2006033281

ISBN13: 978-0-415-77068-2 (hbk)
ISBN13: 978-0-415-99989-2 (pbk)
ISBN13: 978-0-203-94079-2 (ebk)

For Brian Peter Glenney

Contents

Acknowledgments ix

Introduction: Multilingual transnationalisms: Nathaniel Hawthorne, Charlotte Forten Grimké 1

1 Transatlantic education: Phillis Wheatley's neoclassicism 37

2 The blanched Atlantic: James Fenimore Cooper's "neutral ground" 61

3 American world literature: Margaret Fuller's particular universality 91

4 Literary exemplarity: Walt Whitman's "specimens" 111

5 Intellectual property: Harriet Beecher Stowe's copyright 127

Notes 151
Works Cited 175
Index 191

Acknowledgments

At its most idealistic, this book celebrates writing as an interpersonal dialogue. That idealism springs from and was sustained by the communities and the people who have shaped, questioned, and nurtured my efforts.

When I first began thinking about translation, the English Department at the University of Chicago provided a rigorous environment in which I constantly found myself challenged to refine my thoughts and their expression. I am deeply grateful to my dissertation director, Bill Brown, and my two readers, Lauren Berlant and Jim Chandler, for their intellectual generosity and personal support. Ken Warren, Bill Veeder, Beth Helsinger, Eric Slauter, Katie Trumpener, Hilary Justice, Sam Baker, Andrew Hebard, Matt Hofer, Sabine Haenni, Brad Evans, Angela Sorby, and Mary Helen McMurran were valued interlocutors who challenged me to refine my conceptual frames. I owe a special debt to Martha Bohrer for her friendship, which sustained me throughout this project.

Joseph Roach and Diane Jowdy made me feel welcome when I unexpectedly returned to my alma mater, Yale University. I am grateful to Wai Chee Dimock and Alan Trachtenberg for reading early chapter drafts. Thanks to Matthew Pearl and Leslie Eckel for sharing with me their own perspectives on Longfellow and Fuller. A special thanks to Aaron Santesso for keeping me laughing.

When I joined the English Department and the Women's and Gender Studies Program at Dartmouth College in Autumn, 2001, I was welcomed by a distinguished group of colleagues who are extraordinarily generous. For their tireless support, I thank Donald Pease, Ivy Schweitzer, and Barbara Will. I am also grateful to Marty Favor, Lou Renza, Bill Cook, Peter Travis, Silvia Spitta, and Roxana Verona for their mentoring. Matthew Rowlinson helped me think through notions of Romantic fragmentation, and Patricia McKee helped me refine my discussion of race. For their friendship and support, I thank Veronika Fuechtner and Katie-Louise Thomas, as well as Paula Sprague, Francine A'ness, Eleonora Stoppino, Leslie Butler, Klaus Milich, Michael Chaney, Jeffrey Santa Ana, George Edmondson, Mary Coffey, and Klaus Mladek. I am also grateful to the many colleagues and graduate students whom I encountered at Dartmouth College's American Studies Summer Institute over the years, and to Donald Pease for providing a stimulating environment in which to be an Americanist. Special thanks to Elizabeth Dillon, Robyn Wiegman, and Russ Castronovo for their probing questions.

At Routledge, Susan Castillo supported this project with enthusiasm and warmth. My two anonymous reviewers provided helpful insights that I did my best to incorporate. Terry Clague, Katherine Carpenter, Max Novick, and Michael Davidson have been generous and patient in working with me to see this book into print.

This project has benefited from numerous sources of financial support. I am grateful for the generous fellowships I received from The University of Chicago and the Mellon Foundation. The Marcia Tillotson Travel Award and Florence Adams Award at the University of Chicago, as well as the Burke Junior Faculty Grants at Dartmouth College supported my travels to conferences where I met important interlocutors: thanks especially to Chris Gair, Susan Manning, Joel Pace, Lance Newman, and Paul Giles for sharing their knowledge of transatlantic scholarship. The Leslie Humanities Center at Dartmouth College generously supported my research with a faculty fellowship in 2002; special thanks go to Jonathan Crewe. That fellowship allowed me to travel to New York City where I used the archives at the Schomburg Center Library for my research on Phillis Wheatley. The Friends of the Longfellow House awarded me the Diane Korzenik fellowship in 2003, which allowed me to travel to Cambridge, Massachusetts, to research parts of chapter four. The John Sloane Dickey Center for International Understanding at Dartmouth College generously provided the funds for a manuscript review at a crucial stage of revision. I thank Priscilla Wald and Elizabeth Dillon for reading the manuscript in its entirety, and for providing me with candid, helpful feed-back. I am grateful to Dartmouth College for a junior faculty fellowship and a sabbatical leave that allowed me to revise and complete this book.

In consulting archives for this work, I have incurrent several debts. At the Longfellow House, Anita Israel and Jim Shea patiently and enthusiastically supported my work. Jackie McKiernan was exceptionally friendly and helpful at the Stowe Center Library. Stacey Bredhoff and Gail Farr at the National Archives helped me locate the legal documents for Stowe's suite to which Simon Stern at the Yale Law School first pointed me. My thanks also go to the staff at the Beinecke Library, Yale University, where I researched the chapter on Margaret Fuller, and to the librarians at the Regenstein Library, University of Chicago. At Dartmouth College, I thank Dr. Laura Braunstein and Bill Fontaine for their help.

An earlier version of chapter three appeared as "Margaret Fuller's American Translation" in *American Literature,* (March 2004), 76(1), 31–58, and is reprinted here with permission of Duke University Press. An earlier version of chapter four appeared as "Specimens of Translation in Walt Whitman's Poetry" in *Arizona Quarterly,* (Autumn 2002), 58(3), 33–56, and appears here by permission of the Regents of The University of Arizona. Thanks to the Harriet Beecher Stowe Center Library in Hartford, Connecticut, for permission to reproduce the bill of sale for *Uncle Tom's Cabin.*

To the extent that all academic work is autobiographical, my interest in transatlantic matters stems from the bicultural and bilingual home in which my mother, Ursula Boggs, and my father, Paul Boggs, nurtured my intellectual growth. I am grateful to them and to my brother, Sean Boggs, as well as my deceased grandmother, Annemarie Klemme. My cats Kaya and Peevish ensured that my long hours at the desk never got lonely. My son Noah was born as I was completing this manuscript, and added tremendous joy to my life in the final stages of proofreading. Above and beyond all, I thank my husband, Brian Peter Glenney, whose love and patience I have tried beyond endurance, only to find that both are beyond measure. They are comparable only to his intelligence, his humor, and his kindness. With gratitude and love, I dedicate this book to him.

Introduction
Multilingual transnationalisms: Nathaniel Hawthorne, Charlotte Forten Grimké

The nation is the site where the fractures of globalism become visible. The scholarly database www.ethnologue.com records that over 6,900 main languages (not counting dialects) were spoken worldwide in 2006. Given the fact that approximately 230 nation-states existed at the time that means there were about thirty times as many languages as there were states. For the Americas, ethnologue documents the use of 1,013 living languages (15 percent of the languages actively spoken worldwide), and the United States alone was home to 176 of those languages. These statistics call into question the idea, associated with Johann Gottfried Herder's brand of European nationalism, that a single nation speaks a single language, and that there is some organic connection between linguistic and national identity. On the contrary, these figures demonstrate that multilingualism is the statistical norm, and that national identity crosses linguistic boundaries. Although nationalism and monolingualism may be linked ideologically, practically speaking multilingualism and translation lie at the core of national discourse.

Because of the variety of indigenous, immigrant, and imperial languages that have competed and continue to compete in the Americas, assuming a link between language and nation is particularly inappropriate for the study of American literature. Far from being a melting pot or crucible in which all citizens become monolingual speakers of English, the United States is currently and has historically been a multilingual country in which languages other than English thrive.[1] The statistics gathered by the Bureau of the Census "refute the common misconception that most persons with non-English language backgrounds in the United States are foreign born" (Waggoner 1980: 499).

Yet the census also engineered that misconception, which thrives on the changing definition that "mother tongue" has undergone since the census first began recording that data in 1910. Whereas the census initially referred to the mother's tongue, that is, to the "usual language of their [the census participants'] parents' homes in the old country" (Waggoner 1980: 487), the census of 1940 defined the mother tongue as the language a person spoke him- or herself in earliest childhood. For many people surveyed, this change in definition separated their mother's tongue from their mother tongue, and belied their complex relationship to different linguistic contexts. The census made a maternal model of language central to the nation. At the same time, it obfuscated the mother's language and the respondent's own multilingualism.

When American literary studies first became a scholarly and academic discipline, between 1920 and 1940, the number of people reporting English as their mother tongue rose dramatically because of this change in definition (Waggoner 1980: 487). But even as a nominally unified and unifying national language, English carries the traces of the United States' internal multilingualism and of that multilingualism's transnational ties. As Mikhail Bakhtin has argued, "two myths perish simultaneously: the myth of a language that presumes to be the only language, and the myth of a language that presumes to be completely unified" (Bakhtin 1981: 68). Because the statistically engineered Anglophone nation does not reflect the multilingual complexity of the United States, the very fiction of monolingual national identity requires the constant use of translation, between and within languages.

Taking writings in English as my point of departure, I examine the fractured processes and fragmented encounters of American literature to understand how literary nationalism negotiates its relationship to linguistic pluralities. Framed by Phillis Wheatley's invention of transatlantic literature (1773) and that transatlantic literature's foreclosure by international copyright laws (1892), this book narrates a dramatic tale of competing visions and develops a chronological history.[2] There were two schools of thought on the role of language in American literature, which I take up in this introduction through the examples of contemporaries Nathaniel Hawthorne and Charlotte Forten (later Grimké).[4] Hawthorne thought that American literature needed to be written in a single language, English, which would take precedence over all other languages within the Americas. Translation could make texts sound as though they had originally been written in English, and would unify the multilingual nation on the basis of a single shared language. But Forten turned to translation to explore the insight that "transculturation and rearticulation ... are always bi-directional" (Lenz 1999: 17). As a black abolitionist, she imagined a cross-linguistic, cross-cultural intimacy with others that offset the racist and sexist paradigms of slavery. Drawing on Wheatley, she experimented in her diaries with multilingual translation, and defined transatlanticism as an important political strategy for engaging the nation critically.[3]

Forten's approach speaks to recent scholarship, which has begun to put pressure on national constructs: American literary studies entered a "transnational era" (Wald 1998: 199) in the late 1990s. Within this larger debate over transnationalism, the transatlantic has emerged as a subfield on which inquiries, including my own, into the discursive contexts of eighteenth and nineteenth century literature center. Yet what transnationalism is and what it does to the study of American literature remains subject to debate, especially as the emerging field of transnational studies tries to differentiate itself from American studies and cultural studies. The desire to rethink the paradigms of American literature has established a false dichotomy between nationalism and transnationalism. The assumption that American literature has become transnational only recently — that there is such a thing as an "era" of transnationalism — marks a blindness to the intrinsic transnationalism of American literature.

Transnationalism and American Literature: Literary Translation 1773–1892 locates transnationalism in the practice of linguistic translation, which lies at the core of American national discourse. Instead of seeing nationalism and transnationalism as alternatives to one another, I argue that they are related discursive strategies for negotiating the linguistic plurality that confounds state boundaries and complicates identity formations, especially when it comes to race and gender.

In his groundbreaking essay, "'Paradigm Dramas' in American Studies" (1979), Gene Wise pointed out that "symbol-myth-image" scholarship had given the study of American literature pedagogical coherence from the 1930s into the 1960s.[5] Wise thought that the decline of this school of thought would enable cross-cultural scholarship, but he wondered what the scholarly methodology for such an approach might be. The generation of scholars that emerged around the time of Wise's writing abolished the field's foundational investment in white male exceptionalism. By emphasizing race and gender, they made multicultural difference the field's guiding paradigm. But their work has now itself come under scrutiny, primarily from European scholars, for focusing on America's internal multiculturalism without recognizing America's relationship to external cultures. Paul Giles has criticized the field of multicultural American literary studies for replicating the logic of U.S. nationhood (Giles 2001: 188). To abolish the myopia of this multicultural turn, Giles suggests that we read literature beyond the geo-political confines of the nation state. Yet Giles' brand of transatlanticism, which focuses on the relationship between Britain and the United States, has come under attack from American scholars suspicious of "the limits of current foreign humanities scholarship on the United States. Most of it now falls into three categories: immigrant topics, U.S. influence, or comparative analogies" (Desmond and Dominguez 1996: 484). I broker a dialogue between these approaches by locating the United States' internal and external complexity in its linguistic diversity.

Surprisingly little attention has been paid to linguistic mobility in a field that reconceptualized national geographies as discursive spaces, and that challenged the usefulness of the nation form as an analytic unit. Since Paul Gilroy's book *The Black Atlantic: Modernity and Double Consciousness* (1993) helped inaugurate the field, transatlantic studies has blurred the boundaries between what counts as internal and external to (a) culture.[6] Gilroy argued that the slave trade gave rise to cultural modernity. He conceived of the Atlantic as a space where different cultures came into being through their relationship with each other. Rejecting cultural essentialism, Gilroy insisted that no single culture of origin holds explanatory power for the cultures that emerged as a result of the admittedly uneven relationships aboard slave ships.[7] Yet Gilroy did not examine the transatlantic as a space of linguistic encounter, but anglicized the cultures of the black Atlantic.

As a racial formation, the Atlantic was foundational for a nation inaugurated in slavery, but the Atlantic also provided an imaginary alternative to the pro-slavery brand of nationalism. The Atlantic appealed to a number of black and white writers critical of slavery because it functioned in their cultural imaginary as a utopic space beyond racial difference. This blanched Atlantic, as I call it, was premised on a notion of abstraction. David Kazanjian documents how that abstraction occurred when mercantilism "transformed the late eighteenth- and early nineteenth-century North Atlantic by simultaneously consolidating national economies, entrenching the codification of racial and national identity among North Atlantic subjects, and facilitating the emergence of formal and abstract equality among white U.S. citizens" (Kazanjian 2003: 30). Arguing that "the modern nation form is always also a racial formation" (Kazanjian 2003: 4), Kazanjian shows how the Atlantic initially appealed to blacks because it afforded them opportunities that they did not have on land. He also chronicles how black mariners were "increasingly, systematically, and ritually barred from the formal and abstract equality" that the Atlantic offered whites (Kazanjian 2003: 39).

As black sailors saw themselves pushed out of the transatlantic trade, Kazanjian claims, they witnessed the "feminization of their labor" (Kazanjian 2003: 31). Valuable as Kazanjian's attention to gender is in a field that has paid little attention to the subject, he problematically resuscitates the argument that two separate, gendered spheres came into existence in the early nineteenth century when he masculinizes the Atlantic and feminizes the nation.[8] Because transatlantic studies implicitly defines itself in relation to a normative male subjectivity and as an area of literary inquiry *in English*, and *only* in English, the field is replicating some of the most entrenched assumptions of American exceptionalism. I resist the resurgence of frontier masculinity and the equation between language and nation by demonstrating that we should understand American literature through the complexity of its gendered linguistic contacts.

Despite the fervor of scholars who celebrate the transatlantic as an alternative to nation-based paradigms of literary study, the nation and the transatlantic are deeply implicated in one another. The transatlantic can be a more useful category for analysis when we distinguish it from the transnational. The term "transnational" was coined in 1916 by Randolph Bourne to celebrate the complex ethnic, racial and national affiliations of American immigrants (Bourne 1916). That definition still has some critical purchase — for instance, Robert Gross argues that transnationalism "captures a world of fluid borders, where goods, ideas, and people flow constantly across once sovereign space" and where "newcomers sustain a cosmopolitan consciousness, while older minorities, notably African Americans, re-conceive themselves in international terms" (Gross 2000: 378). If such usage suggests that the national and the transnational are implicated in each other, as I argue they are in the transatlantic, the critical trend has been to separate them. Gross' reference to *"once* sovereign spaces" is indicative in this regard: it maps a historical time line from nationalism to transnationalism. In this sense, "transnational" and "postnational" function as synonyms for one another. For the nineteenth century, that can mean two things: one, as an era of nationalization, it is an object of a different order against which transnational scholarship defines itself, or two, the postnational emphasis on things other than the nation frees up scholarship to inquire into nineteenth century literature from a new vantage point. In his call for *The New American Studies* (2002), John Carlos Rowe uses the term postnational to refer to scholarship that has moved away from an exclusive analytic focus on the nation state towards comparative methodologies that *engage* but are not *limited* to the nation (Rowe 2002: xiv–v). Rowe argues that the postnational is not a historical marker, but calls for the kind of methodological intervention I undertake through an inquiry into language.

In the turn to multiculturalism that preceded and enabled transatlantic studies, literary canons changed dramatically, but they have not been altered significantly by transatlantic studies. That's not necessarily a bad thing, *if* it indicates that transatlantic studies is more concerned with methodologies — with the *processes* of literary inquiry — than with canons — the objects and *traits* of literature. The term "transatlantic" is ideally suited to do that kind of critical work. In its historical definition, the term points to a process of dislocation that allows us to conceptualize American literature through its fractured methodologies. The shift in focus to multilingual exchange enables the transatlantic to be more than a theme — indeed, to take on the makings of a methodology. I examine the transatlantic as a mode of bringing certain texts and certain aspects of texts into view. In other words, I understand the transatlantic as a methodology that focuses on the multilingual dimensions of texts that show us how international national American literature has always been.

Americanists have a special provenance — though by no means an exceptionalist provenance — when it comes to the transatlantic. The term came into use during the American Revolution. Samuel Johnson's dictionary does not include the word because the term did not yet exist in 1750; the *Oxford English Dictionary* records the earliest use of "transatlantic" in 1779. Noah Webster defines "transatlantic" as: "lying or being beyond the Atlantic. When used by a person in Europe or Africa, transatlantic signifies being in America; when by a person in America, it denotes being or lying in Europe or Africa. We apply it chiefly to something in Europe" (Webster

1828). The "transatlantic" envisions literature in relationship to an always distant yet ever proximate other. "Transatlantic" defines what is American and what it means to be in America. But if "transatlantic" is a synonym for American, American is not a synonym for "transatlantic." "Transatlantic" means "being in America" only when one is not in America; it defines a location that is always elsewhere. When one is in America, "transatlantic" no longer means being in America but being in Europe or Africa. The term operates in relation to and yet independent of any definitive locus; it is only secondarily a geographical marker, and first and foremost a term that defines relationships. I argue that those relationships are linguistic, and that we need to think of the transatlantic as a discursive site of linguistic exchange, by which I mean translation.

Practices of translation reflect the immanence of the transatlantic in the nation, and of the nation in the transatlantic. My central claim in this book is that American writers conceptualized and practiced translation *as* American literature, and vice versa, that they understood American literature as a form of writing that was always in translation. The writers who interest me most are those who embraced translation as a model for their own literary creativity. Far from fetishizing an isolated literary "originality," they imagined the mark and measure of literary innovation to lie in practices of translation. By being deliberately fragmentary and downright ineloquent at times (when judged by standards of English composition), these American translators allowed their readers to encounter what was unfamiliar in other languages and cultures. That unfamiliarity served purposes of linguistic and literary innovation in American literature. English did not take precedence over or erase those other languages, but functioned as a *lingua franca* that facilitated their coexistence in a fractured transatlantic nation.

Transnationalism and American Literature: Literary Translation 1773–1892 examines American literature through the verbal mobility of translation, and in the process redefines what we might mean by "American": that term functions as "a staging point for ideological contestation by many forces that are asynchronous and multilocal" (Aravamudan 1999: 15). I argue that translation was not a peripheral exercise that occurred separate from the writing of an American national literature, but that translation was the fundamental methodology — even for writers such as Hawthorne who tried to deny its relevance — through which national American writers understood their literary practice.

I.

Jacques Derrida has taught us to understand in theoretical terms the connection between different registers of linguistic complexity through his readings of biblical allegory.[9] Even before the fall from grace, the entry of Adam into language shattered the word-as-object of God and separated signifier from signified, thus making inaccessible the *Ding-an-sich*.[10] This division of the signifier from the signified finds an analogy in the distinction between monolingualism and multilingualism that occurs at the second linguistic fall, the fall of the tower of Babel. Eden and Babel stand for different orders of fracture: Eden marks the fragmentation of all language, whereas Babel represents the additional fragmentation of all languages from one another. Yet the diversification of languages also generates the idea of Edenic linguistic unity. The fragmentation of all languages from one another makes it possible for language to function in seeming coherence as "a" language: after the diversification of languages at Babel, the fragmentation of Eden looked unified. Monolingualism is conceivable only from a multilingual perspective; it is an artificial construct that articulates its coherence through the exclusion of other languages and the denial of its own artificiality and incoherence. Babel creates an epistemology of language that enables the invention of linguistic ontology where word and being coincide, even though such unity was already denied Adam. National languages are back-formations of multilingual fragmentation. That does not make monolingualism the origin or the telos of multilingualism: the Derridean model and the statistics on language use suggest that monolingualism functions as a supplement to multilingualism, whose traces it carries.

In Bakhtinian terms, that relationship between the linguistic supplement and the linguistic trace is expressed in his notions of polyglossia and heteroglossia. As supplements, monolingualism and multilingualism relate to one another through polyglossia, that is, through the translation between different languages that are understood to be distinct from one another. As a trace, multilingualism becomes visible in monolingual texts as heteroglossia, that is, as the diversity within a language that is understood to be self-contained. Neither the supplement nor the trace, the polyglossic nor the heteroglossic text are conceivable separately. By that token, translation is not just the practice that occurs between different languages, but also the practice that is inherent in all language, and we will have to understand multilingual translation in relation to a similar practice that occurs within a single language.

Implicated as Eden and Babel, heteroglossia and polyglossia, are in one another, each also functions as a different claim that writers such as Hawthorne and Forten can make about the workings of language and its intersection with national literature. I begin this inquiry with a look at Hawthorne's construction of a monolingual ontology that constantly strains against its multilingual contexts. Then I turn to Forten's multilingual praxis which strains against monolingual confines. What particularly interests me in these writers is the way in which their different linguistic methodologies allow them to frame the relationship between the nation and its transatlantic contexts.

Hawthorne and Forten were both writing and thinking about language at roughly the same time, around 1850. In the work that inaugurated and for several decades defined American literary studies, F. O. Matthiessen described that period as an *American Renaissance* (1941). Although Matthiessen had earlier published a book on translation in the Elizabethan Renaissance (Matthiessen 1931), his work on American literature reflects the English-only nationalism of the early 1940s in that it brackets the importance of multilingual translation for the American scene. Instead of analyzing the multilingual displacements of American literature, Matthiessen hoped to naturalize a monolingual literature when he set himself the task of illuminating how "Emerson's organic theory of language and expression" shaped the works of Hawthorne, Melville, Thoreau, and Whitman (Matthiessen 1941: xviii). In arguing that Emerson's linguistic theory shaped American literature, Matthiessen's account omitted the fact that Emerson was responding to and contending with Margaret Fuller, as I discuss in chapter three. Fuller rejected the equation between language, nature and nation for which she faulted Emerson, and instead located American literature in practices of multilingual translation.

I want to begin by identifying and contextualizing with each other these two different models of language, the model of "organic" monolingualism (Matthiessen 1941: xviii), which I take up here through the case of Hawthorne, and the model of translational multilingualism, for which Forten serves as my example. Initially, I discuss Hawthorne and Forten as opposites to each other; I pit Hawthorne's conception of an American Eden against Forten's explorations of an American Babel, so to speak. But given what I have already said about the way these two positions are implicated in each other, from a Derridean and Bakhtinian perspective, I also consider how these two very different linguistic models of American literature function as supplements to one another, supplements that carry each other's traces. I return in the final section of this introduction to the methodological implications of my case studies for the field of American literature. Let's begin then with Hawthorne.

In *The Scarlet Letter* (1850), Nathaniel Hawthorne constructs national monolingualism within a field of transatlantic exchange. He formally, thematically, and linguistically stages the question of how adulterous genealogies can produce cultural legitimacy. To achieve a sense of cultural legitimacy, Hawthorne draws on two strategies. One, he excludes linguistic, cultural, and racial "others" from his account of an Anglo-American literature founded in New England. Yet given the dependence of monolingualism on multilingualism, those others keep cropping up in his narrative. Two, he reconstructs alterity along homogenizing lines. He develops a strategy of twice-telling that mimics translation and that gives Anglo-American literature a sense of coherence because it linguistically links the past and the present.[11] By naturalizing English as the mother tongue of American literature, Hawthorne turns linguistic aporia into linguistic tautology. He replaces America's epistemic multilingualism with an ontological monolingualism that defines American literature in terms of a single language, a "mother tongue."

Hawthorne introduces his concern with the coherence and authenticity of American literature as a formal problem. *The Scarlet Letter* (1850) consists of two parts: "The Custom House," a novella (or framing narrative) set in Salem, Massachusetts, in the late 1840s, and a historical novella, set in Boston in the 1640s. How these two pieces relate to one another and whether they jointly amount to a novel has elicited much critical commentary.[12] Hawthorne's work anticipates and invites such formal inquiry. In the "Preface" to the second edition, Hawthorne contemplates removing or at least revising the "Custom House" sketch. He dramatizes his work's reception when he claims that his "sketch of official life" (Hawthorne 1980: xiii) has created a "violent" outcry of "public disapprobation" that "weigh[s] very heavily on him" (Hawthorne 1980: xiii). Since the "Custom House" sketch is "frank," "sincere," and marked by the "general accuracy" of his descriptions, Hawthorne chooses to dismiss partisan bickering — which he himself humorously denies participating in — and to republish the work unaltered so as to retain its lively "effect of truth" (Hawthorne 1980: xiii). His refusal to cut the opening sketch establishes Hawthorne's novel as a twice-told tale, in two ways: one, he retells Surveyor Pue's account of Hester's tale, and two, by refusing to abolish the custom house sketch, the second edition of his novel replicates the exact words and language of the first edition.

Through this strategy of twice-telling, Hawthorne achieves a sense of linguistic continuity and stability: in the "Preface" to the second edition he insists on republishing "his introductory sketch without the change of a word" (Hawthorne 1980: xiv). Whereas the first edition of his work consisted of words on the page that were uniform between different imprints of the same edition, Hawthorne now establishes a linguistic continuity across different editions and printings. The second edition enacts linguistic continuity between the different temporalities and spaces in which Hawthorne's work has appeared. Because the hallmark of multilingualism and translation is the change of words, that is, the shift in signifiers, Hawthorne articulates through the act of twice-telling a logic of monolingualism that thrives on repetition yet occludes variation. Twice-telling mimics the logic of translation in that it expresses again and in another context something previously expressed. But it also fundamentally denies the basic practice of translation, which is the shift in signifier. Twice-telling allows Hawthorne to imagine a literature that consists of and constructs itself around the repetition of signifiers that gain stability and become signs through the act of repetition.

The preface in that sense mimics and teases out the formal logic of his work's division into two novellas. The novellas are set in different places (Salem, Boston; the United States, the British colonies) at different times (1840s, 1640s). But for Hawthorne, those geographical differences generate a coherent space, New England, and the temporal settings jointly amount to a "history of New England" (Hawthorne 1980: 57). The very differences between settings for Hawthorne are building blocks for a geographical and temporal relationship that exceeds the local and momentary and gains unity through its linguistic consistency. As he makes clear when he repeatedly refers to the United States in his opening sketch, and claims that his "native town" made him a "public functionary of the United States" (Hawthorne 1980: 23), Hawthorne uses the disjointed formal structure of his work to construct a national literature that emerges from and exceeds its constituent differences.

What interests me is that this coherence stems from Hawthorne's invention of American literature as monolingual. As its space changes across different temporalities, New England retains its identity by remaining "New England," that is, by remaining a verbal signifier that is stable and stably English. According to Hawthorne's account of America's literary and linguistic genealogies, "New England" remains the same even if New England the place changes over settings and time. In Hawthorne's verbal economy, "New England" can circulate in different registers, elicit various connotations and shifting associations, and yet enact an American geographical and historical continuity. The novel's coherence comes from the linguistic continuity of English, which allows Hawthorne's work to be monolingual even when he internationalizes American literature by sending Pearl to England at the narrative's end. Hawthorne's model is simultaneously isolationist and imperial. The efficacy of Hawthorne's linguistic construct depends on the transparency of his language, which does not acknowledge the presence of competing languages in the American scene and thereby naturalizes English as *the* language, that is, as the *only* language of American literature. It is that ability of language to function as an essence and to obscure the alterity from which it emerges that I refer to as linguistic exceptionalism, and that I argue is founded on the simultaneous invocation of a mother tongue and occlusion of the mother.

The Scarlet Letter's odd formal structure demonstrates that difference itself does not yet tell us anything about diversity. On the contrary, Hawthorne invokes difference to occlude diversity. To establish cultural and historical cohesion, Hawthorne expels indigenous, African-American and Latin American peoples from the colonial past and develops a strategy of twice-telling that constructs a racially and linguistically homogeneous American literature. Hawthorne opens his historical novella with a "vagrant Indian ... [who] was to be driven with stripes into the shadow of the forest" (Hawthorne 1980: 57). Hawthorne excludes indigenous peoples from participating in both the historical past and the cultural present. Similarly, Hawthorne invokes yet banishes African-Americans and Latin Americans. Although he remembers a time "before the last war with England, when Salem was a port by itself," and recalls the bustle of a morning "when three or four vessels happen[ed] to have arrived at once — usually from Africa or South America" (Hawthorne 1980: 17), he insists that the wharf is no longer the site of such commercial exchange. By banishing ethnic, racial, and linguistic "others" from his account, Hawthorne constructs a coherently Anglophone, Anglo-American literature. But excluding these others also acknowledges their presence; his work carries the traces of an alterity that he exposes in the very process of banishing it from his account of literary identity. In his study of colonial conquest, Tvetan Todorov suggests that, "at the same time that it was tending to obliterate the strangeness of the external other, Western civilization found an interior other" (Todorov 1984: 248). Hawthorne's novellas replace the external other with an interior other, whom he identifies as female. By recalling Surveyor Pue's account of Hester Prynne and Pearl, by twice-telling their story, Hawthorne is able to give his work a sense of familiarity that can contain cultural alterity and create a feminized "internal other" which will in turn be subsumed to a homogenizing monolingualism, represented in the novella by the letter of the law that Hester carries on her breast.

Monolingualism strains against the multilingualism and the practice of translation that haunts Hawthorne's enterprise and that concerns me in this book. As Srinivas Aravamudan has said in the context of colonial attempts to define the self against the other, the "trope is transitive, it swerves from self-adequation to surplus" (Aravamudan 1999: 1).[13] Hawthorne tries to contain the surplus of the transitive trope — by which I mean the recalcitrant transatlanticism and multilingualism of American literature — within a logic of self-adequation by carefully constructing a closed economy of national signs. In that closed economy of national signs, literature circulates as a fetishized object.[14] By literalizing the signifier (as the embroidered scarlet letter), Hawthorne makes monolingualism the object and the essence of American literature. But the very need to fetishize monolingual national literature, that is to put in place a "blocking and fixating function" (Apter 1991: xiii), returns it to the multilingual, transatlantic surpluses of its cultural production.

In "The Custom House" sketch, Hawthorne tries simultaneously to banish and internalize what is foreign by playing out the logic of national monolingualism in the register of economic exchange. He enacts his linguistic exceptionalism by troping on the meanings of "custom." According to the *Oxford English Dictionary*, "custom" refers to a place where an economic activity is performed: "customs" is an area of a seaport where goods are examined and customs duties are levied, and it is in this sense that Hawthorne first uses the term when he describes the custom house overlooking the "dilapidated wharf" in Salem (Hawthorne 1980: 16). The goods that custom house officials assess are imports from or exports to foreign countries. In a national economy, all domestic products are free of customs, and only foreign products are subject to them. Hawthorne's insistence that the wharf has become "dilapidated" and that there is no longer much to be done in the custom house casts Salem as a place where foreign goods no longer enter the national market. Instead, a second kind of "custom" has taken hold in the place: Hawthorne draws on the definition by which custom refers to a "habitual or usual practice; common way of acting; usage, fashion, habit (either of an individual or of a community)" (Simpson, Weiner, and Oxford University Press 1989). The two artifacts he finds, the embroidered letter and the written narrative, add another dimension to this second definition: Hawthorne's description of Hester's exacting needlework — by which "each limb [of the 'A'] proved to be precisely three inches and a quarter in length" that revealed it had been "intended ... as an ornamental article of dress" (Hawthorne 1980: 41) — reminds us that custom (especially in combination with made, fitted, built, or tailored) also designates an article "made to measure or to order, or places where such articles are made" (Simpson et al. 1989). Thus, in this second extended sense, "custom" designates the local place and production of specific domestic and literary artifacts. By troping on the multiple definitions of custom, Hawthorne turns Salem from a site of international trade into a site of national literary production.

Hawthorne marks his custom house as a space that authenticates and is authenticated by artifacts and by historical documentation: Hawthorne insists that the pages he found alongside the embroidered letter provide "truth of the authenticity of a narrative" contained in his work (Hawthorne 1980: 16). Hawthorne tropes on "custom" to suggest a closed economy of linguistic signs: although the term takes on different signifieds, the linguistic signifier itself remains stable throughout the sketch, thus ensuring the continuity of the American sign even in its relation to Puritan ancestors who considered themselves English. Hawthorne in effect resolves the paradox of national identity by turning English from a term that refers to another nation to a linguistic term that defines American literature, and that thereby can subsume even other nationalities (the English) under its verbal economy without becoming unrecognizable or unstable.

In "The Custom House" sketch, Hawthorne examines what kind of object national literature is and how cultural circulation works. After his dismissal from the patronage appointment that he held in the custom house, Hawthorne imagines himself to be writing from a position of exile — as a "citizen of somewhere else," dwelling among "other faces" than "these familiar ones" (Hawthorne 1980: 53). That position of exile functions as a transcendent national site. Hawthorne differentiates the literary objects he creates for the nation from the goods circulating in the commercial world of international trade. The custom house is dominated by the fluctuations of political patronage, and thrives on governmental calculations of goods' exchange value in an international economy. This complex process of international mediation is antithetical to the role that Hawthorne envisions for literature in a transcendent national economy. He says that during his time in the custom house, "Literature, its exertions and objects, were ... of little moment in my regard. I cared not, at this period, for books; they were apart from me. Nature — except it were human nature — the nature that is developed in earth and sky, was, in one sense, hidden from me" (Hawthorne 1980: 35). The transcendent "objects" of "literature" cannot exist for Hawthorne in the international trade economy where commercial objects crowd them out. Literature is for Hawthorne an object of a different order, as his structural homology between literature and nature makes clear. As Lauren Berlant has argued, Hawthorne performs in this text "a linkage between naturalization and nationalization" (Berlant 1991: 4). Hawthorne discounts the incessant displacement and mediation within verbal economies of literary objects, and argues instead for the reified stability that literary objects draw from "Nature." By imagining literature removed from the instabilities of the market economy, Hawthorne tries to control the excess of his tropes as part of national literature's self-adequation, and to contain linguistic and national surplus.

Surplus value paradoxically becomes the mark of self-adequation as Hawthorne fetishizes the American book. Hawthorne constantly shows his fraught relationship to commercial exchange by having to resort to the logic of fetishization. Hawthorne plays out this argument when he imagines the scarlet letter and *The Scarlet Letter* as overdetermined objects. In the first instance, the scarlet letter is Hester Prynne's embroidered cloth, which Hawthorne recovers in the attic of the custom house: "the object ... was a certain affair of fine red cloth, much worn and faded" (Hawthorne 1980: 40).[15] Unsure how to read Hester's scarlet letter, Hawthorne finds a document by Surveyor Pue that "authorized and authenticated" Hawthorne's own account (Hawthorne 1980: 42). Although Hawthorne's *Scarlet Letter* is a twice- or even a thrice-told tale, he argues that the act of literary transposition and circulation produces an increased stability that amounts to a literary object: Hawthorne emphatically insists in the "Preface" to the second edition on republishing "his introductory sketch without the change of a word" (Hawthorne 1980: xiv). Even as his novel goes through various editions, it retains its identity by incessantly replicating itself linguistically. Hawthorne's refusal to change "a word" stabilizes and reifies the literary object. Those reiterations create a circulation that is always self-referential. If the incessant circulation of goods through the nation's docks and warehouses marks the custom house as a site of international exchange, Hawthorne argues for a different kind of national custom that defines itself through the circulation of a stable language. Language becomes the locus and the modus of Hawthorne's national imaginary.

By literalizing the signifier as the scarlet letter, and then replicating that literalized signifier, Hawthorne imagines a literature whose coherence and identity is established in the repetition of signifiers and the exclusion of differences. The signifier becomes its own signified: *The Scarlet Letter* refers to the embroidered scarlet letter that Hawthorne finds in the custom house. That scarlet letter is the signified of the signifier, *The Scarlet Letter*. And yet Hawthorne's signified, the embroidered scarlet letter, is also a signifier:

it stands for Hester's adultery, that is, it stands for an unruliness that it returns to submission under the letter of the law. Hawthorne creates a loop by which the signified of the American sign constantly shifts. And yet each signified turns out itself to be a signifier: the signifier (*The Scarlet Letter*) refers to another signifier (the scarlet letter which stands for Hester's adultery — which in Pearl's reading becomes yet another signifier, as I discuss below). Because the signified always turns out itself to be the signifier, and a signifier that infinitely reproduces itself in the exact same way without linguistic alteration, the American sign remains consistent and self-referential in spite of and because of its seeming multiplicity. Thanks to Hawthorne's monolingual construction of American literature, the "contradictory interpretations of a sign" do "*not* call into crisis the meaning or function of that sign, or of the system that authorizes it" (Berlant 1991: 7). We will see presently how multilingual translation calls forth that crisis.

In Hawthorne's work, the signified of American literature is signification. The incessant repetition of the signifier achieves two purposes: one, it occludes linguistic and cultural "others" from American signification, and two, it constructs a coherent American literary identity around the repetition and consistency of the signifier. But Hawthorne's use of repetition also develops a particular argument about translation. If multilingualism and translation are marked by shifts in signifiers, Hawthorne fantasizes about a monolingualism in which each shift in the signifier reinforces that signifier. In the sense that monolingualism constructs itself through acts of verbal repetition, it mimics the methodology of multilingual translation while negating its fundamental premise, that is, the shift in signifiers. Hawthorne draws on acts of reiteration to define translation as a carrying over (which is the literal, etymological meaning of "translation") of the signifier from one context to another. Through these acts of twice-telling, Hawthorne ultimately establishes a claim for American literature's untranslatability: he anticipates Walter Benjamin's argument that "translation, ironically, transplants the original into a more definitive linguistic realm since it can no longer be displaced by a secondary rendering. The original can only be raised there anew and at other points of time" (Benjamin 1969: 75). For Hawthorne, translation — in its limited definition as a carrying over of language from one printing to another, from one novella to another, from one English telling to another English telling — does not negotiate between different linguistic contexts but helps to establish a more authoritative cultural essentialism.

As we saw above, twice-telling establishes the "truth of the authenticity of a narrative" (Hawthorne 1980: 16). Implicitly, then, Hawthorne recognizes that translation does not just replicate an original, but that translation also creates an original. Through his use of twice-telling, of carrying linguistic signifiers from one context to another, Hawthorne develops an argument for American literary identity: by Hawthorne's account, the significance of American literature lies in it being self-referential. Hawthorne converts the aporia of language into a tautological argument for monolingual coherence. From the Babel of translation that he invokes and recodes in the "Custom House" sketch, Hawthorne reconstructs an Eden of linguistic unity in the "Scarlet Letter," where the American sign coheres in a relation of stable signifiers. No matter how much the signified shifts, that shifting signified itself always turns out to be another signifier, and that signifier is always stably the scarlet letter of *The Scarlet Letter*.

In the historical novella, Hawthorne plays out his linguistic argument when he replaces the adulterous mother with the unadulterated mother tongue. After playing on the beach, Pearl returns with a green letter of seaweed pinned to her breast. Hester contemplates Pearl's letter, and asks her if she knows "what this letter means which thy mother is doomed to wear" (Hawthorne 1980: 171). Pearl's association with the letter is literary, as she makes clear when she answers: " 'Yes, Mother, ... It is the great letter "A." Thou hast taught me in the hornbook'" (Hawthorne 1980: 171).[16] Pearl's response plays out the logic of linguistic repetition: her mother has instructed her to replicate the letter from the "hornbook," that is, from the primer with which colonial children were instructed to read and to write letters on erasable horn. Pearl has in fact performed just such duplication by recreating the green letter on her own bosom: she has retraced a letter that is infinitely reproducible as a signifier. And yet Pearl does not recognize what Hester knows, that Pearl herself is the letter's signified. That lack of recognition is striking: what Pearl would have read in the hornbook when encountering the letter "A" is that "In Adam's Fall, We Sinned All." Pearl fails to understand the letter A in its significance for a fall from Edenic innocence into carnal sin. What she does recognize is the hornbook's linguistic instruction, by which Adam's fall is a fall into monolingualism. Although the adage points to a fall into language, that language is imagined as unified and unifying: the "A" explicated here refers equally to "Adam" and "All," and creates a sense of linguistic coherence, in which Pearl participates through her act of replicating the scarlet letter.

At the crucial moment when Hester reveals her sin to her daughter, Hawthorne shifts from the register of paternity to the context of language pedagogy, that is, he shifts from the logic of the signified to the logic of the signifier. Exasperated by Pearl's response, Hester restates her question and asks her daughter whether she knows "wherefore thy mother wears this letter" (Hawthorne 1980: 171). By the logic of the historical scene that Hawthorne constructs, Pearl's answer is utterly enigmatic —she clearly does not know that Dimmesdale is her father, and yet she answers: "for the same reason that the minister keeps his hand over his heart" (Hawthorne 1980: 171). This answer makes sense only if we read the scarlet letter as a signifier for American language, both written and spoken. Pearl's relationship to the letter plays out the definition that Noah Webster provides for "A" in the 1828 edition of *An American Dictionary of the English Language*:

> A is the first letter of the Alphabet in most of the known languages of the earth ... It is naturally the first letter because it represents the first vocal sound naturally formed by the human organs: being the sound uttered with a mere opening of the mouth without constraint, and without any effort to alter the natural position or configuration of the lips. Hence this letter is found in many words first uttered by infants; which words are the names of objects with which infants are first concerned, as the breast, and the parents. Hence in Hebrew ... am, is mother, and ab, is father. (Webster 1828)

Hawthorne draws on the letter's association with mother and father to construct Pearl's ability to read the signifier correctly. Although for Hester the "A" signifies her adultery, and "Adam's fall," Pearl's responses demonstrate that for the next generation, the scarlet letter marks a linguistic relationship: the infant's recognition of her parents is naturalized and inseparably linked, by Webster's definition, to the infant's initiation into language. Confronted with her daughter's confident reading of the letter as a linguistic marker, Hester is silent for the first time about the moral significance of the letter and allows it to stand as a linguistic signifier, thus becoming complicit in this linguistic turn.

In this key instructional scene, then, Hester's silence shows us that Pearl's knowledge of her mother is primarily a knowledge of her mother tongue. Hawthorne constructs that association through Pearl's literary initiation into language at her mother's breast. Hester recalls that "Pearl's inevitable tendency to hover about the enigma of the scarlet letter seemed an innate quality of her being" (Hawthorne 1980: 173). This description reminds us that Pearl grew up in the presence of her mother's letter, and that her oral development — at her mother's breast — was directly tied to her initiation into literacy; orality and literacy are not separable for Pearl, and both are marked by a letter that conflates and then replaces her mother with her mother tongue. Pearl's schooling replicates a standard trope of nineteenth century nationalist literature that evokes and denies its multilingual orality by reinscribing itself in a monolingual print culture. As Deirdre Lynch has said of the monster in Mary Shelley's *Frankenstein* (1818), his education (like Pearl's) "elides the distinction between the phonetic and the alphabetic ... such an elision suggests that language is always already alphabetized, a denatured combination, for it casts the native speech at the novel's center as reinvented transcription" (Lynch 2002: 215). Pearl is an illegitimate child, but she becomes the locus of a literary legitimacy that Hawthorne carefully constructs as monolingual and written.

Hawthorne sets up in Pearl's reading of her mother's letter a "fetishism of reading" (Apter 1991: xi) that performs an "incremental fragment cathexis whereby individual parts eventually crowd together and usurp the original whole" (Apter 1991: xi). As Michael Ragussis has suggested, "Hester is, in the educative system I am describing, the teacher of the mother tongue" (Ragussis 1991: 321). But Ragussis' point needs to be carried even further: Hester herself is ultimately elided when the adulterous mother is replaced with the unadulterated mother tongue. Especially if Ragussis is right in thinking that "despite all the methods of parental and social control exerted over her," Pearl represents "an alien other to be feared" (Ragussis 1991: 323), it is important to recognize that the alien other has been eliminated as an external threat and recreated internally, in the role of a child. The infantilized alien is inscribed in a linguistic negotiation that sustains its authoritative and authorizing frame through its monolingualism. By recreating cultural dialogue formally, thematically and linguistically as Anglo-American monologue, Hawthorne turns the external other into an internal other and argues for an American identity based on English as a mother tongue. But for all Hawthorne's efforts, that monolingualism remains in competition with and constituted by the multilingual American and transnational scene, to which I now turn.

II.

In the multilingual diversity of the signifier, the nation strains beyond its homogenizing frames towards multilingual pluralism. But what might such multilingual unframing look like? A contemporary of Hawthorne's in Salem, Charlotte Forten, provides us with a sophisticated answer to that question when she imagines multilingualism as a way of opposing slavery while expressing her national idealism. Instead of locating American literature in a colonial past that is reconstructed along Anglophone lines, Forten envisions a transatlantic American literature that relies on multilingual translation to unsettle ontological claims. In her diaries, Forten locates herself in a field of transatlantic exchange that draws on translation to engage an "other" who remains external. To achieve a sense of cultural diversity, she draws on two strategies. One, she includes linguistic, cultural and racial "others" in her account of Anglo-American literature. Two, she reconstructs alterity along heterogeneous lines and develops a strategy of translation that unsettles the seeming coherence and language-based identity of Anglo-American literature. Far from fetishizing American origins and originality, Forten examines cultural contexts in their domestic and transatlantic complexity. Whereas Hawthorne is concerned with identifying American literature in terms of its traits — of monolingual originality — Forten explores the multilingual processes and methodologies by which American literature operates. Pointing out that the very notion of a naturalized mother tongue functions as a metaphor that obscures the wrongs of the middle passage, Forten examines the possibility of drawing on linguistic alienation to critique such metaphoricity. By unsettling English as the mother tongue of American literature, Forten turns linguistic tautology into linguistic aporia. She replaces ontological monolingualism with America's epistemic multilingualism and defines American literature in terms of its linguistic plurality.

Far less known than Hawthorne in her own time and ours, Charlotte Forten requires a short introduction: she was born in 1837 into a prominent black family in Philadelphia. She lost her mother at the age of three, and although her father remarried, the family never regained its stability.[17] Growing up without a mother, Forten reconfigured her sense of intimacy to encompass a wider circle of family and friends. In 1853, Charlotte moved to Salem, where she lived with the abolitionist Charles Lenox Remond and his family. A month before graduating from the Salem Normal School in 1856, Charlotte became a teacher at the Epes Grammar School, a post that she held (intermittently because of her bad health) throughout the next six years. During this time, she published poetry in the *Liberator* and the *National Anti-Slavery Standard*. Following the advice of John Greenleaf Whittier, one of her many prominent friends, Forten set out in 1862 for Port Royal, South Carolina, to teach contraband slaves. The *Atlantic Monthly* published her account of that endeavor in 1864 in a two-part essay entitled "Life on the Sea Islands." In addition to the successes she achieved in magazines, Forten's literary accomplishments included her translation of Emile Erckmann and Alexandre Chatrain's novel *Madame Thérèse; or, The Volunteers of '92* which was published by Scribner's in 1869 with a foreword by Colonel Thomas Wentworth Higginson; but Forten is known today chiefly for the rich journals she kept from 1856–92. After marrying Francis Grimké in 1878 (and serving as guardian to his niece Angelina Weld Grimké from 1894–98), Charlotte Forten Grimké helped to found the National Association for Colored Women in 1896; she died in 1914.

Forten's journals reveal a very different Salem from the one we encounter in Hawthorne's "Custom House" sketch.[18] Rather than inhabiting a space that has become "dilapidated" (Hawthorne 1980: 16), Forten shows what an intellectually vibrant community Salem was in the 1850s. In a journal explicitly kept to record and recall at a later time "much-loved friends" and the "interesting books that I read" (Forten 1988: 58), Forten conflates the personal and the textual when she refers to her studies as her "closest friends" (Forten 1988: 24). This conflation of people and texts makes sense when we look at her circle of acquaintances, a veritable who's who that mingles literary with political prominence: William Wells Brown was a family friend, as were John Greenleaf Whittier and Thomas Wentworth Higginson. Although Forten largely led a domestic life, her engagement with questions of burning national interest — especially abolition and what we would today call gender politics — constantly drew her out of the home and into the lecture hall: she attended lectures by virtually all the prominent abolitionist speakers of the day, including William Lloyd Garrison (on the twentieth anniversary of British emancipation), Wendell Phillips (on Toussaint L'Ouverture, among other topics), and Henry Ward Beecher (on patriotism). But Forten was equally eager to encounter literati such as

James Russell Lowell (whom she heard on "the imaginative faculty" in English poetry and on Dante), and Ralph Waldo Emerson (who spoke, on separate occasions, about France, time, and the true beauty of Nature). These political and literary activities went hand in hand for Forten: her attendance of abolitionist lectures educated her in the issues of the day, but she worked out her own political positions in her literary responses, and especially in her relationship to language. What makes Forten's journals so compelling is that she develops a vision of a multilingual literature that presents us with a historically available alternative to Hawthorne's fetishized monolingualism.

Like Hawthorne, Forten examines her relationship to language through the dual trope of the mother/mother tongue. Forten expresses what we might identify as a feminist response to Hawthorne when she associates the loss of the mother with the fetishization of patriotism. That critique emerges in entries like the one recording her attendance at Theodore Parker's lecture (January 30, 1855) on the "The Anglo-Saxon Race," whose superiority in practical applications he praised, and whose lacking imagination he criticized. Forten's record of Parker's speech seems to express first and foremost her own convictions: she had "long wished very much to see and hear this remarkable man, and my pleasant anticipation were [sic] fully realized" (Forten 1988: 125). Referring to the Anglo-Saxon race as "they," Forten records that Parker

> spoke of their aggressive spirit, which continually prompted them to make war upon and exterminate other races, and to take possession of their country, and of their strong love of individual liberty; but described them as too selfish to be fond of equality. One of their greatest failings is a lack of conscientiousness — they are *downright* before *men* but *not upright* before God. This somewhat exemplified by pauperism in England and slavery in America. Every eighth man in England is a pauper — he does not own the hands with which he works — the feet upon which he stands. Every eighth woman in America does not own herself nor the child upon her bosom. (Forten 1988: 125)

Hawthorne's image of the mother as the locus for a community's moral, intellectual, and literary self-definition takes on a new dimension when Forten examines the importance of race for patriotism. In a society where individualism negates equality, the "possession of their country" by white men depends on the conversion of black women into chattel; her journal critiques a patriotism that relies on objectification. But Forten also understands racial and gender oppression as part of a broader power dynamic when she includes male English paupers in her consideration. By combining issues of race and gender with questions of class, and by expanding her focus from the national to the international scene, Forten introduces empire into her considerations. She critiques an imperialism that poses as nationalism but that negates the very ideals of community and equality on which, she argues, nationalism should be founded. She portrays this brand of patriotism as one that "take[s] possession" and in that act of conquest establishes a claim that appropriates land as "country."

Forten also develops an important understanding of the role that gender plays in these transatlantic power relationships. Her diaries enable us to recognize how current transnational scholarship neglects questions of gender and language, of mothers and mother tongues. Arguing that an irresolvable tension between national consciousness and race consciousness emerges in the middle passage, Paul Gilroy demonstrates that the black Atlantic marks the emergence of new subjectivities and temporalities, and the irrecoverable loss of old ones. That dimension of loss is particularly important if we are to understand the black Atlantic as a gendered space. One of the most compelling arguments about the losses of the transatlantic remains Hortense Spillers' essay "Mama's Baby, Papa's Maybe" (1987), where she demonstrates that in the middle passage, "motherhood as a female bloodrite is outraged, is denied, at the very *same time* that it becomes the founding term of a human and social enactment" (Spillers 2003: 228). Yet drawing on Spillers as a supplement to Gilroy raises the problem of pitting female embodiment against male consciousness. To avoid replicating that model of gender ascription, we need to turn to language as a field of inquiry in which the gender politics of the transatlantic can be negotiated discursively.

Concerned about an imperial politics that belies the democratic ideals it purports to espouse, Forten looked for a way of separating patriotism from wage, race and gender slavery. To establish the efficacy of nationalism in protest against such repressive state formations, Forten locates her sense of authenticity in personal and textual relationships. These relationships thrive on mediations that are always in excess of what is being mediated. Whereas Hawthorne imagines replacing the customs of international exchange with the customs of fetishized nationalism, Forten shows the incessant interpenetration between the international and the national in the vibrant space of cultural and intellectual circulation that she inhabited in Salem. To imagine a brand of nationalism critical of imperialism, Forten continuously breaks with frames of self-adequation: she imagines nationalism as a form of mediation and a kind of relationship that is partial and fragmented.[19] For her, the literary and the political are inseparable but not coextensive.

Forten initially worked out her literary and political agenda through her reading. She was an avid reader, and the volumes she consumed made up the popular national and international canon of her age. Among the writers she most admired and most closely emulated was Margaret Fuller — who had served Hawthorne as a model for Hester Prynne (Bercovitch 1991: 352). By resurrecting Fuller as Hester, Hawthorne drew on the scandalized speculation that Fuller's infant child (who drowned with her in 1850) may have been born out of wedlock. But his attack on Fuller is even more far-reaching when he turns her, in her guise as Hester, into the chief pedagogue of American monolingualism: Fuller was best known during her lifetime as an accomplished linguist and translator (as I discuss in chapter three), and it is that legacy in particular that Hawthorne's novel tries to suppress. Through her engagement with Fuller, Forten developed a gendered methodology for reimagining the national frame linguistically. Inspired by Fuller to read Goethe, Forten complains of Thomas Carlyle's *Wilhelm Meister* (2 vols.; 1824, 1827) and of works in general that they lose "very much of their beauty by translation. Oh, when shall I be able to read them in the original. I do most earnestly desire to" (Forten 1988: 154). Translation created in Forten a desire to study German — perhaps not surprisingly, given that in the nineteenth century United States, "German [was] by far the largest single non-English language group," as reflected by its predominance "among American imprints" from that time (Assing 1999: xi). Instead of foreclosing an interest in other languages because texts were readily available in English, translation on the contrary inspired Forten to become multilingual: reading works in English translation drew Forten to the study of other languages, and she did indeed start learning German shortly after reading Fuller and Carlyle (Forten 1988: 286).

German was not the only non-English language that Forten learned — she studied the ancient (Latin) as well as the modern (German and French) languages most widely taught at the time. Moreover, practice in languages and translation was readily available in the abolitionist press. For instance, the *Liberty Bell* for 1851 contained an essay in French on "Influence de L'esclavage sur les Maîtres" (Souvestre 1851: 231–34), alongside five of Emerson's translations "from the Persian" (Emerson 1851: 78–82, 156–7). Throughout Forten's accounts of abolitionist and literary lectures run entries in which she records turning "to my Latin which I like better than anything else; and which will, I know, be still more interesting to me when I commence to translate. I love to master 'Virgil's lay' and Livy's 'pictured page'" (Forten 1988: 155). Forten's use of the word "master" in this context is striking: Forten pictures language study as a way in which she can accomplish a degree of mastery. In the process, she recodes mastery and turns it from a form of oppressive linguistic imposition into one of affective linguistic agency — as she tells us, mastery for her is about "love." Instead of imagining language exclusively as an oppressive force, Forten argues that linguistic pluralism allows for affective engagements that lie at the core of a non-coercive relation to alterity.

By studying other languages, Forten offsets the self-adequation of monolingual nationalism: if the American sign in Hawthorne attains its stability through the incessant recirculation of stable signifiers, Forten's linguistic engagement imagines the substitution of other linguistic signifiers within the national symbolic economy. But to achieve such a goal, it was not enough to multiply monolingualisms. Forten was not just interested in accumulating languages and putting English next to Latin, French, and German. She was also interested in multilingualism as a way of relating languages to one another and achieving a linguistic mobility that unsettles the stability of the signifier and unhinges monolingualism's self-adequation. Her desire to conceptualize multilingualism as a relational methodology emerges in her complex thoughts on translation. If we look again at the two passages cited above, it initially seems unclear what Forten means by and makes of translation. She complains that beauty gets lost in translation when she worries about Carlyle's inadequate rendering of Goethe's work, and yet she suggests that her Latin texts are enhanced — they will "be still more interesting to me when I commence to translate" (Forten 1988: 155). Her views on translation seem antithetical: in the instance of Carlyle, translation is a loss, in her own endeavors translation is a gain of linguistic and textual meaning. How are we to understand that contradiction?

In a different context, Arjun Appadurai has made a distinction that is useful for addressing this question: he argues that,

> as scholars concerned with localities, circulation, and comparison, we need to make a decisive shift away from what we may call 'trait' geographies to what we could call 'process' geographies. Much traditional thinking about 'areas' has been driven by conceptions of geographical, civilizational, and cultural coherence that rely on some sort of list — of values, languages, material practices, ecological adaptions, marriage patterns, and the like. However sophisticated these approaches, they all tend to see 'areas' as relatively immobile aggregates of traits, with more or less durable historical boundaries and with a unity composed of more or less enduring properties. (Appadurai 2001: 7)

Forten distinguishes between translation as an object marked by traits and translation as a process. This distinction was theorized by Friedrich Schleiermacher (1768–1834), who differentiated between language as a condition (*Gegebenheit*) and as an act (*Tat*).[20] Forten dismisses translations that have themselves become reified texts, and praises the process of translation for enhancing her linguistic appreciation. Translation as an object diminishes the literary text in that it newly reifies language and limits linguistic mobility — as we saw with Hawthorne. By studying the languages involved in translation, Forten is not merely able to reclaim the "original" as an object; she is able to read the text "in the original," that is, in the medium in which it was composed (Forten 1988: 154). The distinction is crucial: by saying that she will be able to read the text "in the original" (instead of saying she will be able to read the original) Forten places an emphasis on language and on her desire to read the text in a symbolic economy different from her own. In dismissing Carlyle's translation, she is not trying to replace one object — the translation — with another object — the original. Instead, she is imagining a different kind of translation that is not first and foremost a literary object but a linguistic process. For

Forten, translation as a process becomes the privileged methodology for offsetting fetishistic self-adequation and for unsettling the American sign. As process, translation requires a bilingual readerly and authorial capacity whose intertextuality is not contained within the tautological frame of fetishized monolingualism but broadens its self-contained dialectic into a pluralistic, multilingual dialogic.[21] Forten imagines a nation that defines itself through its relationships to others. By emphasizing process, she is able to tolerate competing originals.

Thinking of translation as a process challenges our understanding of the cultural identities that translation reflects and generates. And yet for the study of American literature, such an emphasis on process must always carefully negotiate its relationship to traits. After all, the notions of manifest destiny and of vernacular literature that lie at the heart of American exceptionalism reify process as trait and invoke alterity only to banish it. As we have seen in the instance of Hawthorne, process (reiteration) can lend itself to the construction of traits (fetishized monolingualism). The question becomes how process can function and can keep functioning as process, can be and remain a "flow" without becoming a structure or a trait (Appadurai 2001: 5–6).[22] The answer to that question lies in conceptualizing translation as a process without end. In her recent work, *Mother Tongues: Sexuality, Trials, Motherhood, Translation* (2002), Barbara Johnson interprets Walter Benjamin as saying that

> translation ... is 'a somewhat provisional way of coming to grips with the foreignness of languages.' Only through translation does an original *become* an original. In saying this I think that Benjamin does not — or not only — mean to say that the original acquires some new authority from the process, but that the idea of the original is a back-formation from the difficulties of translation. Until one sees that from which something deviates, one does not think of that thing as a starting point. The trajectory from original to translation mimes the process of departing from an origin and thus enhances the belief that there *is* an origin. What translation allows us to see is also a fantasy language uniting the two works, as if all translations were falls away from some original language that fleetingly becomes visible. But nothing proves that this is not another back-formation from the difficulties of translation. (Johnson 2003: 16)[23]

A text is simply a text. But when we imagine that a text is an original text, that claim to originality paradoxically makes the text a secondary object. A text can be defined as an original only through the conceptual availability of something that is other-than the original, such as a translation. But for an original to be other-than a translation, this other category of translation had to be there in the first place. Translation is not the afterthought of originality — the original can only be conceived of in relationship to its translation. At the very moment that a claim to originality is made, it makes possible not only a future translation, but already draws on a translation that had to be there for the conceptual transformation of the text into an original. In translation, national literatures and languages engage the unfamiliar. But translation remains a process only when we acknowledge that the familiar and the unfamiliar are not a priori categories, and that they emerge through the process of translation.

Hawthorne's cultural fantasy depends on the a priori existence of self and other before colonial contact. This model of separating different cultures from one another and imagining them as hermetically coherent before their contact with each other has long informed scholarship on American literature; it expresses itself, for instance, when Tvetan Todorov's refers to "the discovery *self* makes of the *other*" (Todorov 1984: 3), and when he treats both parties of an encounter as having pre-existing forms of identity. In the 1990s, this model for understanding cultural identities came under scrutiny. Examining the complexity of Circum-Atlantic culture, as he calls it, Joseph Roach argued that moments of contact are transformative for all parties involved. In this model, modern individuals and cultures do not exist a priori but emerge through acts of cultural performance. What Roach has said of cultural performance holds true for a literature that understands itself in relation to translation: "the key to understanding how performances worked *within* a culture, recognizing that a fixed and unified culture exists only as a convenient but dangerous fiction, is to illuminate the process of surrogation as it operated *between* the participating cultures" (Roach 1996: 5).[24]

Although Forten never fully explores the theoretical insights of her linguistic practice, there are moments in the journals where we can glimpse its implications for cultural identities that are never fixed or complete but always standing in for each other as fragmented surrogates. One way in which translation achieves force for Forten as a multidirectional activity becomes obvious when she tells us, that, while teaching contraband slaves in the South, she

> Finished translating into French Adelaide Proctor's poem 'A Woman's Question,' which I like so much. It was an experiment, and I assure you, *mon ami*, tis a queer translation. But it was good practice in French. (Forten 1988: 398)[25]

Forten draws on translation to practice her proficiency in non-English languages by translating from and into them. When she addresses herself to her diary as "*mon ami*," Forten's entry enacts what it reports on: she herself is translating her work into French, and vice versa, is translating from French into English. Forten unsettles her and our relationship to the language we are in: we are not sure if the passage is in English or French originally. Moreover, we are not just left wondering what language we are actually in, but may also question whether we are suddenly experiencing a compound language — a French-English or Franglais of sorts.²⁶ Forten may be mimicking a particular publishing practice here by which an original and a translation were published side by side. As I discuss at greater length in chapter one, that practice was popularized by John Clarke (1687–1734), a devoté of John Locke's educational philosophy, who published introductory Latin texts side by side with their English translations, and whose textbooks were widely used in "American grammar schools and were required for admission into colleges" well into the nineteenth century (Winterer 2002: 38). As Yota Batsaki has shown, "the choice of bilingual versions facing each other seems to subordinate the relationship between originality and faithful reproduction (the thorniest of issues in theories of translation) to a scheme of equivalence" (Batsaki 2002: 63). Rather than imagining the study of language and the act of translation as something that familiarizes the foreign, Forten revels in the possibility that language may defamiliarize the domestic and erode the very borders of linguistic distinction. This defamiliarization also points to the inadequacy of gendered tropes to account for this linguistic practice. Instead of engaging with mothers or mother tongues, Forten imagines queering the "Woman's Question." Forten's linguistic dualism exceeds the ontological categories of her engagement: the "Woman's Question" becomes addressed to a man (*mon ami* is in the masculine gender). The resulting translation is "queer" in that it unsettles our relationship to nationally bounded language and confounds the gendered trope of the mother tongue. The mother tongue is no longer a familiar certainty but an alien possibility.

That sense of translation's alien possibility was borne out by Noah Webster's 1828 definition of what it means to translate:

> translate: 1. to bear, carry, or remove from one place to another. ... 2. to remove or convey to heaven, as a human being, without death. 3. to transfer, to convey from one to another. 4. to cause or remove from one part of the body to another, as to translate a disease. 5. to change. 6. to interpret; to render into another language; to express the sense of one language in the words of another 7. to explain (Webster 1828)

Webster begins his definition with a literal sense of conveyance: translation means movement across space. The term has geopolitical (and as the fourth definition reminds us, biophysical) dimensions that make it akin to diaspora: translation marks a physical, bodily, at times pathological movement from one place to another. The second definition expands on this sense of removal but relinquishes the territoriality that adheres to diaspora. Instead, the second definition envisions an extra-territorial transcendence that extends beyond the physical to the spiritual realm. The cultural logic of translation, then, might surprise us for joining two seemingly incommensurate strands of American history and literature: by these first two definitions, the middle passage and transcendentalism are part of the same linguistic logic. If both initial definitions partake of geopolitical or religious power, and if the second definition establishes a vertical hierarchy, in the third definition, to translate becomes a way of imagining reciprocity between "one" and "another." Far from being repetitive or homogenizing, that reciprocity generates innovation (change) and exegesis (explanation and interpretation). This reciprocity also scrambles the ability to discern which component in this interpretive relationship is the original and which is the translation. Given his use of "one" and "another" in the third definition, Webster's sixth definition suggests that the act of translation does not replicate "one" at the cost of "another," but that on the contrary, the act of translation allows for the defamiliarization that comes with rendering "into another language" as opposed to rendering into one's own language. By Webster's definition, translation is not a movement of the foreign towards the familiar, but a movement from the familiar to the foreign.

Forten explores this insight and reminds us that in the Americas, "English" itself is always a dislocated language. Instead of imagining the nation in relation to itself, as contained by its own processes of mediation and its own structures of temporality and locality, Forten envisions a transatlantic nation that is in dialogue with others who remain geographically and temporally distant. Paradoxically, that distance is a prerequisite for the kind of intimacy she imagines, as becomes evident when Forten privileges translation as a form of mediation, but rejects the newly available global media. In a journal entry for August 17, 1858, Forten records:

> I suppose I ought to rejoice to-day for all the city seems to be rejoicing. The Queen's message arrived safely through the wonderful submarine telegram, the bells are pealing forth merrily. But I cannot rejoice that England, my beloved England should be brought so very near this wicked land. I tremble for the consequences, but I will hope for the best. Thank God for *Home!* (Forten 1988: 332)

Forten clearly desires a relationship with her "beloved England," but she worries about a mode of communication that makes what is distant proximate to "this wicked land." She rejects technologies of communication that familiarize what is foreign and wishes instead to defamiliarize the domestic scene. As with her queer translation, Forten imagines intimacy as an approximation but not an appropriation.

Yet how exactly Forten envisions geotemporal relationship seems enigmatic when she refers to "this wicked land" yet celebrates "home." Forten constructs the nation in transatlantic terms that echo Phillis Wheatley, whose work she greatly admired. As I indicated above, the term "transatlantic" came into use during the American Revolution. Samuel Johnson's dictionary does not include the word. The *Oxford English Dictionary* records the earliest use of "transatlantic" in 1779, when the word denoted a "passing or extending across the Atlantic Ocean" (Simpson et al. 1989). The term came to designate a location on the other side of the Atlantic when Thomas Jefferson asked in 1782 "whether nature has enlisted herself as a cis- or trans-Atlantic partisan" (Simpson et al. 1989). Although Jefferson uses the word to refer to Europe, "transatlantic" became a synonym for "American" in the late eighteenth century, when it meant "situated or resident in, or pertaining to a region beyond the Atlantic; chiefly in European use: = AMERICAN" (Simpson et al. 1989). As I discuss in chapter one, this dimension of the term emerged in the work of Phillis Wheatley — whom Jefferson summarily dismissed when he said that "Religion indeed has produced a Phyllis Whately [sic]; but it could not produce a poet" (Jefferson 1982: 140). Yet Wheatley's definition of the word evidently made it into the American vocabulary quickly. Noah Webster records the word in his 1828 dictionary, where "transatlantic" means

> lying or being beyond the Atlantic. When used by a person in Europe or Africa, transatlantic signifies being in America; when by a person in America, it denotes being or lying in Europe or Africa. We apply it chiefly to something in Europe. (Webster 1828)

The "transatlantic" imaginary enacts spatially what translation establishes linguistically: it envisions literature in relationship to an always distant yet ever proximate other. "Transatlantic" defines what is American and what it means to be in America. But if "transatlantic" is a synonym for American, American is not a synonym for "transatlantic." "Transatlantic" means "being in America" only when one is not in America; it defines a location that is always elsewhere. When one is in America, transatlantic no longer means being in America but being in Europe or Africa. The term operates in relation to and yet independent of any definitive locus; it is only secondarily a geographical marker, and first and foremost a term that defines geography as a space of relationships.

Instead of drawing on the transatlantic as a geographical term, then, I argue that we need to think of the transatlantic as a multilingual discourse. Drawing on Saskia Sassen's claim about spatiality and temporality, I suggest that transatlantic literature belongs "to both the global and the national, if only in part. This 'in part' is an especially important qualification, as in my reading the global is itself partial, albeit strategic .... the global and the national ... significantly overlap and interact ... the dynamics of interaction ....operate both within the global and the national and between them" (Sassen 2001: 260—1).[27] The term "transatlantic" provides a way of thinking space relationally, but frames those relationships unevenly: by Webster's definition, "transatlantic" privileges European-American connections over African-American and African-European contexts. The relationship between Europe and America becomes the primary relationship of cultural context and translation, and yet that context is haunted by the African translation — literally, by the middle passage, and metaphorically, by the way that violent displacement creates an extra-territorial literature.[28] Because translation is not just an object but also a process, it functions both as an instance of cultural relations, and as their political unconscious.[29]

The groundwork for an unsettling of linguistic exceptionalism has been laid through the efforts of Werner Sollors, Marc Shell, and the Longfellow Institute at Harvard University. They have published an anthology of American texts written in languages other than English, and two companion volumes of essays.[30] For the colonial period, a similar anthology exists (Castillo and Schweitzer 2001), with a companion essay collection (Castillo and Schwetizer 2005). Yet this interest in multilingualism raises the question how viable this model of American literature can be, given that even the most erudite individual reader has human limitations when it comes to the acquisition of languages. By locating multilingualism in translation, my work provides an answer to that problem without reifying English as the default language of American literature.

By imagining her relationship to England — and English itself — through geographic (the Atlantic) and linguistic (*mon ami*) distancing, Forten allows us to answer the question I raised above, and to imagine what multilingual unframing might look like when, through multilingualism and geotemporal displacement, the nation strains beyond its containable interpretative pluralism. Forten points to the immanence of the transatlantic in the national, and vice versa: the very concept of American literature emerges at the site of translation, and yet translation also continuously challenges and unsettles what we might mean by American literature.

III.

Given this interplay, it is evident that casting Forten's multilingual translation and Hawthorne's monolingual reproduction in antithetical terms belies their shared sense that language in general and translation in particular matter immensely for conceptualizing American literature. Different as their arguments about and use of language seem, Hawthorne and Forten are in fact working within the same literary frame: Hawthorne's fetishization of authenticity and Forten's acts of translation are not (only) opposites of but (also) supplements to one another. According to the model I have been tracing, translation is a general frame, a specific position within that frame, and a process that exceeds the positions within the frame. Useful as poststructuralist analysis is for understanding the complexities of translation, there are several problems with this theoretical model that the historical practice of translation allows us to address. If all language is in translation, then how can we distinguish literature that explicitly engages textual, linguistic and cultural alterity from literature that eliminates differences and constructs coherence? For all its investment in différance, the poststructuralist model of translation collapses diversity. The immanence of translation in originality, and vice versa of originality in translation, makes all alterity interior. That internalization of alterity becomes particularly troubling given the reliance of the Derridean model on Western allegories and biblical exegesis. Clearly this model itself is culturally specific in its universalizing claims. But precisely that recognition, that claims to universality are themselves culturally specific and reflect a particular position, is possible only from the vantage point of a historically produced understanding of translation that emerged in its full complexity in the time period this book considers.

In outlining the practices and ideologies of Western translation theory, Hugo Friedrich details three stages that he periodizes as Roman, Renaissance, and Romanticism. I demonstrate in the chapters that follow how these different models of translation spoke to and competed with one another in the American context. For the Romans, translation meant "the appropriation of the original without any real concern for the stylistic and linguistic idiosyncrasies of the original: translation meant transformation in order to mold the foreign into the linguistic structures of one's own culture" (Friedrich 1992: 12). This model of *translatio imperii et studii* amounted to a form of cultural domination in which scholarship went hand in hand with imperial appropriation.[31] In the only book-length study to date that examines the role translation plays in American cultural formation, Eric Cheyfitz defines translation in these terms, as a form of conquest, and Hawthorne has served in this introduction to exemplify how such a model operates.[32]

Useful as it is to point out how imperialism draws on translation, one cannot infer that all translation is imperialist. Friedrich reminds us that even the Romans had other models of translation that became particularly relevant when the Renaissance rediscovered the texts and methodologies of antiquity. The Romans also saw translation as "a contest with the original text," and from this second type of translation grew a desire to go "beyond the appropriation of content to a releasing of those linguistic and aesthetic energies that heretofore had existed only as pure possibility in one's own language and had never been materialized before" (Friedrich 1992: 13). As F. O. Matthiessen argued about the English Renaissance (Matthiessen 1931), this desire to enrich one's own language and culture became the primary aim of Renaissance translations. The Renaissance also developed a distinction between three different methodologies of cultural enhancement: John Dryden's preface to his Ovid translation became the *locus classicus* for the distinction between metaphrase, paraphrase, and imitation. In metaphrase, a translator attempts to reproduce the original as closely as possible by replicating its syntax, sounds, and word order, even if that means violating accepted standards of grammatical and literary correctness in English. In paraphrase, the translator tries to find English stylistic equivalents while generally maintaining the sense and, where compatible, the style of the original. In imitation, only a loose general outline of the original remains. All three of these strategies had for their primary aim the cultural enrichment of the language into which texts were translated, but they were aimed less at gaining an appreciation of the language and culture from which the translations were drawn.

During the Romantic period, the goal of translation shifted once again when "a totally new type of translation and of translation theory emerged that ran parallel to the increased tolerance of cultural differences" (Friedrich 1992: 14).[33] As Frederic Jameson has argued, "it is from 'Romanticism' itself in the most general sense ... that the concept of Comparative Literature springs in the first place" (Jameson 1987: 16). A new "respect for the foreign" emerged that made it possible for translation "to move toward the foreign — yet obviously not with the argument of *iure victoris*" (Friedrich 1992: 15). The importance of translation for Romantic literature has virtually been erased by accounts that universalize Hawthorne's postures of originality and argue for the "romantic dissociation of authenticity from imitation" (Giles 2002: 14). In practice, if not always in ideology, Romantic authors embraced translation. They found it desirable to adapt themselves to the linguistic subtleties of other languages, and saw translation as a source of innovation. Through this shift in translation strategies, untranslatability takes on a different meaning than the one Hawthorne gave it as pointing to a cultural essence. Instead, untranslatability marks the limitations of universalizing claims. Only when translation is not always already an act of imperial appropriation can the notion of a failed or incomplete translation exist.

This Romantic understanding of translation has most recently been adapted by Mary Louise Pratt (Thomas 2000: 5). Pratt questions the very telos of empire by suggesting that contact is always reciprocal, even where that reciprocity is uneven or denied. Drawing from linguistic theorists the concept of a "contact language," Pratt redefined colonial frontiers as "contact zones" in

> an attempt to invoke the spatial and temporal copresence of subjects previously separated by geographic and historical disjunctures, and whose trajectories now intersect. By using the term 'contact,' I aim to foreground the interactive, improvisational dimensions of colonial encounters so easily ignored or suppressed by diffusionist accounts of conquest and domination. A 'contact' perspective emphasizes how subjects are constituted in and by their relations to each other ... often within radically asymmetrical relations of power. (Pratt 1992: 6–7)

Useful as Pratt's definitions are, spatializing contact languages as contact zones generates two problems. First, Pratt does not allow us to imagine what contact would look like that was not personal and immediate, but contact that was impersonal and mediated. Meredith McGill's work on the culture of reprinting is particularly important for suggesting how contact occurs outside of zones, and in a print culture that is deeply national in its transnationalism and transnational in its nationalism (McGill 2003). Second, by locating contact and linguistic reciprocity in zones, Pratt's work ultimately homogenizes the cultural spaces that are beyond the zone of interaction. As Susan Friedman has pointed out, although Pratt "acknowledges the way in which the dominant culture is itself hybridized in the process of transculturation," her work "discusses hybridity only in the context of colonialism, focusing upon cultural exchanges in the contact zones characterized by asymmetrical power relations" (Friedman 1998: 91). My book argues that translation allows for the "dominant culture" itself to be hybridized and transculturated.

Amy Kaplan's recent work recognizes and redresses the problems that arise from locating transculturation exclusively in contact zones. She points out that "domestic and foreign spaces are closer than we think, and that the dynamics of imperial expansion cast them in jarring proximity" (Kaplan 2002: 1). Kaplan draws attention to the "ambiguities and contradictions of imperial relations in the formation of a national culture" to explore "how international struggles for domination abroad profoundly shape representations of American national identity at home, and how, in turn, cultural phenomena we think of as domestic or particularly national are forged in a crucible of foreign relations" (Kaplan 2002: 1). Kaplan's work is particularly useful for suggesting how contact occurs in nominally homogeneous cultural spaces that are far removed from direct zones of interaction. But Kaplan shares with Pratt the basic assumption that cultural relations occur within an imperial power matrix. By reclaiming contacts that are not recognizably imperial (such as the American fascination with German Romanticism), I ask how transnational models of world literature and of belletrism differ from or relate to explicitly imperialist and nationalist undertakings.

The writers on whom I focus were not located in Pratt's contact zones. For them, contact was mediated by print, and they acquired their multilingualism through literary study. The importance of multilingualism and translation for the American publishing industry seems almost incomprehensible from a contemporary American perspective. Currently, the relevance of translation to the publishing industry marks one of the central divisions between the United States and European countries: as the *New York Times* recently pointed out, citing the National Endowment for the Arts, "about 3 percent of the books published in the United States ... [are] translations, compared with 40 to 50 percent in Western European countries" (Salamon 2004). That statistic speaks to the way in which American literature has become nationalized as monolingual and self-referential, but it belies the profound relevance of multilingualism that informed American literature: between the passage of the first American copyright law in 1790 and the first international copyright laws in the 1890s, translations held a large market share in the American book trade that trumps current European statistics. By one estimate, translations from languages other than English and reprints of English works jointly held a market share of 70 percent in 1820 and 30 percent in 1850.[34] Even when the percentage in overall market share declined at mid-century, translations maintained pre-eminence in the book trade in that they regularly numbered among the best sellers in America: for example, translations of such French novels as Victor Hugo's *The Hunchback of Notre Dame* (1834), or Alexandre Dumas' *The Three Musketeers* (1844) achieved top sales.[35] Yet current accounts of the link between print and nation by and large overlook the historical relevance of multilingualism and translation and replicate instead our current association of print with nationalism.[36] Asking how our notion of U.S. nationalism might be different when we take these factors into account provides a way "to assess critically the construction of nationhood and regard the constitution of 'the United States' as the object of study in these investigations as a provisional way of denoting a national entity which is never historically stable nor innocent. It is obviously part of our goal to turn a self-reflexive eye at that formulation" (Desmond and Dominguez 1996: 488). Since translation itself is inherently comparatist, it provides a particularly useful way of turning that "self-reflexive eye" at American literature and for understanding the relevance that multilingual translation plays in the construction and the deconstruction of the nation.

Translation enables a field imaginary while also continually challenging the frames of that field. In that sense, translation enacts the kind of American literary studies that is no longer "founded upon the study of national cultures and their histories" (Rowe 2002: xiv) and yet can make sense of them. Benjamin Lee has articulated usefully how we can imagine a scholarly approach in which

> universals emerge only out of comparison, and cannot be grounded except through radical comparisons, that is, by looking for maximal differences within an analytic framework. Comparisons do not presuppose that any universals will necessarily emerge. Instead of universals, comparisons may disclose only a set of linkages. However, the fact that any judgment must be made 'somewhere' does not preclude the possibility of universals. Just as a comparative approach does not presuppose a non-empirical justification of relativism, since comparison may reveal some universal regularities in cultural form. ... A comparative approach does not assume either the existence of normative universals, or the unlimited critical power of relativism. (Lee 1995: 578–9)

My book embraces these paradoxes. This project's most ambitious aim is to redefine American literature as American translation, that is, to redescribe the very framework within which paradigms of American literature emerge. And yet I am deeply wary of my own claim that all American literature is translation because I do not want to erode the very process of differentiation (i.e., the translation and the transatlanticism) through which relativism and universalism become possible. For that reason, this book also has a far less ambitious agenda: I wish simply to recover translation as an area of American literary activity that has received little critical attention. This second aim is limited in scope. In discussing translation in this book, my concern has not been to provide a comprehensive overview of the translation activity that took place during my historical time frame; I have done so elsewhere (Boggs 2006). Here, I focus on translations that frame their projects in relation to a transatlantic, alphabetized print culture. My emphasis on alphabetized print culture explains why Native American traditions of oral translation are absent from my discussion. My aim has been to take up different theoretical, historical, linguistic cases to identify the conceptual problems of American literature that translation calls forth and addresses.

In chapter one, "Transatlantic education: Phillis Wheatley's neoclassicism," I take up the question to what extent translation establishes cultural parity, and what the racial and gendered limitations of that parity might be. I begin with Wheatley's invention of a transatlantic American literature and argue that she responded to the forceful loss of her African mother and mother tongue in the middle passage by acquiring not only English, but also Latin. For her, neoclassical translation provided a way of protesting the forceful exclusion of Africa from the transatlantic imaginary, and a means of authorizing herself as an American poet. I demonstrate that we must understand the transatlantic in relation to its lost maternal genealogies, but I also argue against figuring those losses as feminine in any essentialized way.

Writing in response to the emancipation of slaves in the West Indies (1807) and to the Missouri crisis (1820–1), James Fenimore Cooper envisioned the American frontier as a discursive site where transatlantic problems became negotiable.[37] Building on Wheatley's understanding of what it meant to lack a mother tongue, Cooper rejected the idea that language was genealogically conditioned, and conceptualized language through its translatability as non-essentialist and blended. Cooper located his vision of American literature in a theory of language that he drew from Adam Smith and the Celtic fringe novelists (especially Sir Walter Scott). By imagining translation as occurring in a "neutral ground" that is the linguistic analogue to Smith's "impartial spectator," Cooper invented an American literature whose cultural originality emerged in translation. As I show in chapter two, "The blanched Atlantic: James Fenimore Cooper's 'neutral ground,'" this model of cultural diversity leaves out those aspects of language and culture that are so specific as to resist translation. Under slavery, such anti-essentialism is itself a white privilege. Ultimately, Cooper performed a blanching of the Atlantic that, at its best, imagined translation as an egalitarian practice, and at its worst made translation a white prerogative.

Chapter three, "American world literature: Margaret Fuller's particular universality," takes up the question, raised by Cooper's novels, how cultural identity can emerge from the negotiation between universality and particularity. In response to theoretical challenges from Emerson, Fuller developed a model of empirical translation that protected national diversity and literary globalism from homogenizing universality. Fuller conceived of world literature in terms of constituent particulars that resisted wholeness. For Fuller, cultural identity was not solipsistically original but intimately relational, and translation was the linguistic equivalent of that contingency. Fuller developed a feminist strategy of fragmentation and a mode of reciprocity; translation enabled her to define cultural identity as a model of personhood that depends on a dialogue with others in a nation whose culture emerges in global contexts.

For literature to function as representative, some notion of exemplarity needs to exist. But how can there be exemplarity when language itself constantly shifts its representational contexts — when language and cultural relations are, as Fuller sees them, iterative and dialogic, not ontological and fixed? These questions about linguistic representation and literary exemplarity lie at the heart of Whitman's and Longfellow's engagement with translation. Chapter four, "Literary exemplarity: Walt Whitman's 'specimens,'" explores the contours of the unlikely attachment between translation and the American vernacular. Drawing on the discourse of a specific kind of literary anthology, the specimen collection, Longfellow and Whitman invoked and unsettled Emersonian paradigms of linguistic naturalism: they understood "specimens" by their botanical definition, as examples of variation within a given species, and conceptualized translation as representing the linguistic diversity within national genera.

The final chapter, "Intellectual property: Harriet Beecher Stowe's copyright" reexamines the argument — advanced most influentially be Benedict Anderson — that print, nationalism and monolingualism enable one another and go hand-in-hand. By examining the legal standing of translation under copyright law, I recover nineteenth-century attitudes towards print as a medium that facilitated transnational and multilingual dissemination. In 1852, Stowe sued F. W. Thomas in Circuit Court, claiming that the unauthorized German translations of *Uncle Tom's Cabin* (1852) that Thomas had published in *Die Freie Presse*, a Philadelphia newspaper, violated the legal property she held in her literary work. Whereas the history of her novel's circulation illustrates the importance of translation for the antebellum literary market, Stowe herself tried to restrict the free translation of her work. In *Uncle Tom's Cabin*, she developed a theory of national literature that hinged on iconic translation, a form of translation by which a text maintained its linguistic and national identity even as it passed into other languages. Stowe's theory was fraught with anxieties over the instability of texts and the effect that immigrants — among whom Stowe numbered slaves — would have on American literary identity. Stowe's lawsuit sought to redress those anxieties: she argued that national literature was inalienable, and that consequently Thomas' translation amounted to an unauthorized copy that infringed on her sales. The lawsuit called into question what it meant to think of print as a commodity, and pitted the circulation of books as fixed objects against the free linguistic circulation of ideas. Although Stowe lost her suit, the case inaugurated legal reforms that eventually ended the culture of translation I outline in this book.

The questions I pose in these chapters are admittedly grand: how are we to understand the "nature" of American literature and the metaphoricity of naturalizing claims in relation to the empirical existence of multilingualism? What role does exemplarity play for American literature in global contexts? How does language negotiate national identity, difference, diversity? As far as this book offers a grand historical narrative, that narrative argues that multilingual translation was once an integral part of American literature, and that historical changes in the educational, social, intellectual, and legal climate of America have obscured our understanding of its relevance as a cultural process. One way in which I locate that larger claim is by tracing throughout this book the theme of pedagogy. In the nineteenth century, a profound shift took place: whereas instruction in Latin and Greek had been and continued to be an important staple of university education, the languages of antiquity began competing in the 1820s with the modern languages for curricular space and academic resources. The study of literature was first introduced to students at American universities through the study of languages, and it is that nexus between language and literature that I investigate here. That nexus became lost to Americans and Americanists in the twentieth- and twenty-first centuries. As I discuss in a coda to the final chapter, the repressive language politics that were part of the xenophobic backlash against World War I had a lasting effect on the American pedagogical landscape. Although the Supreme Court eventually overturned laws prohibiting the instruction in languages other than English, the damage to American multilingualism that was done in the 1920s has been remarkably persistent, and has become further entrenched by the ongoing disputes over bilingual education. Although the authors whom I discuss in this work saw bi- and multilingualism as an important form of cultural capital, multilingualism is now largely stigmatized along racist lines that normalize Anglo-American linguistic exceptionalism: bilingualism is often treated as a scholarly deficiency. It is time to look at historically available alternatives to such restrictive definitions of what it means to be educated in America. If the chapters in this book amount to "only a set of linkages" (Lee 1995: 578–9), I hope that they follow Benjamin Lee's injunction that we articulate and offset universalizing aspirations. It is my hope that this work maintains the very fragmentation that allows for difference to be the hallmark of America's tremendous literary, linguistic, and cultural diversity.

1 Transatlantic education
Phillis Wheatley's neoclassicism

In *Beloved* (1988), a novel known for the lyrical beauty of its language, one of the most poignant moments occurs when Sethe tries to remember the stories her surrogate mother Nan told her about her enslaved, branded, dead African mother: "What Nan told her she [Sethe] had forgotten, along with the language she told it in. The same language her ma'am spoke and which would never come back. But the message—that was and had been there all along" (Morrison 1988: 66). In Morrison's historical recreation, the middle passage over the Atlantic stands for two deaths: the death of the mother accompanies the death of the mother tongue. Morrison imagines that Africans become African-American through the loss of African languages, whose use was forbidden in slave states, and which often died out with the first generation of African slaves. Yet even without remembering the language in which Nan spoke, Sethe recalls the language-transcending "message" passed on to her. In Morrison's account, the loss of African origins calls forth African-American translation: Sethe remembers stories whose originals are lost to her, and which exist only in her translation.[1] Like the ghosts that haunt 124 Bluestone Road, language is an absent-presence and a present-absence, continuously subject to mediations that invoke but never recover the lost mother and the lost mother tongue.

Morrison's novel lyrically captures the loss of African languages and the being-in-translation that inaugurated the poetry of Phillis Wheatley.[2] Like Sethe, Wheatley lost her mother's tongue (the language her mother spoke) and her mother tongue (the language she herself spoke in earliest childhood) in the middle passage. Consequently, the language in which Wheatley spoke and wrote, English, was an acquired secondary language that was always in translation from a lost linguistic original and a lost cultural origin. Unable to reverse or recover her losses, Wheatley experimented with translation to make those losses visible in a culture that relied on yet negated the horrors of the middle passage. Wheatley modeled her poem "On Being Brought from Africa to America" on contemporary dictionary definitions of translation. She explicated what it meant to be in English translation without recourse to non-English origins and originals, and argued that a larger cultural tautology constructed itself around the linguistic and ethnic occlusions of the middle passage. By portraying America as a site simultaneously of cultural knowledge and amnesia, Wheatley tried to offset the tautology and the teleology of the transatlantic voyage.

Figuring translation as a trope proved inadequate for Wheatley's construction of a cultural alternative. By learning a second language, Latin, Wheatley created a double translation — from a lost African original into English, and from Latin into English — that allowed her to relativize and contextualize English as one language among others. Writing neoclassical verse from the marginal position of "an Ethiop" opened up textual and theoretical space for linguistic proliferation. In poems such as "To Maecenas" and "Niobe in Distress for her Children slain by Apollo, from Ovid's Metamorphoses, Book VI. and from a view of the Painting of Mr. Richard Wilson," neoclassical translation provided a means for Wheatley to authorize herself as a poet. And yet her choice of Latin to achieve such ends should give us pause: what did Latin offer her? Latin offered Wheatley two things: as the language of antiquity, Latin enabled Wheatley to rewrite the racial politics of empire. As the site of eighteenth century pedagogical debates, Latin gave Wheatley the opportunity to participate in the subject formation normally reserved for white men. Wheatley drew on educational theories and translation practices to experiment with making language a field of contestation, in which definitions of identity and alterity were negotiated in racial, ethnic, and gendered terms. She made linguistic acquisition generally and translation specifically the locus of American literary formation. By practicing translation in a way that created cultural distance and linguistic difference, Wheatley developed a methodology of alienation and excess. By that methodology, she could imagine an American literature that — even when written in English — always remained partially foreign to itself and that allowed her to participate in yet remain estranged from Western discourse. In the process, she invented a transatlantic American literature that reflected the diversity of its differently empowered parts, and that figured the emerging nation as a site of global fracture and fragmentation.

I.

The letter from John Wheatley that accompanies Phillis Wheatley's *Poems on Various Subjects, Religious and Moral* (1773) catalogues the three stages of the young slave's education. Phillis Wheatley was "born on the West Coast of Africa, most probably along the Gambia River ca. 1753–1754" (Thomas 2000: 203). After being brought to America from Africa in 1761, as a seven-year-old child orphaned by slavery, Wheatley quickly, thoroughly, and without formal schooling "attained the English Language, to which she was an utter Stranger before" (Wheatley 1988: 6). Second, "her own Curiosity" prompted Wheatley to learn how to read and to write (Wheatley 1988: 6). Third, John Wheatley tells us, "she has great

Inclination to learn the Latin Tongue, and has made some Progress in it" (Wheatley 1988: 6)³ Throughout these linguistic initiations, Wheatley contemplated translation as a means of expressing her coerced losses, and as a tool for crafting her role in American letters. Wheatley's best-known and most often anthologized poem, "On Being Brought From Africa To America," commemorates the first stage of her education, her forceful entry into English, through a sustained meditation on what "to translate" means in English:

On Being Brought From Africa To America.

'TWAS mercy brought me from my *Pagan* land,
Taught my benighted soul to understand
That there's a God, that there's a *Saviour* too:
Once I redemption neither sought nor knew.
Some view our sable race with scornful eye,
"Their colour is a diabolic die."
Remember, *Christians, Negros*, black as *Cain*,
May be refin'd, and join th' angelic train.

> [written 1768; listed in her 1772 book proposal as "Thoughts on Being Brought From Africa to America;" published in the 1773 *Poems on Various Subjects Religious and Moral*]

This poem explicates what it means to translate. According to Noah Webster's *Dictionary* (1828), the verb "to translate" carried the following definitions:

> 1. to bear, carry, or remove from one place to another. ... 2. to remove or convey to heaven, as a human being, without death. 3. to transfer, to convey from one to another. 4. to cause or remove from one part of the body to another, as to translate a disease. 5. to change. 6. to interpret; to render into another language; to express the sense of one language in the words of another 7. to explain (Webster 1828)

Webster could have drawn this definition from a reading of Wheatley's poem, so closely do the two texts parallel one another. Webster begins his definition with a literal sense of conveyance: translation means movement across space. The term has geographical (and as the fourth definition reminds us, biophysical) dimensions that define translation as a physical, bodily, at times pathological movement "from one place to another." That teleological movement for Wheatley seems to be the middle passage: she describes what it means to be "brought from Africa to America." Her poem's title captures the sense of removal from one place to another that Webster outlines; it reads the middle passage as a translation in the geographical and physical sense of that term.

But the title's investment in geography is at odds with the poem's original title and its opening lines. Wheatley charts the middle passage as an initiation into a new kind of knowledge. Her original title, "Thoughts On Being Brought From Africa To America," reflects her emphasis on cognition by invoking "thoughts" on the middle passage rather than the literal transportation Wheatley experienced. The content of the poem bears out this desire to see translation first and foremost in cognitive and didactic terms. In the poem itself, Wheatley is not "brought from Africa to America." Instead, she is brought from her "*Pagan* land" to be "taught" and "to understand" — the expected reference to America is missing here. The poem reconfigures the transatlantic voyage, and turns it from a geographical movement into an intellectual process. America is not a place, but an episteme for Wheatley.

Wheatley's poem investigates what kind of episteme America is, and inquires into the tropological construction of that episteme. In the poem's opening lines, translation becomes Wheatley's trope for troping.[4] Wheatley is experimenting with two genres, the conversion narrative and the captivity narrative that both hinge on the word "redemption" as a trope for translation. She portrays the middle passage as a process of coming "to understand" what it means for the "benighted soul" to seek "redemption." Her religious imagery plays with the idea that to translate means, in Webster's second definition, "to remove or convey to heaven, as a human being, without death." Read as a conversion narrative, Wheatley's poem defines translation as spiritual salvation. And yet Wheatley ties that notion of spiritual transcendence to her own reification in the verbal economy of empire. According to the *Oxford English Dictionary*, redemption is not only a religious term that denotes "deliverance from sin and its consequences by the atonement of Jesus Christ" (Simpson, Weiner, and Oxford University Press 1989) The word also refers to "the action of freeing a prisoner, captive, or slave by payment; ransom," and denotes "the fact of obtaining a privileged status, or admission to a society, by means of purchase" (Simpson et al. 1989). By invoking this second aspect of redemption, Wheatley demonstrates that the verbal economy of slavery draws on the register of spirituality to turn her into chattel. Wheatley's status as a captive in need of redemption tropes on Webster's third definition of translation: she can be transferred or conveyed from one owner to another. In the closing lines of her poem, Wheatley teases out the logic of this verbal economy. As James Levernier has pointed out, her references to "die," "Negros," and "Cain" designate the indigo dye, slaves, and sugarcane that were exchanged in the transatlantic trade between North America, Africa, and the West Indies (Levernier 1981: 25–6). Wheatley makes clear that, in the instances where it is a reified form, the trope is itself complicit with the slave system.

Wheatley's poem demonstrates that the logic of her captivity — that is, the logic of the reified trope — depends on the ability of English to function as a self-referential episteme by occluding other languages. In the second half of her poem, she explicates what it means to be in English translation without recourse to other languages. In lines 5–6, ("Some view our sable race with scornful eye,/'Their colour is a diabolic die'"), Wheatley shifts the vocal register of her poem from a first person individual voice ("brought me," "taught my," "once I") to a third person collective perspective ("some," "their," "Christians, Negros"). She uses a direct quote to represent the shift to a collective discourse and to a discourse of collectivity. Direct citation was one of Wheatley's favorite strategies, and she drew on it to accomplish three goals.[5] One, citation inscribes orality within print culture and allows both to coexist. That coexistence disrupts the linear move from orality to literacy that John Wheatley outlines as part of Wheatley's educational "Progress." Two, although translation is always implicitly citational, direct quotation draws attention explicitly to the citationality of all language. Third, direct citation makes visible the linguistic construction of cultural epistemologies. In this poem, she uses the quote to demonstrate how an ascriptive racism uses language to objectify (through the materiality of "die") and demonize slaves (refers to them as "diabolic"). For Wheatley, such racism depends on epistemes that are linguistically self-referential.

She establishes this linguistic self-referentiality in the next lines: "Remember, *Christians, Negros*, black as *Cain*, / May be refin'd, and join th' angelic train." Wheatley demonstrates what it means to be in English translation without recourse to non-English origins and originals. The line is poignant for its use of the word "remember," which portrays America simultaneously as a site of cultural knowledge and amnesia. The remembrance that Wheatley invokes here is not one of her home in Africa, nor of her voyage across the Atlantic. What she remembers is the need for redemption, in both senses I outlined above. She is in need of redemption by virtue of being a slave cut off from any other kind of remembrance. She does not "remember" so much as remind Christians of their own preachings. These lines are powerful as a moment of inversion, where she is turning around the conversion imposed on her. But ultimately, her intervention into racism exhausts itself in reminding her readers of their own tropological investments. Exploring what "to translate" means in English inscribes Wheatley within the very hermeneutic circles she critiques. She shows that a larger cultural tautology constructs itself around the linguistic and ethnic occlusions of the middle passage.

In response to this problem, Wheatley again shifts the register of what she means by translation. Her inability to step outside her construction as a slave hinges on her entrapment within a linguistic system that has turned translation into a self-referential and reifying enterprise. What seems to be missing from the poem is Webster's definition by which to translate means "to render into another language; to express the sense of one language in the words of another" (Webster 1828). Given that Wheatley has outlined America's epistemic construction in English, that part of Webster's definition raises the possibility that a shift in language will go hand in hand with an epistemic shift. By his definition, to translate becomes a way of imagining reciprocity between "one" and "another." Far from being repetitious or homogenizing, that reciprocity generates innovation (change) and exegesis (explanation and interpretation). This reciprocity also scrambles the ability to discern which component in this interpretive relationship is the original and which is the translation. Webster's definition suggests that the act of translation does not replicate "one" at the cost of "another," but that on the contrary, the act of translation allows for the defamiliarization that comes with rendering "into another language" as opposed to rendering into one's own language. By Webster's definition, translation is not a movement of the foreign towards the familiar, but a movement from the familiar to the foreign.

If epistemes are linguistically constructed, then invoking another episteme will challenge the meaning that "words" carry in constructing the language of "another." Wheatley imagines just such a possibility when she suggests at the end of her poem that she could become "refin'd" and "join th' angelic train." By "train," she presumably means a host of angels: according to the *Oxford English Dictionary*, a train is the "succession of persons" (Simpson et al. 1989). But the odd expression, "angelic train," also enables another reading. The word "train" means "training, education" (Simpson et al. 1989), and with the adjective "angelic," the expression comes to mean training in divinity. So Wheatley ends her poem by requesting a particular educational training. That reading is substantiated by her desire to become "refin'd": the word tropes on refining sugar cane but also imagines that educational training provides an as yet unspecified escape from such reified tropes.

The connections I am drawing here will seem tenuous for now, especially since Wheatley does not work them out in this particular poem, but in her other works. It will not be immediately apparent how her desire to be "refin'd" and "join the angelic train" fits in with translation in Webster's definition of a relationship between languages, nor how such translation can reform Wheatley's subjectivity and allow her to reclaim the memories of her losses, from which translation in English separates her. It will be the task of the next section to establish those connections in a broader cultural and historical context, before I return specifically to Wheatley's Latin translations in the final section of this chapter.

II.

Much has been made of Wheatley's examination by a group of Boston's elite, and in the context of eighteenth century racist ideology, the implications of that examination seem all too clear. But little attempt has been made to understand that scene in its broader social context, by which

Wheatley was actually not singled out as much as admitted to a certain type of pedagogical examination — especially if, as Henry Louis Gates speculates, she was asked "to conjugate a verb in Latin or even to translate randomly selected passages from the Latin" (Wheatley 1988: viii). Having to prove one's linguistic ability was standard procedure in academic circles. In the eighteenth century, students "translated, turning Latin into English and then English back into Latin" (Winterer 2002: 11) as early as grammar school. Students entering Harvard "had to demonstrate their ability to 'read Tully [Cicero], or such like classicall Latine Author ex tempore & make & speak true Latin in verse & prose, suo (ut aiunt) Marte' [by his own exertions]" (Winterer 2002: 12).[6] By demonstrating "great Inclination to learn the Latin Tongue," and making "some Progress in it" (Wheatley 1988: 6), Wheatley created for herself an opportunity usually afforded only male, white entrants into Harvard.

But Wheatley was also subject to an examination that such white Harvard men would not have the opportunity to undergo for another century: by being asked to demonstrate her understanding of versification, she was the first person to sit for an examination in English literature at an American institution of higher learning. Wheatley not only discredited the racist assumption that slaves lacked the linguistic and reasoning abilities manifest in her poems. Her performance also admitted vernacular literature into the academy and was the harbinger of a significant shift in educational policy. Bill Readings has argued that modern university education underwent three phases: it was guided by "the Kantian concept of reason, the Humboldtian idea of culture, and now the techno-bureaucratic idea of excellence" (Readings 1996: 14). Phillis Wheatley stood at the nexus of this educational investment in reason and culture. By pointing to the tension between universalizing claims and racist exclusions in poems such as "On Being Brought from Africa to America," she demonstrated that reason was itself a cultural performance. Her examination was the first instance of the university's explicit engagement with an "idea of culture" (Readings 1996: 15), in "the dual sense of culture as both product and process, as general object and individual cultivation" (Readings 1996: 74). By that very token, the culture that enters the academy with Wheatley cannot be understood exclusively in relation to "the production and circulation of national self-knowledge" (Readings 1996: 15): Wheatley inscribed the emerging nation's culture within the contexts of its transatlantic slave trade.

Wheatley's double examination in Latin and in English situates her at the fulcrum of educational changes in colonial America, changes in which cultural subjectivity was being negotiated in its individual and collective, as well as its national and transatlantic contexts. In his *Thoughts Concerning Education* (1693), John Locke had offered something very appealing to American reformers: a means of acquiring an independent cultural subjectivity through acts of translation. Locke had taken up the question of what constituted a mother tongue, and had argued that it was not biologically determined (by the mother's tongue) but socially transformative (by one's acclimatization to or deliberate acquisition of a mother tongue). He had suggested that learning a foreign language should be like learning a mother tongue: instead of teaching students grammar, he believed they should learn a language by hearing it spoken, or when that was not possible (as in the case of Latin) by reading and themselves writing literal translations (Locke 1968: 267–83). Arguing that languages should be studied comparatively through translation so as to produce an analytically discerning intellectual subject, Locke had made linguistic circulation crucial for "typifying the acts of understanding in which ... [he] had anchored consent, the political principle by which a people forms and authorizes its government" (Brown 2001: 4). Locke's pedagogical philosophy sparked a debate among educators that revolved around two questions: one, whether modern languages (among them English) should be taught as separate subjects alongside the ancient languages (especially Latin) that dominated curricula, and two, what methodology — instruction in grammar or memorization by means of translation — should be adopted for teaching languages. Pedantic as these questions may seem, at stake in this discussion was the formation of American cultural subjectivity, and the production of American cultural memory. Both hinged on understanding the importance of multilingualism and of translation as a multilingual methodology.

For us, the Classics have become synonymous with canonicity, that is, with a set of literary objects that claim to hold universal humanist appeal. But for the eighteenth century, the Classics were first and foremost a discipline of linguistic instruction that had come to serve two purposes by the time of Wheatley's writing: one, it made accessible linguistically remote intellectual content, and two, it elicited cultural innovation as translators expressed foreign content in their own linguistic contexts. John Locke's educational philosophy achieved wide circulation through the efforts of John Clarke (1687–1734) and Benjamin Franklin (1709–1790). Clarke published textbooks for language instruction based on Lockean methods of translation. His works enjoyed tremendous success in America, with the third edition of *Corderii Coloquiorum centuria selecta* appearing in 1724, and the twentieth edition appearing in 1770. He remarked at the comparative ease with which boys attained modern languages by translation, and he complained that they were taught Latin by grammatical instruction. Clarke commented on the "Want of [...] Literal Translations" in Latin classes, and argued that language education would be rendered "more Easy and Delightful" by providing a "Literal Translation of the easier Authors in the Latin Tongue for the Use of Beginners" (Clarke 1724: i–ii). Clarke went on to specify what he understood by literal translation: he argued for publishing "the Latin and English each in their distinct Pages or Columns. For whilst the Latin Words are in the same Order with the English, and the corresponding Words in each Language in the same Character, the Scholar is in no danger of mistaking" one for the other (Clarke 1724: iii). Although in Clarke's textbooks the modern English texts translated the ancient Latin texts, for English-speaking students, the English text was the primary text from which they turned to the Latin. For a student first coming to these texts, this publishing practice reversed the relationship between original and derivation, and turned the Latin into the translation of the English text. Yet as students worked increasingly to gain competency in Latin, the English text could also become the secondary text, read after the Latin text, and critiqued for its successes and failures by the standards of the Latin. With Latin and English eliciting one another, and with texts translated into English but also into neo-Latin, Clarke turned language into a relationship.

Evidently, Benjamin Franklin was quite familiar with these practices: he composed the manuscript of his memoirs in the fashion outlined by Clarke. He divided his manuscript sheets in half along vertical axis, then drafted text on one side of the crease, leaving the other side blank (Looby 1986: 89). Like Clarke, Franklin thus created textual space for the kind of juxtaposition requisite for linguistic comparison and innovation. Franklin was among the most prominent public figures to elevate Locke's language theory into a programmatic call for educational reform. In his essay on "The Education of Youth in Pensilvania [sic]" (1749), Franklin took up the first question raised by Locke's writing, which languages should be taught, ancient or modern, and to what end. Franklin argued that

> all intended for Divinity, should be taught the *Latin* and *Greek*; for Physick, the *Latin, Greek*, and *French*, for Law, the *Latin* and *French*; Merchants, the *French, German*, and *Spanish*; and though all should not be compelled to learn *Latin, Greek*, or the modern Languages, yet none that have an ardent Desire to learn them should be refused; their *English*, Arithmetic, and other studies absolutely necessary, being at the same time not neglected. (Franklin 1936: 204–5)[7]

Franklin's recommendations distinguish three educational purposes. One, he concerns himself with the training of professionals (clergymen, doctors, lawyers) for whom Latin is important. Wheatley's examination situates her in this group and its engagement with the discourse of reason. Two, he thinks about the utility of languages for merchants, and reveals what he saw to be the predominant trade and language patterns by emphasizing the importance of French, German, and Spanish. But third, departing from Locke, Franklin moves away from a purely utilitarian understanding of language training when he imagines that nobody with "an ardent Desire to learn" should be prevented from acquiring a language. By revealing "great inclination" to learn Latin, Wheatley participates in this belletristic language study, and situates herself in relation to a cultural desire.

Nominally, his trade as a printer explains Franklin's interest in language study. Situated in the heavily Germanophone port city of Philadelphia, multilingualism was a commercial necessity for Franklin. His imprint appeared for the first time on a German book, the *Mystische und Sehr Geheyme Sprueche* by Conrad Beissel (Winterich 1935: 83), and publications in languages other than English at times made up the bulk of Franklin's trade. For instance in the year 1742, Franklin published a total of nineteen books, eleven in German, six in English, and one in Latin.[8]

Franklin made a name for himself as a printer and laid out his cultural agenda with the translations he published. *M.T. Cicero's Cato Major, or his discourse of old-age* (1744) was immensely popular, judging by the reprints that appeared in London (1750; 1778), Glasgow (1751; 1758), and Philadelphia (1758; ca. 1812) (Campbell 1918). Franklin articulated in this work a vision of the transatlantic culture he imagined would emerge from multilingualism in general and from translation in particular. In his foreword to the text, Franklin refers to the publication as the "first Translation of a *Classic* in this *Western World*," and expresses the hope that it "may be followed with many others, performed with equal Judgment and Success; and be a happy Omen, that *Philadelphia* shall become the Seat of the *American* Muses" (Logan 1744: v–vi).[9] By imagining that the publication of this translation makes Philadelphia the "seat of the *American* Muses," Franklin argues that translation inaugurates American literary creativity. And yet such a claim seems paradoxical: if translation is on some level a textual repetition, how does Franklin work out his relationship to originality?

To answer that question, we must take up Franklin's engagement with the second concern raised by Locke's writing. Franklin considered very carefully what methodology was appropriate for language study, and in the process revised the concept of *literal* translation. In his most sustained reflection on languages and translation, his posthumously published *Memoir* (1791) now known as the *Autobiography of Benjamin Franklin*, Franklin explores questions of linguistic methodology in two ways.[10] Much like Wheatley, he examines the importance of memory for his English compositions, and he develops a process of translation that draws on other languages to achieve epistemic innovation.

When he records his experimentation with English prose style, Franklin describes a process of methodological and linguistic inquiry:

> About this time I met with an odd Volume of the *Spectator*. [...] I thought the Writing excellent, and wish'd if possible to *imitate* it. With that View, I took some of the Papers, and making short Hints of the Sentiment in each Sentence, laid them by a few Days, and then without looking at the Book, try'd to compleat the Papers again, by expressing each hinted Sentiment at length and as fully as it had been express'd before, in any suitable Words, that should come to hand. Then I compar'd my Spectator with the Original, discover'd some of my Faults and corrected them. But I found I wanted a Stock of Words or a Readiness in recollecting and using them, which I thought I should

have acquir'd before that time, if I had gone on making Verses, since the continual Occasion for Words of the same Import but of different Length, to suite the Measure, or of different Sound for the Rhyme, would have laid me under a constant Necessity of searching for Variety, and also have tended to fix that Variety in my Mind, and make me Master of it. Therefore, I took some of the Tales and turn'd them into Verse [...] By comparing my work afterwards with the original, I discover'd many faults and amended them; but I sometimes had the Pleasure of Fancying that in certain Particulars of small Import, I had been lucky enough to improve the Method or the Language and this encourag'd me to think I might possibly in time come to be a tolerable English Writer, of which I was extreamly [sic] ambitious. (Franklin 1964: 62)

Like Wheatley and like Morrison's Sethe, Franklin imagines an initiation into a language that is not his own. Franklin marks down "short Hints of the Sentiment in each Sentence," and thus records the language-transcending message of the text. After an interval, he tries to express that message in language that is newly varied. The language itself undergoes a transformation in the process of composition, and that transformation constitutes both a linguistic and methodological improvement. The very act of textual repetition for Franklin is tied to a sense of linguistic mastery from which originality emerges.

With over fourteen editions of Franklin's work published before 1800, the *Autobiography* achieved this kind of originality in that it became a paradigmatic text for the literary formation not only of an individual but also collectively of the young republic. As Christopher Looby has argued, the *Autobiography* is

in large part an explicit record of an individual's accession to language. However, because Franklin claims a representative status for himself, presenting his life as an allegory of American national experience, it is also an account of the nation's self-constitution in language. For just as Franklin encountered language as the vehicle of a social given — a complete system of relationships and values, a symbolic order into which he was required to enter in order to acquire individuality — so too did the American colonies struggle to achieve, largely by means of rhetorical assertions and semantic transformations upon a previously existing system, the singularity and autonomy that are, for nations as well as persons, largely the effects of language. (Looby 1986: 73)

Useful as Looby's claim is for assessing the intersection between linguistic and cultural construction, his argument needs to be revised by a crucial semantic shift. For Franklin, "language" was not a single semantic system, nor did "language" and the nation constitute one another. Instead,

Franklin thought of languages, in the plural, in terms that relied heavily on multilingual translation, and the *Autobiography* imagined literature — and conceived of itself as literature — in transatlantic contexts.

Whereas Locke had advocated the use of literal translation as a pedagogical tool, Franklin developed a methodology of paraphrastic translation. Thereby, he situated himself in relation to the guidelines that John Dryden had established in the *locus classicus* of neoclassical translation theory, the preface to his translation of *Ovid's Epistles* (1680). Dryden had distinguished between three categories of translation:

> First, that of metaphrase, or turning an author word by word, and line by line, from one language into another. [...] The second way is that of paraphrase, or translation with latitude, where the author is kept in view by the translator, so as never to be lost, but his words are not so strictly followed as his sense; [...] The third way is that of imitation, where the translator (if now he has not lost that name) assumes the liberty, not only to vary from the words and sense, but to forsake them both as he sees occasion. (Dryden 1992: 17)

For Dryden, the only form of translation permissible from a literary perspective is paraphrase. He argued that "it would be unreasonable to limit a translator to the narrow compass of the author's words" so as to hinder his own freedom of expression (Dryden 1992: 21). But Dryden was also attentive to the fact that equal freedom be afforded the translated author: by means of paraphrase, he believed, "the spirit of an author may be transfused, and yet not lost; [...] for thought, if it be translated truly, cannot be lost in another language" (Dryden 1992: 21). That liberty in Dryden's description simultaneously invokes the translated author as a ghostly specter, and contributes to the translator's formation as a linguistically independent subject. Dryden explicitly figures such translation as an act of resistance against slavery. He writes that translation is an "art so very useful to an enquiring people, and for the improvement and spreading of knowledge, which is none of the worst preservatives against slavery" (Dryden 1992: 30). By Dryden's argument, paraphrastic translation was the paradigmatic methodology for establishing liberated subjectivity while granting others that same freedom.

Franklin picked up on that argument when he engaged with the importance of linguistic plurality and translation in the *Autobiography*. In his recollection of his language study in the 1730s, Franklin writes:

> I soon made myself so much a Master of the French as to be able to read the Books with Ease. I then undertook the Italian. An Acquaintance who was also learning it, us'd often to tempt me to play Chess with him. ... I at length refus'd to play any more, unless on this Condition, that the Victor in every Game, should have a Right to impose a Task

either in Part of the Grammar ... or in Translation, &c. ... As we play'd pretty equally we thus beat one another into that Language. I afterwards with a little Painstaking acquir'd as much of the Spanish as to read their Books also. ... which encouraged me to apply my self again to the Study of it [Latin, which he had briefly studied as an adolescent], and I met with the more Success as those preceding Languages had greatly smooth'd my Way. (Franklin 1964: 168)

Franklin, who visited Phillis Wheatley in London in 1773, casts his description in terms and imagery that closely resemble the account John Wheatley gives of her.[11] As Franklin describes his acquisition of linguistic and literary skill, he infantilizes himself through his repeated references to "play." Whereas play is originally a temptation, Franklin's refusal "to play any more" transforms chess, a game that pits black and white figures in a game of strategic opposition, into a form of enforced labor. That labor is cast in terms of violence: he and his partner "*beat* one another into that Language," and his acquisition is "*Pains*taking." If Franklin casts himself in the role of the slave child, he also portrays translation as a means to emancipatory, intellectual mastery. Surprisingly, the violence described in this scene is reciprocal in that Franklin and his partner "Play'd pretty *equally*" and "beat *one another*" into an understanding of Italian. By submitting to the role of the slave child, Franklin imagines a transformation of that role: he understands the relationship between language acquisition and literacy in terms of a process by which he makes himself "a Master," that is, an autonomous person who reads books in multiple languages. That process centrally hinges on translation, as a mode of language practice and acquisition. John Wheatley's account of Phillis literalizes this trope of language acquisition: if Franklin metaphorically infantilizes and enslaves himself, Phillis is literally the slave child who reads English and Latin.

Franklin's passage anticipates by over one hundred years Ferdinand de Saussure's use of chess in the *Course in General Linguistics* (1915). Saussure avails himself of a comparison with chess to explain the difference between internal and external linguistics, that is, between synchronic language states and diachronic language development. In the *Course in General Linguistics,* he writes that

> in chess, what is external can be separated relatively easily from what is internal. The fact that the game passed from Persia to Europe is external; against that, everything having to do with its stem and rules is internal. If I use ivory chessmen instead of wooden ones, the change has no effect on the system; but if I decrease or increase the number of chessmen, this change has a profound effect on the 'grammar' of the game. One must always distinguish between what is internal and what is external. In each instance one can determine the nature of the

phenomenon by applying this rule: everything that changes the system in any way is internal. (Saussure 1959: 22–3)

Franklin's passage anachronistically adds an important dimension to Saussure's comparison. Instead of focusing on chess as a system and bracketing questions of intentionality, as Saussure does, Franklin focuses on the players' subjectivity and their relationship to language. By casting the game of chess, that is, Saussure's very image for synchronic linguistics, in terms of a master-slave dialectic, Franklin points to the violence that is implicit in "language-states"(Saussure 1959: 81) — an expression that I read to refer also to state-languages, since Saussure's expression in French (*états de langue*) bears out that reading. Franklin points out that the linguistic game does not occur only between equal chess partners, but also along an emerging power differential. Yet Franklin wants to subvert that differential: the loser, abjected as a slave, becomes the linguistic master.[12]

That mastery seems to be part as much of the game's external as its internal relationships. Franklin had written an essay "On the Morals of Chess" (1779), that explicitly imagined what Saussure describes as the external dimension of chess. The essay continued to be reproduced in chess manuals such as George Walker's *The Chess Player* (1840) well into the nineteenth century. For Franklin, chess was a cultural artifact shared between individual players and different countries. Franklin claimed that "Chess is the most ancient and most universal game among men; for its origin is beyond the memory of history, and it has, for numberless ages, been the amusement of all civilized nations of Asia, the Persians, the Indians, and the Chinese. Europe has had it above a thousand years; the Spaniards have spread it over their part of America, and it begins lately to make its appearance in these States" (Walker 1840: 7). Franklin antiquates chess while refusing to produce a narrative of origins: it is "most ancient" and "most universal" precisely because it does not have an originary moment in time but emerges from the "beyond" of "memory" and "history."

As a cultural artifact, Franklin locates chess and language in a "beyond" that resonates with Homi Bhabha's conceptualization of that term as "neither a new horizon, nor a leaving behind of the past. … What is theoretically innovative, and politically crucial, is the need to think beyond narratives of originary and initial subjectivities and to focus on those moments or processes that are produced in the articulation of cultural differences" (Bhabha 1994: 1). By Franklin's account, translation becomes the privileged mode of what Bhabha calls the "interstitial passage between fixed identifications … [and] the possibility of a cultural hybridity that entertains difference without an assumed or imposed hierarchy" (Bhabha 1994: 4). Bhabha celebrates that site of difference as one of connection. His emphasis on hybridity adapts Derrida's concept of "*différance*." Derrida uses *différance* to explain the synchronic relationships between signs, that is, the way in which they *differ* from each other, but he also points to the diachronic way in which they constantly *defer* significance to what he calls the "becoming-sign" (Derrida 1997: 47) of the symbol. Derrida conceptualizes this process through the image of the hinge. For Derrida, the hinge has a double meaning: it is not just the joint, but also the break, the brisure, the "breach, crack, fracture, fault, split, fragment" (Derrida 1997: 65).

Franklin does not privilege a sense of hybridity but one of profound cultural alienation, and sees the hinge to be functioning as a break. When he imagines his knowledge of Italian to be the result of his game, he ironizes an opposition that does not result so much in dialectic resolution or a Hegelian *Aufhebung* as in a linguistic acquisition that is simultaneously a linguistic alienation. Franklin turns a binary language game into the site of knowledge that exceeds its own dialectic, where language functions as both the mark of that binary relationship and the marking of its excess. Moreover, Franklin applies this concept of the brisure, of the fragment, to the linguistic subject he imagines. Instead of thinking merely of himself as a student of language, he imagines two students of language.

I want to read that doubling along the lines that Michael Warner proposes in his discussion of Franklin's "Remarks Concerning the Savages of North-America" (1783). Warner insists that Franklin critiques "two elements that have been taken as central to modernity: the self-present individual and Western progress. With its dependence on custom and mediation, Franklin's politeness refuses the usual transcendence of reason. ... Because the other *is* the reference of your being, you are both strangers" (Warner 1993: 87). Franklin imagines a relationship not between self and other, but between other and other. Because the subjects who acquire foreign languages through translation are themselves fragmented, language and subjectivity exceed both a narrative of origins and a telos. Translation draws on both, and yet becomes neither; it is a profoundly alien third category, a *tertium quid*.

III.

In paraphrastic translations such as "To Maecenas" and "Niobe in Distress for her Children slain by Apollo, from Ovid's Metamorphoses, Book VI. and from a view of the Painting of Mr. Richard Wilson," Wheatley invented a transatlantic American literature that reflected the diversity of its differently empowered parts through an act of triangulation. By learning a second foreign language, Latin, in addition to English, Wheatley created a double translation that could address the loss of her African home *as a loss*. According to educators like Locke and Franklin, acquiring a foreign language by means of translation was *like* acquiring a mother tongue. But for Wheatley, this educational simile had no referent: as someone who no longer had a mother tongue, acquiring a language *like* a mother tongue made loss the simile's referent. Yet the very notion that one could acquire more than one language as one would acquire a mother tongue also held out the possibility of addressing that loss by creating a relationship among simulacra. For Wheatley, translation amounted to an originality of lost origins that in her poetry shaped the memories and cultural subjectivities of the transatlantic.

Wheatley enacts, theorizes, and thematizes the translation between languages for us throughout her extant writing. In an early letter to the Countess of Huntington, dated 25 October 1770, Wheatley writes on the occasion of the Reverend Mr. Whitefield's death: "The Tongues of the Learned are insufficient, much less the pen of an untutor'd African, to paint in lively character the excellencies of this Citizen of Zion!" (Wheatley 1988: 162). The sentence sets up and deconstructs a set of binary pairs: the "Tongues" and the "pen," the "Learned" and the "untutor'd," the "African" and the "Citizen." Wheatley marks her supposed insufficiency by comparing the "tongues," that is, the act of speaking as well as a multiplicity of languages, to the "pen," that is, the act of writing as well as the ability to write. That comparison not only reverses the trope by which orality is the slave's provenance and by which literacy is the master's domain; Wheatley also invents an aporia that hinges on translation. The contrast between "Learned" and "untutor'd" emphasizes language acquisition. The "tutor" whom Wheatley lacks is precisely the person who would have instructed her in the classical languages – in the tongues of the learned. And yet his absence points not so much to a lack of mastery on her part, but to the absence of a master. She is untutor'd in the sense that she is her own linguistic master. The "Tongues of the Learned" that are insufficient turn out to be Wheatley's own: she herself knows those languages just as she knows how to write. Nominally, Wheatley has the skills of a cultural subject, yet they prove "insufficient": she examines the relationship between language and the politics of subject formation when she imagines being able to "paint" a "character," or rather, not being able to paint the character of a "Citizen." Instead of being a "Citizen," she is an "African" slave who is barred from citizenship, but who imagines translation between languages as a way of participating in the discourse of subject formation. The translation that she cannot perform is Whitefield's religious translation, that is, his "removal from earth to heaven, *orig*. without death, as the translation of Enoch" (Simpson et al. 1989). It is such religious translation, that is, such a transcendence of the linguistic into a realm of pure signification, that Wheatley cannot produce upon the occasion of Whitefield's death. Instead of embracing a model of transcendence in which differences and particularities no longer matter, she indicates in this passage the difficulty and necessity of producing translation in a realm of fragmented and differential signification. In this letter, then, Wheatley points to her insufficiency in religious translation but also privileges linguistic translation over other kinds of translation.

For Wheatley, linguistic translation must engage with but can never draw on her African mother tongue. By casting herself as an "untutor'd African" removed from "Zion," Wheatley emphasizes her alienation from both the African and the American context. She maintains that alienation throughout her writing, but transforms it into a position of transatlantic subjectivity. Her earliest biographer, Margaretta Matilda Odell, inaugurated a long line of attempts to repatriate and reparent Wheatley. Odell wanted to recover African sun rituals in Wheatley's poetry, and wished to link them to Wheatley's memories of her mother (Odell 1838: 12). But Wheatley herself rejected attempts to reinscribe her within her lost maternal genealogies. She experimented with translation as a way of expressing the importance of her loss without reclaiming her mother and mother tongue from within slavery's cultural parameters.

Wheatley's sense of linguistic alienation becomes obvious in a letter to the Reverend John Thornton, dated 30 October 1774. Thornton had apparently proposed that Wheatley should join missionaries bound for Africa, and she responded:

> You propose my returning to Africa with Bristol Yamma and John Quamine ... but why do you hon'd sir, wish those poor men so much trouble as to carry me so long a voyage? Upon my arrival, how like a Barbarian should I look to the Natives; I can promise that my tongue shall be quiet/ for a strong reason indeed/ being an utter stranger to the language of Anamaboe. (Wheatley 1988: 184)

Wheatley rejects the simple equation of blackness with all things African, that is, she rejects an essentialized understanding by which language, culture, race, and ethnicity go hand in hand. Instead, she performs a remarkable dual-act of linguistic alienation in this passage. She imagines that she would be silenced by a return to Africa, that her *"tongue"* — that is in this instance the English she is accustomed to speaking — would be silenced, and that she would be an "utter stranger" because she does not know the *"language* of Anamaboe." For her, there can be no repatriation. Instead of juxtaposing the self and the other, she imagines a relationship between herself as an other, and her African interlocutors as another other. She imagines Africa as the site of linguistic alienation, but of a linguistic alienation that is reciprocal: Wheatley pictures the response of the "Natives," and in a remarkable move, reverses the logic of empire. Instead of viewing them as barbarians, she imagines that they would think of her as a "Barbarian." She uses the word in the original Greek sense, as someone who speaks a different language — and thus imagines the Africans in the role of the Greeks, who are confronting foreign intruders. At the very moment, then, when she imagines herself *in* Africa, Wheatley's self-stylization as an "African" turns out to hinge on a profound sense of linguistic alienation. By casting Africans in the role of Greeks, that alienation also claims Africa as the site of classical antiquity.[13] Yet Wheatley's understanding of translation as the site of alienation allows her to work out her relationship to Africa and America in a way that avoids a potential pitfall, a pitfall that Anthony Appiah has "called 'the Naipaul fallacy': 'The post-colonial legacy which requires us to show that African literature is worthy of study precisely (but only) because it is fundamentally the same as European literature'" (Gates 1988: xx). Instead of emphasizing similarity, translation enables Wheatley to think productively about differences.

For those differences to remain operative in the face of the middle passage, Wheatley reconstructs the imperial space of the transatlantic as a fragmented discourse. As I discussed in this book's introduction, during the American Revolution the term "transatlantic" came to mean

> lying or being beyond the Atlantic. When used by a person in Europe or Africa, transatlantic signifies being in America; when by a person in America, it denotes being or lying in Europe or Africa. We apply it chiefly to something in Europe. (Webster 1828)

By this definition, "transatlantic" is a synonym for American, American is not a synonym for "transatlantic." "Transatlantic" means "being in America" only when one is not in America; it defines a location that is always elsewhere. The term operates in relation to and yet independent of any definitive locus; it is only secondarily a geographical marker, and first and foremost a term that defines geography as a space of relationships. But Webster's definition frames those relationships unevenly: "transatlantic" privileges European-American connections over African-American and African-European contexts. In Wheatley's writing, the relationship between Europe and America becomes the primary relationship of cultural context, and yet by casting that relationship in terms of a translation that is always in excess of itself, that cultural context is never independent of but always haunted by Africa.

Wheatley drew on practices of translation to invent a transatlantic American literature that reflected its differently empowered parts. In one of her longest poems and her most explicit translation, "Niobe in Distress for her Children slain by Apollo, from Ovid's Metamorphoses, Book VI. and from a view of the Painting of Mr. Richard Wilson," Wheatley chose to translate a poem in which Niobe's desire to enter into a relationship of verbal equality with the gods results in her and her children's silencing. In her translation of Ovid, Wheatley powerfully imagines the mother's loss as the loss of the mother tongue. Niobe incurs Venus' wrath when she disobeys the prohibition against comparing human beings to the gods. Niobe's hubris lies in the fact that she "spoke. The Theban maids obey'd" her and failed to make offerings to Venus (Wheatley 1988: 105). In response, "The angry goddess heard, then silence broke// on *Cynthus*' summit, and indignant spoke" to Apollo (Wheatley 1988: 106). Venus says of Niobe that "her tongue rebels," and it is that rebellion that Apollo sets out to avenge. His actions amount to a silencing of Niobe's children: we find out that "then didst thou, *Sipylus*, the language hear/ Of fate portentous" (Wheatley 1988: 107) and that Niobe's daughters were "struck dumb" (Wheatley 1988: 111). In the final stanza, Niobe's "tongue, her palate both obdurate grew ... A marble statue now the queen appears/ But from the marble steal the silent tears" (Wheatley 1988: 113). In this poem, "motherhood as a female bloodrite is outraged, is denied, at the very *same time* that it becomes the founding term of a human and social enactment" (Spillers 2003: 228). Because "the 'feminine,'" is cast as "a corporeality turned trope" (Spillers 2003: 145), the poem reveals the construction of "a patriarchalized female gender, which from one point of view is the only female gender there is" (Spillers 2003: 216). In the logic of patriarchy, the silencing of the mother goes hand in hand with the silencing of the mother tongue: Apollo's actions accomplish both, they destroy Niobe and her offspring. By that token, Apollo's patriarchal intervention also plays out a drama of genocide by means of linguistic control. But because of that connection, recovering the mother tongue cannot be Wheatley's objective if she wishes to avoid tropes of reification. As she made clear in "On Being Brought from Africa to America," the reified trope constructs itself around an exclusive relationship to language that can only be offset by multiplying linguistic frames and keeping them constantly in play. Wheatley understands that her poetry must dwell in translation to escape the logic of the reified trope.

Wheatley explored her relationship to reification by experimenting with paraphrase, and by constantly displacing her verbal referents. By turning to Latin, Wheatley creates a translation between two languages, yet uses those two languages to gesture at a third entity, a lost language that they can engage only through its traces, that is, the "silent tears" made eloquent by Wheatley's poem. We may ask whether Wheatley undercuts her desire to dwell in translation by reifying her poetry in producing a book. That question warrants further discussion, which I provide in chapter five, when I discuss how Harriet Beecher Stowe compared the commoditization of books and slaves. But for now, I want to explore how Wheatley negotiates dwelling in translation on the level of her poetry's theoretical and practical engagements with language.

Wheatley fully worked out her thoughts on translation in the crucial final stages of composing her *Poems on Various Subjects, Religious and Moral* (1773). She had unsuccessfully tried to get her poems published in Boston in 1772, and we have the prospectus for that volume. When she failed to find support in Boston, Wheatley sailed to London and met with success there. Under the Patronage of the Countess Huntington and the Earl of Dartmouth, her *Poems* were published in September 1773. The London volume includes several poems that were not part of the Boston prospectus: "To Maecenas" (a poem contemporary papers widely reprinted), "On Imagination," "To S.M. a Young African Painter," and "Niobe in Distress for her Children slain by Apollo, from Ovid's Metamorphoses, Book VI. and from a view of the Painting of Mr. Richard Wilson" were apparently all composed during Wheatley's time in London. All of these poems highlight issues of language and translation.

So why this intensified interest in translation? During Phillis Wheatley's stay in Britain, the Earl of Dartmouth presented her (in July 1773) with a five volume set of Alexander Pope's translation of Homer's *Iliad* (1715).[14] Those volumes are now housed in Rauner Library at Dartmouth College.[15] Although the gift volumes contain no marks in her hand, the impact they had on Wheatley is inscribed in the poems she composed. The opening poem, "To Maecenas," thanks the Earl of Dartmouth thematically and methodologically for the gift he made her of Pope's translation. "To Maecenas" repeats the dedication of Horace's Book I, Ode I to the patron of Roman Arts, and the opening stanzas sound like a translation from the Latin:

> Maecenas, you, beneath the myrtle shade,
> Read o'er what poets sung, and shepherds play'd.
> What felt those poets but you feel the same?
> Does not your soul possess the sacred flame?
> Their noble strains your equal genius shares
> In softer language, and diviner airs.
>
> While *Homer* paints lo! circumfus'd in air,
> Celestial Gods in mortal forms appear; [...]
> And, as the thunder shakes the heavn'ly plains,
> A deep-felt horror thrills through all my veins.
> When gentler strains demand thy graceful song,
> The length'ning line moves languishing along. (Wheatley 1988: 9–10)

In the poem's first stanza, "Maecenas" is presumably the Earl of Dartmouth who gave her the translation of Homer's poetry, which she describes in the second stanza. Yet the second stanza then also makes "Maecenas" a composite figure of Dartmouth, Pope, and Homer himself. Her reference to the "gentler strains" echoes the opening line's reference to the "noble strains" that Maecenas' "equal genius shares" and conflates the giver with the gift. Wheatley not only thematizes the gift of the translated volume in the poem, but she also acknowledges Pope's translation in her prosody. She writes in iambic pentameter with rhyming couplets, that is, in the meter and with the rhyme schemes of Pope's *Iliad* translation.

Certainly, Wheatley's engagement with Pope does not come as a surprise. Evert A. Duyckinck argued in his 1856 assessment of her poetry, "Phillis Wheatley is a very respectable echo of the Papal strains. In the first poem of the volume, addressed *To Maecenas*, she writes of Homer with an eloquence evidently derived from the glowing translation of the bright-eyed little man at Twickenham" (reprinted in Robinson 1982: 75). Duyckinck comes very close to calling her a mockingbird poet, and given the tenor of his "Young America" agenda, his claims are most likely meant to dismiss her neoclassicism as utterly unoriginal and derivative. Yet Duyckinck misses the linguistic complexity of Wheatley's work. He fails to explore his own insight that her poem sounds like a translation.

Wheatley creates multiple layers of paraphrase: she is paraphrasing Pope who is paraphrasing Homer, and she is creating these paraphrases in a poem that invokes Horace. She had similarly scrambled her reference points in "Niobe in Distress for her Children slain by Apollo, from Ovid's Metamorphoses, Book VI. and from a view of the Painting of Mr. Richard Wilson" — the title casts the poem as a translation of Ovid, methodologically invokes not only Ovid in general but more specifically Dryden's Ovid, yet also appears to be a description of Wilson's painting.

Recognizing the complexity of Wheatley's compositions, her contemporary black writer Ignatius Sancho arrived at an assessment very different from Duyckinck's. Far from seeing her work as derivative, Sancho insisted that "Phillis' poems do credit to nature — and put art — merely as art — to the blush" (in Robinson 1982: 36). Sancho reads Wheatley as producing both an organic form of expression (nature) and stylization (art). He sees her poems as reflecting and constructing artistic contexts — as doing justice to an original, nature, while producing their own originality, art. Moreover, Sancho's comment captures an argument about translation that Wheatley herself stages: she creates in Maecenas himself a figure of the paraphrastic translator. Wheatley turns Maecenas into a translator who does not just "feel the same" but is able to express poetry — the "sacred flame" — in a way that improves on the original and expresses it "in softer language, and diviner airs."

Wheatley stages the poem as a paraphrastic translation. Yet if we reach through the layers of paraphrase, she also refuses us the ability to trace her poem back to a definitive origin. Although Dryden would want to think of such a translation as an imitation, Wheatley consistently evokes an original that she is paraphrasing, only to reveal that no such original exists. I will demonstrate that Wheatley developed her model of paraphrastic translation through her engagement with Pope. But I also propose that Wheatley radicalizes Pope's insights, and that she imagines creating a translation that refers back to an original which will always remain elusive or lost.[16]

If Wheatley is paraphrasing, the closest passage to her opening lines that I have been able to locate comes at the end of Horace's Ode — in Charles Bennet's Loeb Classical Library translation:

> Me the ivy, the reward of poets' brows, links with the gods above; me the cool grove and the lightly tripping band of the nymphs and satyrs withdraw from the vulgar throng, if only Euterpe withhold not the flute, nor Polyhymnia refuse to tune the Lesbian lyre. But if you rank me among lyric bards, I shall touch the stars with my exalted head. (Horace 1988: 5)

Wheatley uses her translation to fashion a public, not a private persona for herself. While she invokes the "noble strains" of Horace's "flute" and "Lesbian lyre," the "diviner airs" she builds up to are decidedly not those of the "lyric bards," but of the epic, of Homer. Phillis Wheatley does not use the first person singular, but instead ends her opening invocation of the second person singular, Maecenas, with his participation in the second person plural, "their." The opening paragraph invokes the lyric only to reject the lyric persona. That rejection occurs precisely at the moment where Wheatley reflects on language: she uses the comparative to refer to a "softer language," and thereby suggests a comparatist approach to language — rather than Horace's exalted removal.

For that matter, she refers to language throughout the poem in comparative terms. The comparison enables Wheatley to omit a narrative of origin and to resituate Maecenas in a mode of sympathy and reciprocity. Whereas Horace refers in the opening line to Maecenas as "sprung from royal stock" (Horace 1988: 3), Wheatley replaces this narrative of origin with an emphasis on feeling. In a line that seems to repeat itself, she asks "What felt those poets but you feel the same?" She has exchanged "royal stock" for a moment of feeling, where sentiment is the great equalizer — structurally and in terms of content, she creates a repetition. Yet she both imagines a sameness, and in the same instance, calls into question whether there is such a thing as feeling "the same." Wheatley invokes and questions the possibilities of a sympathetic identification that would collapse the position between the self and the other. She repeats this query later in the poem:

> Great *Maro's* strain in heav'nly numbers flows,
> The *Nine* inspire, and all the bosom glows.
> O could I rival thine and *Virgil*'s page,
> Or claim the *Muses* with the *Mantuan* Sage;
> Soon the same beauties should my mind adorn,
> And the same ardors in my soul should burn:
> Then should my song in bolder notes arise,
> And all my numbers pleasingly surprise;
> But here I sit, and mourn a grov'ling mind
> That fain would mount and ride upon the wind.
>
> Not you, my friend, these plaintive strains become,
> Not you, whose bosom is the *Muses* home;
> When they from tow'ring *Helicon* retire,
> They fan in you the bright immortal fire,
> But I less happy, cannot raise the song,
> The fault'ring music dies upon my tongue. (Wheatley 1988: 10–1)

Wheatley imagines that she could participate in "the same beauties" as Virgil and the "same [poetic] ardors" to let her "song in bolder notes arise."

While translation holds out the possibility of participating in the "same beauties" and "the same ardors," Wheately finds herself excluded from this discourse of sameness. Although she wishes to be the "same," she finds herself in a position where she mourns and where she is "less happy, [and] cannot raise the song,/ The fault'ring music dies upon my tongue." Her comparisons do not resolve themselves in sameness, but instead result — as they did for Niobe — in mourning and in the silencing of her "tongue." Important as affect is for Wheatley, it does not have the efficacy of translation for critiquing her losses and generating cultural alternatives.

Wheatley's translation offsets the silencing she invokes, as becomes evident when we examine her methodology in relation to the translation theory that Alexander Pope developed and that Wheatley explores in this poem. Reading the opening as a paraphrastic translation may seem to contradict Pope's view of translation. In his preface to his translation of the *Iliad*, Pope states that "It is certain no literal Translation can be just to an excellent Original in a superior Language; but it is a great Mistake to imagine (as many have done) that a rash Paraphrase can make amends for this general Defect" (Pope 1969: 452). Pope rejects the very notion of sameness that Wheatley was invoking, and suggests that translation will always be different. Pope's seeming rejection of paraphrase underscores his emphasis that "it is the first grand Duty of an Interpreter to give his Author entire and unmaim'd; and for the rest, the *Diction* and *Versification* only are his proper Province; since these must be his own, but the others he is to take as he finds them" (Pope 1969: 452). His desire to represent the author "entire and unmaim'd" indicates that he resists the violence — the maiming — that can come with temporal, linguistic, and cultural transposition.

Yet he also wishes to understand translation as a mode of original composition when he insists that the "diction and versification" of the translation are the translator's own. If the translator is derivative and imitative of the original in terms of content, it is language that remains or becomes "his own." Pope explicates this point when he says: "I know no Liberties one ought to take but those which are necessary for transfusing the Spirit of the Original, and supporting the Poetical style of the Translation" (Pope 1969: 452). In a curious way, Wheatley, Morrison, and Pope turn out to be surprisingly close in their claims about language. Pope proposes a model that reflects on the violence of changing idioms, and that tries to offset that violence in a way that agrees with Morrison's understanding that the "message" was there all along even as the language changed. Niobe's "silent tears" carry a message that her tongue can no longer formulate but that finds expression in the new tongue of Wheatley's poetry. For Wheatley as for Pope, language becomes the site of loss and alienation, but also of linguistic originality: the very loss of an origin marks language's capacity to function originally.

The ability to function originally in translation marks Wheatley's invention of a transatlantic literature. The Boston Brahmins who examined

Wheatley for her linguistic abilities wrote a letter that was published with her *Poems* (1773) so "that none might have the least Ground for disputing their [the poems'] *Original*." The very men who tested Wheatley's capacity as a translator designated her poems original compositions. Although that designation might strike us as contradictory, it articulated the cultural logic of transatlantic literature.

Wheatley conceptualized originality through the losses, but also the gains, of her transatlantic translations. Far from fetishizing an isolated literary "originality," Wheatley conceptualized and practiced translation *as* American literature, and vice versa, understood American literature as a form of writing that was always in translation from a lost mother and mother tongue. For Wheatley, translation was not a peripheral exercise, but the fundamental methodology through which she understood her literary practice. Wheatley imagined a literature that would always remain partially foreign to itself as it identified with cultural alterity. She conceptualized American literature through the verbal mobility of translation, and defined what we might mean if we understand "American" as "a staging point for ideological contestation by many forces that are asynchronous and multilocal" (Aravamudan 1999: 15). In translation, she invented a transatlantic American literature that reflected the diversity of its differently empowered parts.

2 The blanched Atlantic
James Fenimore Cooper's "neutral ground"

On February 25, 1852, William Cullen Bryant addressed, at New York City's Metropolitan Hall, an assembly gathered *in memoriam* of the recently deceased James Fenimore Cooper. In a self-defining moment for the United States' literary elite, Bryant assessed Cooper's controversial literary achievement. Cooper had garnered international and national censure for his vituperative political writings in which he had tried to vindicate "his country from various flippant and ill-natured misrepresentations of foreigners ... [and] to save her from flatterers at home" (Bryant 1873: 63). But Cooper had also built another kind of reputation with the Leatherstocking tales. Transcending geopolitical factions, Cooper wrote "for mankind at large," and produced "one of the noblest, ... most striking and original creations of fiction" in Natty Bumppo (Bryant 1873: 57). Bryant credited Cooper with having crafted world literature.[1] He argued that Cooper's works managed to span the globe and exceed their own contexts because

> All his excellences are translatable — they pass readily into languages the least allied in their genius to that in which he wrote, and in them he touches the heart and kindles the imagination with the same power as in the original English. Cooper was not wholly without humor; it is sometimes found lurking in the dialogue of Harvey Birch [*The Spy*], and of Leatherstocking; but it forms no considerable element in his works; and if it did, it would have stood in the way of his universal popularity, since of all qualities, it is the most difficult to transfuse into a foreign language. Nor did the effect he produced upon the reader depend on any grace of style which would escape a translator of ordinary skill. ... Cooper's genius ... may remain the delight of the nations ... after the English language and its contemporaneous form of civilization shall have passed. (Bryant 1873: 87–91)[2]

Cooper could not have wished for a more astute reader than Bryant. Throughout his career, Cooper found himself captivated by practices of translation because he found in them a means of locating cultural differences in negotiable linguistic plurality. Cooper showed his characters performing translations, but he also imagined himself to be writing in translation. He created for his readers the illusion that passages and even whole novels were written in translation.[3] Picking up on this practice, Bryant praises Cooper's works for being translatable, that is, for having an intrinsic quality that allows them to transcend existing linguistic, temporal and cultural contexts.[4] Although translations are subject to the misrepresentations that "a translator of ordinary skill" might produce, Cooper's works can withstand the loss of humor and stylistic refinement because of their sentimental appeal: even in bad translations, Cooper "touches the heart."

Building on the earlier work of Ann Douglas, Cathy Davidson, and Jane Tompkins, critics in the 1990s, such as Julia Stern and Elizabeth Barnes, made sentimentality and sympathetic identification veritable shibboleths for reading American fiction.[5] They demonstrated that, under the influence of such seminal works as Adam Smith's *The Theory of Moral Sentiments* (1759), literature from the late eighteenth through the nineteenth century worked out its relationship to racial and political difference through a theory of sympathetic identification. Smith had argued that moral judgment occurred by way of an "impartial spectator," that is, an abstract figure who mediates between an individual man and collective "mankind," and who judges individual acts by a principle of right action. In Smith's model, alterity, and identity went hand in hand: only through a process of self-alienation by which one imagined an "other" did it become possible to "view ourselves" (Smith 1982: 7).

Important as theories of sentimentality have been for explaining a mechanism by which American novels negotiate difference, discussion has focused primarily on the relationship between characters in novels, on the reader's sympathetic identification with those characters, and on the national bond such sympathetic readings foster. That emphasis has led to a tautology: by identifying with characters in novels, readers become part of a national community, and in turn, characters with whom readers identify become national characters.[6] Cooper takes a different approach to the relevance of sentimentality for American fiction: he draws on sentimentality to develop a *linguistic* model for negotiating difference, and his linguistic model does not see the nation as a foregone conclusion. Instead, Cooper thinks of nationalism as a displaced discourse that negotiates its relationship to global as well as local contexts through a process of translation that occurs in a "neutral ground," the linguistic equivalent of Smith's impartial spectator.

Experimenting with the role of language enabled Cooper to explore his relationship to the transatlantic slave system. Writing in response to the emancipation of slaves in the West Indies (1807) and the Missouri crisis (1820–21), Cooper envisioned the American frontier as a discursive site where transatlantic problems became negotiable.[7] Building on Wheatley's understanding of what it meant to lack a mother tongue, Cooper rejected the idea that language was genealogically conditioned. Instead, he conceptualized language by two developmental stages. One, he thought that language underwent a process of abstraction in which expressions that had once been specific to an individual object became generalized and applied to categories. He thought of metaphor as an essential stage in the development of language, and he attributed such metaphoric language primarily though not exclusively to his Native American characters.[8] Second (and this move interests me primarily), he understood each modern language to be blended from multiple metaphoric languages. For him, any modern language was inherently multilingual. Consequently, translation was not just a way of making different languages comprehensible to each other, but also an important mechanism for making language comprehensible to itself. For Cooper, modern national languages are never simply subject to translation; because modern national languages are internally multiple, they themselves exist in translation. He thought of them as contact languages, and the challenge in reading Cooper lies in understanding on what basis and in what registers contact occurs.

For Cooper, translation was not a binary relationship between one language and another language, one culture and another culture. Instead, Cooper developed a theory of triangulation by which translation always involved at least three components: the context from which something is translated, into which it is translated, and the translation itself, which participates in both contexts but is commensurate with neither. Cooper thought of his novels as translations, which he conceptualized as a *tertium quid*, that is, a third entity that continually facilitates and is itself subject to change.[9]

Because translation only engages points of linguistic and cultural overlap, there are always sites of excess that lie beyond it. Cooper's model allowed for an alterity that remains beyond the discursive reach of translation. He acknowledged this realm of difference by theorizing moments when translation fails or succeeds only partially. Cooper's version of translation is anti-essentialist, and leaves out those aspects of language and culture that are so specific as to resist translation. Yet under slavery, such anti-essentialism is itself a white privilege. Ultimately, Cooper performed a blanching of the Atlantic that, at its best, imagined translation as an egalitarian practice, and at its worst made translation a white prerogative.

I.

Language theory became a growth industry in the mid-eighteenth century. As the example of Thomas Jefferson suggests, dabbling in language theory became *de rigueur* for educated men. Jean-Jacques Rousseau, Johann Gottfried Herder, and Adam Smith were among the best known philosophers to weigh in on how language had first come into being, and on what explained linguistic differences.[10] The urgency behind this interest was twofold: in response to colonial contacts with other cultures, philosophers tried to develop models by which to understand non-European peoples. Second, they were interested in applying to autoethnographic purposes the methodologies developed in the study of others.

Beginning with the third edition published in 1767, Adam Smith's *Theory of Moral Sentiments* contained the essay "Consideration Concerning the First Formation of Languages," also known as the "Dissertation on the Origin of Languages," which had previously been published in *Philological Miscellany* in 1761. The first American edition in 1817, which was based on the 12th Edinburgh edition, contained Smith's essay (Smith 1817). In his treatise, Smith developed a linguistic analog to the impartial spectator when he thought about language formation in two ways. One, he imagined the formation of languages as occurring through a move from specificity to universality. For him, all language was initially metaphoric. Two, Smith imagined that modern languages had emerged when different metaphoric languages encountered one another and became blended. Smith did not think of language as the stable trait of a nation; the treatise on language made multilingual contact the privileged site of national emergence, and translation the central mode of national literature. National languages emerged through multilingual contacts; thus, a language became comprehensible to itself through acts of translation.

Smith developed an idealized version by which language formation occurred through non-confrontational acts of social interaction. He claimed that the first use of language was in the "institution of nouns substantive" by which "two savages" would "begin to form that language by which they would endeavour to make their mutual wants intelligible to each other" (Smith 1907: 507). Smith imagined that language arises harmoniously from "mutual wants" that two people make intelligible "to each other" in an equitable fashion. According to Smith, abstract concepts develop on the basis of such reciprocity:

> When they had occasion ... to mention or to point out to each other, any of the new objects, they would naturally utter the name of the correspondent old one, of which the idea could not fail, at that instant, to present itself to their memory in the strongest and liveliest manner. And thus those words, which were originally the proper names of individuals, would each of them insensibly become the common name of a multitude. A child that is just learning to speak, calls every person who comes to the house its papa, or its mamma; and thus bestows upon the whole species those names which it had been taught to apply to two individuals. (Smith 1907: 508)

Language develops as two people conversing with each other apply a specific name to a generic concept. Their intimate relationship to an individual (to "papa, or ... mamma") becomes transferred to a category — the "whole species" takes on the names originally applied to "individuals."

Language extends intimacy; it is tied to social formation, and occurs as speakers negotiate their local contexts in more global terms.

Cooper's desire to be universally comprehensible and nationally specific caused him to develop a comparable way of conceptualizing language. Similarly to Smith, Cooper thought of metaphor as an essential stage in the development of language. He staged the formation of metaphoric language when he explained in his introduction to the 1831 edition of the second Leatherstocking novel, *The Last of the Mohicans: A Narrative of 1757*, that the Native American "draws his metaphors from the clouds, the seasons, the birds, the beasts, and the vegetable world" (Cooper 1986: 5). Although Cooper most often associates metaphoric language with Native Americans, it is not exclusive to them. In a footnote, for instance, Cooper describes the English spoken in the Americas as a metaphoric language when he writes:

> In vulgar parlance the condiments of a repast are called by the American 'a relish,' substituting the thing for its effect. These provincial terms are frequently put in the mouths of the speakers, according to their several conditions in life. Most of them are of local use, and others quite peculiar to the particular class of men to which the character belongs. In the present instance, the scout uses the word with immediate reference to the salt, with which his own party was so fortunate as to be provided. (Cooper 1989: 49)

Cooper imagines a stage of language formation in which the specific has not yet become widely generalized. He himself performs that generalization, and in this passage enacts the process of language formation. Cooper demonstrates that Natty's language is metaphoric (or to be more precise, synechdochal), in that it applies an individual effect to a category of objects. Cooper insists that such categorical designation is "local," "peculiar," and relevant to a "particular class of men." Yet Cooper makes this "vulgar parlance" part of his own novel, and ensures through his explanation that it becomes accessible to a broader readership. Presumably, the local readership Cooper addresses would not require an explanatory note, and indeed, the footnotes in the 1831 edition of Cooper's novel explicitly and implicitly address British readers unfamiliar with American contexts. At the very moment that Cooper is most explicitly developing an American idiom, then, he is addressing himself to a transatlantic readership.

Cooper and Smith thought of metaphor as a first stage in the development of language. Modern languages emerge in a second stage, when different metaphorical languages come in contact with each other. Smith argues that

> Language would probably have continued upon this footing in all countries, ... had it not become more complex in its composition, in

> consequence of the mixture of several languages with one another, occasioned by the mixture of different nations. ... when two nations came to be mixed with one another, either by conquest or migration ... Each nation, in order to make itself intelligible to those with whom it was under the necessity of conversing, would be obliged to learn the language of the other. (Smith 1907: 531)

This model of simple and compound national languages complicates the premise expressed in one of the titles under which Smith's essay was published, "Dissertation on the Origin of Languages." Modern language does not stem from an origin, but results from contact, that is, from an initial social contact that propels people into language, and then from social contacts between groups that had previously been geographically and linguistically separate from each other. Contact necessitates translation between different languages: in order to "make itself intelligible," it becomes necessary for "each nation" to "learn the language of the other" and to negotiate between languages.

Smith suggests that translation becomes internalized as individual languages are altered and become "more complex" by their contact with each other:

> The English is compounded of the French and the ancient Saxon languages. The French was introduced into Britain by the Norman conquest, and continued, till the time of Edward III, to be the sole language of the law, as well as the principal language of the court. The English which came to be spoken afterwards, and which continues to be spoken now, is a mixture of the ancient Saxon and this Norman French. (Smith 1907: 534)

Cooper stages a similar understanding of blended language in a footnote to the first Leatherstocking novel, *The Pioneers, or, The Sources of the Susquehennah* (1823), where he writes: "Sleigh is a word used in every part of the United States to denote a traineau" (Cooper 1991: 17). To explain the Anglophone word "sleigh," Cooper draws on the francophone word "traineau," and expects his readers to be more familiar with the francophone word than the Anglophone expression. For Smith and Cooper, a language such as English carries the traces of its conflicted history, and translation is the mechanism by which a modern people comes to understand itself.

Although Cooper's work closely parallels Smith's linguistic theory, he might not have read *The Theory of Moral Sentiments* and the essay on language formation as primary texts. Most likely, Cooper drew his understanding of Smith's linguistic philosophy from Sir Walter Scott's novel *Ivanhoe* (1819), which Cooper said served him "for a guide" in writing his first works (Cooper and Beard 1960: I.42).[11] Scott's work was published at a crucial moment in the development of the British novel: "between 1760 and 1830, British literature is obsessed with the problem of culture: with historical and cultural alterity, with historical and cultural change, with comparative cultural analysis, and with the way traditional customs and values shape everyday life" (Trumpener 1997: xiv). In his early novels, beginning with *Waverley* (1814), Scott had explored the theme of alterity as it pertained to the act of union (1707) and the effects of English dominion on Scottish identity. But in *Ivanhoe* (1819), his work on Medieval England, Scott explored the foundational role that alterity played in the formation of a single national identity and language.

Scott stages Smith's theory of modern national language formation when he writes: "the necessary intercourse between the lords of the soil, and those oppressed inferior beings by whom that soil was cultivated, occasioned the gradual formation of a dialect, compounded betwixt the French and the Anglo-Saxon, in which they could render themselves mutually intelligible to each other; and from this necessity arose by degrees the structure of our present English language, in which the speech of the victors and the vanquished have been so happily blended together; and which has since been so richly improved by importations from the classical languages, and from those spoken by the southern nations of Europe" (Scott 2001: 31).[12] Scott illustrates how he imagines that mixed language developing. As Saxon serfs, the jester Wamba and the swineherd Gurth are outraged at the repression their Lord experiences at the hand of the Normans. Walking home with a herd of swine, Wamba gives vent to his political feelings by reasoning that the swines' destiny is

' ... to be converted into Normans before morning, to thy no small ease and comfort.'

'The swine turned Normans to my comfort!' quoth Gurth; 'expound that to me, Wamba, for my brain is too dull and my mind too vexed to read riddles.'

'Why, how call you those grunting brutes running about on their four legs?' demanded Wamba.

'Swine, fool — swine,' said the herd; 'every fool knows that.'

'And swine is good Saxon,' said the Jester; 'but how call you the sow when she is flayed, and drawn, and quartered, and hung up by the heels, like a traitor?'

'Pork,' answered the swineherd.

'I am very glad every fool knows that too,' said Wamba, 'and pork, I think, is good Norman-French; and so when a brute lives, and is in charge of a Saxon slave, she goes by the Saxon name; but becomes a

Norman, and is called pork, when she is carried to the castle hall to feast among the nobles. What dost thou think of this, friend Gurth, ha?'

'It is but too true doctrine, friend Wamba, however, it got into thy fool's pate.' (Scott 2001: 35–6)

Whereas Smith thought of language as an equitable exchange, Scott explores how language both reflects and offsets repressive political power. Wamba describes how a Saxon word, swine, is replaced with a Norman-French word, pork. Both words refer to the same thing, but the act of translating swine into pork marks a power differential that expresses itself politically, economically, and linguistically. Wamba's refusal to be inscribed unthinkingly in this new verbal regime indicates how the multiplicity of languages does not just reflect but can also offset such power politics. By examining the linguistic shifts and performing his verbal mobility, Wamba reveals the power dynamics that imperial language masks. Even under conditions of conquest, language for Scott reflects negotiable and pluralistic contact.

In *The Pioneers* (1823), Cooper obsessively stages his relationship to *Ivanhoe*. Much could be said about the similarities and differences between *Ivanhoe* and Cooper's rewriting, but the plot elements are at best of secondary interest to me.[13] What concerns me is the methodology that Cooper adapts from Scott, that is, a way of thinking about translation as a means of forming national languages and negotiating cultural differences. Cooper draws on Scott to adapt Smith's model of linguistic blending so as to accommodate notions of linguistic and cultural alterity.

Cooper humorously invokes Smith's linguistic theory when he imagines a "composite order." He constantly thwarts his readers' understanding of what he might mean by that term. For instance, he tautologically points out that "the composite order ... was an order composed of many others" (Cooper 1991: 43). The term refers most explicitly to an architectural style prevalent in Templeton. the fictive village in which *The Pioneers* is set. That style spatializes and illustrates the linguistic blending that Cooper performs throughout his novel. Ultimately, Cooper's "composite order" amounts to a parody of his own linguistic methodology. He stages that parody when he describes the state of learning in Templeton, He describes that the local "Academy," the chief example of the "composite order,"

for a short time ... employed a graduate of one of the eastern colleges, to instruct such youth as aspired to knowledge, within the walls of the edifice which we have described. ... [The building] contained two rooms, that were intended for the great divisions of education, viz. the Latin and the English scholars. The former were never very numerous; though the sounds of 'nominative, pennaa; genitive, penny,' were soon heard to issue from the windows of the room, to the great delight and manifest edification of the passengers. Only one labourer in this temple of Minerva, however, was known to get so far as to attempt a translation of Virgil. He, indeed, appeared at the annual exhibition, to the prodigious exultation of all his relatives, a framer's family in the vicinity, and repeated the whole of the first eclogue from memory, observing the intonations of the dialogue with much judgment and effect. The sounds, as they proceeded from his mouth, ... were the last that had been heard in that building, as probably they were the first that had ever been heard, in the same language, there or any where else ... from this time until the date of our incidents, the Academy was a common country school. (Cooper 1991: 101–2)

Cooper's description caricatures Smith's theories and the debates over language instruction that I traced in chapter one. Because Clarke's model of instruction depends on translating between English and Latin, and because Smith insists that languages are blended, "penny" becomes a good example of Latin. The absurdity of this declension stems from the fact that it erases cultural differences and allows a word to be transposed historically. The scene's parody depends on the word penny's express modernity — drawing on one of the many Latinate words still current in English would not have accomplished the same comic effect. The instruction in language that takes place at the academy fails to distinguish between Latin as an ancient and English as a modern language. Even though Cooper draws from Smith the notion that language is without origin and is not genealogically conditioned, he suggests that it is important to recognize the history of contact, and to maintain a sense of cultural difference.

Scott provided his readers with a theoretical model for the way in which language worked in relation to historical and cultural difference. He prefaced *Ivanhoe* with a "Dedicatory Epistle" written by the fictional editor Mr. Laurence Templeton. Although Scott ridicules antiquarians for their absurd investment in insignificant detail, the "Epistle" also serves him as a statement of his own literary theory, which hinges on the concept of linguistic and cultural translation.[14] In writing historical fiction, Scott says that he "translated into the manners, as well as the language, of the age we live in" (Scott 2001: xix—xx).[15] He imagines that *Ivanhoe* performs three acts of translation: one, as I have shown, Scott stages scenes of translation in which his medieval characters negotiate their complex relationship to Saxon and Norman-French. Two, Scott portrays Laurence Templeton as drawing on historical documents to perform an act of translation by which he makes the past intelligible to his contemporaries. But three, Scott himself writes a novel in which even the documents upon which Templeton draws are fictional. Absent the existence of "original" documents, Scott creates a text that exists only in his translation.

Scott argues that translation is both the ground for communication and an instance of communication when he locates his work in

> that extensive neutral ground, the large proportion, that is, of *manners and sentiments* which are common to us and to our ancestors, having been handed down unaltered from them to us, or which arising out of the principles of our common nature, must have existed alike in either state of society. ... He who would imitate an ancient *language* with success must attend rather to its grammatical character, turn of expression, and mode of arrangement, than labour to collect extraordinary and antiquated terms, which, as I have already averred, do not in ancient authors approach the number of words still in use, though perhaps somewhat altered in sense and spelling in the proportion of one to ten. What I have applied to *language* is still more justly applicable to *sentiments and manners*. ... His *language* must not be exclusively obsolete and unintelligible; but he should admit, if possible, no word or turn of phraseology betraying an origin directly modern. It is one thing to make use of the *language and sentiments* which are common to ourselves and our forefathers, and it is another to invest them with the sentiments and dialect exclusively proper to their descendants. (Scott 2001: xx, my italics)

For Scott, language does not have its origins in the past. Instead, when he speaks about words that reveal an "origin directly modern," he thinks of linguistic origin as something that arises in the development of language. By translation, then, Scott does not designate an origin and a telos: instead, he imagines translation to occur when language becomes multireferential and belongs to more than one time period and more than one culture. He brackets both explicitly antiquarian and explicitly modern terms from his use, and draws his vocabulary from a pool of shared expressions. Scott puts the past and the present, the familiar and the foreign, on an egalitarian footing in a third time-space: the "extensive neutral ground" is Scott's linguistic equivalent to Smith's impartial spectator. It is a realm of linguistic and sentimental abstraction that provides a meeting ground for cultural negotiation. For Scott, that common realm of shared sentiments and language exceeds momentary stages and social formations. The successful translation of ancient language to a modern audience depends on an imitation of its grammatical character, on finding a shared vocabulary and on eliciting the "principles of our common nature." Scott imagines that national history and culture emerge in acts of translation. The insight that Cooper draws from him is that "translation is the self-realization of a culture" (Homel and Simon 1988: 10).[16] But what exactly it means for Cooper to draw on sentimentality as a linguistic theory and to think of American culture in translation needs clarification.

II.

Cooper invented a model of language that was not genealogically determined, and that defined language as translation.[17] Trying like Wheatley to understand what it meant to lack a mother tongue, Cooper rejected the idea that language was genealogically conditioned. But in the process, he performed two kinds of erasure: he erased the relevance of gender and of race from transatlantic discourse.

Similar to the shifting census definitions in the twentieth century that I described in the introduction, Cooper erased the "usual language" spoken in the "parents' homes in the old country" (Waggoner 1980: 487) from his consideration, and instead focused on the language a person spoke him- or herself in earliest childhood. In the first Leatherstocking novels, *The Pioneers* (1823) and *The Last of the Mohicans* (1826), mothers and mother tongues are conspicuously absent. There are no Native American women in these works who could function as mothers or speak in mother tongues. The female characters who do appear in the novels — Elizabeth Temple, Cora and Alice Munro — neither have nor are mothers. Their relationship to their fathers is not cast in terms of a linguistic genealogy either. Whereas Judge Temple speaks in Quakerisms, his daughter Elizabeth, who has just returned from school, does not share his linguistic quirks. Similarly, the "peculiar accent of Scotland" (Cooper 1989: 149) that resonates in Munro's speech is absent from his daughters' language.

What was primarily at stake for Cooper in imagining the absence of a mother tongue was his relationship to English. In *Notions of the Americans* (1828), Cooper staged what he saw as the key conflicts in the transatlantic relationship between the United States and England some fifty years after the War of Independence. Cooper concerned himself with the way political separation had affected the countries' linguistic and cultural relationship. Troping on the travel guides popular in England at the time, and defying their disadvantageous representations of American life, Cooper imagined an English gentleman to be touring the United States with an American companion.[18] In a key moment, Cooper's American points out that the Englishman "forgets that, when we achieved our independence, we conquered an equal right to the language" (Cooper 1828: I. 434). Cooper's American refuses to consider English an English prerogative: instead of associating language (English) with nationality (Englishness), he argues that language operates independent of any specific nationality, and he unhinges nationality from any specific language. For Cooper, language and cultural identity are mobile and not tied to specific state- and nation-formations. English has become a prerogative that the United States earned alongside political independence from England. Yet how to figure the relevance that English in particular and language in general then had for the American scene proved a challenge for Cooper.

Cooper imagined that America's linguistic originality emerged in acts of translation. In an early scene from *Last of the Mohicans*, David Gamut describes the book of psalms, from which he lyrically performs as

> 'the six-and-twentieth edition, promulgated at Boston, Anno Domini 1744; and is entitled *The Psalms, Hymns and Spiritual Songs of the Old and New Testaments; faithfully translated into English Metre, for the Use, Edification, and Comfort of the Saints, in Public and Private, especially in New England.*' During his eulogium on the rare production of his native poets, the stranger had drawn the book from his pocket, and, fitting a pair of iron-rimmed spectacles to his nose, opened the volume with a care and veneration suited to its sacred purposes. (Cooper 1989: 17)

In this passage, Gamut's "native poets" are the authors of biblical translations. Presumably, these poets are "native" in the sense that they spoke and wrote in English in North America. By that logic, they are then also "his" native poets because David shares their linguistic and geographical affiliation. Yet for the nativism these poets represent, English is not itself the originary language, nor are the poems original in the sense that they were first composed in English. Moreover, as a book expressly written by and for immigrants, the poets' geographical affiliation is not nativist either. To see these psalms as the "production of his native poets," we have to grant translation, as both linguistic and geographical transposition, the status of native composition. Cooper's linguistic nativism then does not differentiate an original from a translation, but on the contrary, suggests that originality emerges in acts of translation.

Cooper explored the relationship between this linguistic model and national identity when he examined the word "Yankee," and argued that it

> has two significations among the Americans themselves, one of which may be called its national, and the other its local meaning. The New-Englandman evidently exults in the appellation at all times. Those of the other states with whom I have come in contact, are manifestly quite as well pleased to lay no claim to the title, though all use it freely in its foreign, or national sense when they travel outside of the United States. (Cooper 1828: I.73)

The democratic idiom could have multiple, local definitions and yet sustain a national meaning — which in some cases even contradicted the vernacular meaning (we can imagine the following syllogism: a Southerner is not a Yankee, a Southerner is an American, an American is a Yankee, therefore, a Southerner is a Yankee). When he enables the word "Yankee" to encompass conflicting meanings, Cooper imagines that the American idiom emerges in translation. Provocatively, Cooper uses the word's "foreign" sense as a synonym for its "national sense." He imagines that foreign translation establishes the American idiom's ability to signify nationally.

Cooper most thoroughly staged his unhinging of nationality from a language of origin in *The Pioneers*. When Judge Marmaduke Temple accidentally wounds Oliver Edwards during a hunt, he takes the young man into his home. Edwards' racial and cultural identity is a mystery to the Judge and his daughter Elizabeth, who suspects that Oliver is Native American. On an excursion, Elizabeth tries to gather information about Oliver when she asks him to interpret their companions' supposedly learned discussion of maple sugar:

'Is this Greek or Latin, Mr. Edwards?' whispered the heiress to the youth, who was opening a passage for herself and her companions through the bushes — 'perhaps it is a still more learned language, for an interpretation of which we must look to you.'

The dark eye of the young man glanced towards the maiden, with a keenness bordering on ferocity; but its expression changed, in a moment to the smiling playfulness of her own face, as he answered —

'I shall remember your doubts, Miss Temple, when next I visit my old friend Mohegan, and either his skill, or that of Leather-stocking, shall solve them.'

'And are you, then, really ignorant of their language?' asked Elizabeth, with an impetuosity that spoke a lively interest in the reply.

'Not absolutely; but the deep learning of Mr. Jones is more familiar to me, or even the polite masquerade of Monsieur Le Quoi.'

'Do you speak French?' said the lady, with a quickness that equalled her former interest.

"It is a common language with the Iroquois, and through the Canadas,' he answered with an equivocal smile.

'Ah! but they are Mingoes, and your enemies.'

'It will be well for me, if I have no worse,' said the youth, dashing ahead with his horse, and putting an end to the evasive dialogue.[19]

With this passage, Cooper puts into play and challenges an ontological view of American culture. Elizabeth is not merely thwarted in her attempts to determine identity by language, but Cooper also demonstrates that she is wrong to equate the two. Oliver's responses demonstrate her error:

Elizabeth tries to determine whether he knows Delaware when she asks if their companions speak "a still more learned language." Her catalogue of Latin, Greek, and Delaware compares the Native American language to the classical languages — the unspoken, "dead" languages. Edwards resists this antiquation when he insists on the vitality of Delaware by saying that he will answer her question after conversing with Mohegan and Leatherstocking. Elizabeth fails to recognize this resistance when she interprets his reluctance to answer as an indication that he is ignorant of "their" language, a language that her exclusion of Oliver from the personal pronoun "their" makes distinct from his identity. Oliver's response is "equivocal" in that it multiplies his linguistic knowledge and cultural allegiances: he indicates that he is familiar with Delaware, English, and French. Again, Elizabeth proves unable to recognize this proliferation when she tries to establish whether he speaks — and whether he is — French. Oliver's reply overthrows her association between language and cultural identity when he explains his knowledge of French by the language's currency among the Iroquois and Canadas. As an emergent American hero, Oliver relates to multiple languages but is not defined by any single one of them.

Exploring what it means to define national literature as emerging in acts of translation lies at the core of Cooper's agenda as a novelist. Cooper imagined himself to be writing in translation: he created for his readers the illusion that he wrote whole passages and even whole novels in translation. For instance, he starts a passage in which the French commander Montcalm speaks by writing in French and then translating into English: "'je deteste ces fripons-la; on ne sait jamais sur quel pie on est avex eux. Eh, bien! monsieur,' he continued, still speaking in French, 'though I should have been proud of receiving your commandant, I am very happy that he has seen proper to employ an officer so distinguished, and who, I am sure, is so amiable, as yourself'" (Cooper 1989: 158). Cooper's translation tries to give the reader a sense of what Montcalm might have said in French. Cooper's word choices establish a close resemblance between French and English: words such as "commandant," "proper," "employ," "officer," "distinguished," and "amiable" would be nearly identical in French. Cooper's strategy is not to replace the language he is translating with English, but to write English in a way that draws on the commonalities between the two languages. Cooper is locating himself in Sir Walter Scott's "neutral ground": he is drawing on shared vocabulary to establish the relationship between Montcalm's speech and his own. Yet Cooper's translation also replicates some of the grammatical structure familiar to French but foreign to English. The translated section of the passage is grammatically choppy, as the five commas make clear that subdivide this partial clause. The effect of Cooper's translation is not only to establish a familiarity, but also to use the "neutral ground" to demonstrate where languages diverge and become dissimilar. In this scene, Cooper's linguistic model relies on a sense of both verbal identity and grammatical alienation. For Cooper, translation simultaneously familiarizes and defamiliarizes its multiple contexts; it establishes a basis for communication, but also ensures the existence of an alterity that remains outside of translation.

By drawing on linguistic commonalities, Cooper is able to defamiliarize English and allow it to reflect the idiomatic differences of other languages. He adopts what Lawrence Venuti calls "a foreignizing method" that exerts "ethnodeviant pressure ... to register the linguistic and cultural difference of the foreign text, sending the reader abroad" (Venuti 1995: 17).[20] Cooper makes explicit his strategy for such foreignizing translation when Natty speaks "in the tongue which was known to all the natives who formerly inhabited the country between the Hudson and the Potomac, and of which we shall give a free translation for the benefit of the reader; endeavoring, at the same time, to preserve some of the peculiarities, both of the individual and of the language" (Cooper 1989: 22). Cooper envisions sections of his novel to be written in translation. He imagines that his text makes intelligible things that were said in another language to readers who do not speak that language. And yet the intelligibility Cooper promises to the readers of his translation into English does not make Native American languages transparent. Instead of familiarizing the "tongue" of the "natives," Cooper promises to acquaint his readers with its "peculiarities." He tries to capture those aspects of this language that are different from English.[21]

The "peculiarities" Cooper invokes are not merely foreign — Cooper uses translation to break down the division between the familiar and the foreign; translation is always both. He accomplishes this goal by pointing out that the "peculiarities" he translates stem from both "the individual," that is from Natty Bumppo, and "the language" he is speaking, Delaware. This emphasis on the speaker and on the language makes clear that the "peculiarities" Cooper's text represents are both familiar and foreign: Cooper is not translating Native American languages *per se*, but specifically translating Natty Bumppo speaking in "the tongue ... known to all the natives who formerly inhabited the country between the Hudson and the Potomac" (Cooper 1989: 22). Paradoxically, Natty serves as an example of linguistic nativism when he is speaking in non-European languages as one of the people who "inhabited the country" (Cooper 1989: 22). The language Cooper represents is "peculiar" by virtue of a double act of translation: Natty is translating himself into an acquired language, and Cooper is writing in translation. The translation itself does not lead back to a cultural source that is distinct from the context into which Cooper is translating; rather, the basis for his translation is a character who is deeply multilingual and transcultural.

Cooper draws attention to a cultural and linguistic blend that is already integral to the language he reproduces. Because of that immanence, Cooper's work is doubly a translation without an original: on a textual level, there is no source from which Cooper can be said to be translating (since we never hear what Natty actually says). On a linguistic level, translation is not the outcome of transposing an original into another language, but rather is already inscribed in the cultural context from which it "originates" and into which it enters. Natty is speaking a native language that is not genealogically "his" — as he constantly reminds us when he describes himself as "a man without a cross" (Cooper 1989: 67). Unpalatable as such invocations of race are, they create a model of acculturation and of foreignization that Cooper enacts linguistically. Because he is not himself a Native American, Natty stands in a translator's relationship to his own acculturation; because of his acculturation, he also stands in translative relationship to his culture of origin. In fact, we see him interpreting Native American culture to European Americans as often as we see him explaining European Americans to Native Americans. These passages in Cooper's work make the multiplicity of languages and cultures translatable, rather than making language and culture racially essential.

Yet in the very process of establishing that anti-essentialism, Cooper relies on the discourse of race, and ultimately resurrects racial divisions. The issue of race crops up throughout Cooper's works. Dana Nelson has read Cooper's depictions of race as a "means to power" by which Anglo-Americans come to dominate Native Americans and consolidate their white racial and national identity (Nelson 1992: 45). Reflecting on the work that language does for Cooper, she draws on Bakhtin's notion of "double-voiced discourse" to argue that the novel is "rooted in heteroglossia ... and is therefore inevitably sedimented with the very social history frontier *tradition* seeks to repress" (Nelson 1992: 60). For Nelson, heteroglossic excess runs counter to the novel's ideological agenda and occurs "despite the author's intentions" (Nelson 1992: 61). By contrast, Jared Gardner argues that discursive displacements play a strategic role in Cooper's works, especially in his dealings with race. Whereas Nelson's comments focus exclusively on the relationship between Anglo- and Native Americans, Gardner takes into account Cooper's relationship to African-Americans. He argues that Cooper tries to "erase race from national identity" (Gardner 1998: 85) by a logic "in which the myth of the Vanishing American brings about the vanishing of slavery, the state of Missouri, and the very fact of racial difference altogether" (Gardner 1998: 102).[22] When Gardner points out that in Cooper's novels "all the talk of race has nothing to do with racial difference" (Gardner 1998: 93), his reference to the "*talk* of race" hints at the important work that discursive displacement itself does for Cooper's novels. Cooper imagines that a particular kind of discourse, that of translation, allows him to set aside issues of race and to imagine differences as verbally conditioned and negotiable.

By separating language from race, Cooper's novel participate in a specific vision of the transatlantic. As I have pointed out, Webster argued that

> when used by a person in Europe or Africa, transatlantic signifies being in America; when by a person in America, it denotes being or lying in

Europe or Africa. We apply it chiefly to something in Europe. (Webster 1828)[23]

Cooper enacts the logic by which Webster's definition frames transatlantic relationships unevenly: "transatlantic" privileges European-American connections over African-American and African-European contexts. In Wheatley's writing, the relationship between Europe and America becomes the primary relationship of cultural context, and yet by casting that relationship in terms of a translation that is always in excess of itself, that cultural context is never independent of but always haunted by Africa. Although Cooper shares key assumptions with Wheatley — such as the absence of a mother tongue, the doubling of translation through the invocation of multiple linguistic contexts, and the sense that translation is always excessive — he capitalizes differently on her model. Whereas for Wheatley translation provided a way of addressing racial inequality and cultural losses, for Cooper, translation holds the possibility of setting aside the issue of race and imagining the proliferation of a pluralistic discourse as a net cultural gain.

One way in which Cooper performs the vanishing of Africa from the transatlantic and of race from the American scene is through his use of characters. In *The Pioneers*, he introduces Agamemnon, an African-American slave whose classic name evokes and whose illiteracy mocks the model of neoclassical translation represented by Wheatley. Cooper invokes Agamemnon only to have him disappear quickly from the novel's action as Oliver Edwards, the white scion of British loyalists, takes center stage.[24] Cooper addresses the issue of slavery most directly in *The Last of the Mohicans*. He racializes Cora by pointing out that "the tresses of this lady were shining and black, like the plumage of the raven. Her complexion was not brown, but it rather appeared charged with the color of the rich blood, that seemed ready to burst its bounds" (Cooper 1989: 10). Surprisingly, discussions of Cora's race are usually absent from Cooper criticism.[25] Most scholars focus on the death of Uncas to illustrate Cooper's complicity with the ideology of Indian removal.[26] Through his portrayal of Cora, Cooper performs the discursive erasure of race and the blanching of the Atlantic.

Her father, Munro, casts Cora in the role of the tragic mulatta when he mistakes Duncan Heyward's preference for Alice as a sign of racial prejudice. In explaining Cora's history, Munro charts the course of the British Empire and makes his daughter an emblematic character for transatlantic slavery:

'I had seen many regions, and had shed much blood in different lands, before duty called me to the islands of the West Indies. There it was my lot to form a connection with one who in time became my wife, and the mother of Cora. She was the daughter of a gentleman of those isles, by a lady whose misfortune it was, if you will,' said the old man, proudly, 'to be descended, remotely, from that unfortunate class who are so basely enslaved to administer to the wants of a luxurious people. But could I find a man among them who would dare to reflect on my child, he should feel the weight of a father's anger! Ha! Major Heyward, you are yourself born at the south, where these unfortunate beings are considered of a race inferior to your own.' (Cooper 1989: 164)

In this passage, Cooper acknowledges the importance of slavery and race not only for Cora specifically, but more generally for the transatlantic. Yet he immediately antiquates race as "remote" even from Cora's dead mother. That antiquation allows Cooper to reinvent the transatlantic, so that it comes to refer "chiefly to something in Europe" (Webster 1828): although the passage is nominally about Cora, she is merely a vehicle for Cooper's reinvention of the transatlantic as the site of a Scottish identity on which American identity will be based. By ending the novel with the union between Heyward and Alice, Cooper imagines a restoration of Scottishness that eliminates the issue of transatlantic slavery and racial difference. Munro and Heyward are both Scottish: Cooper refers to Munro as "the veteran Scotchman" (Cooper 1989: 4), and Munro lets us know that Duncan is "half a Scotsman" himself (Cooper 1989: 156) whose ancestors "were an ornament to the nobles of Scotland' (Cooper 1989: 162). Munro had initially desired to marry Alice's mother, a fellow Scot like himself, but was prevented from entering into that union by her father. Due to paternalistic interventions, he was displaced into imperial relationships at the cost of his domestic bliss. Participating in the course of empire, Munro finds himself in the West Indies, the paradigmatic site of the transatlantic trade in slaves and goods, but also of slave emancipation by the time of Cooper's writing in 1826.[27] Munro's exclamation amounts to a plea for racial tolerance and reconciliation that Cooper himself sees as unrealistic. Instead of imagining racial tolerance, Cooper fantasizes about the abolition of racial difference as he undertakes to rewrite the history of transatlantic relations.

At times, it seems that Cooper's attempts to abolish racial difference go hand in hand with the breakdown of communication rather than with the proliferation of translation. Much of *The Last of the Mohicans* revolves around a desire to set aside words and instead embrace action: for instance, we reach in the novel "a crisis ... when acts were more required than words" (Cooper 1989: 146). At another point, we are told that "it was too obvious now that their situation was imminently perilous to need the aid of language to confirm it" (Cooper 1989: 215). Lora Romero has concluded from these and other moments that Cooper sets up a gender binary by which words are feminized and actions masculinized. She writes that

antebellum discourse ... uses images of the modern proliferation of words as a sign that feminine words have replaced masculine muscle as the basis of authority. Momist imagery of the loss of autonomy resulting from this feminization of power expresses nostalgia for a form of power whose lack of psychic consequences guarantees that it does not compromise the autonomy of the male subject. (Romero 1991: 401–2)

Yet if that logic held throughout the novel, *The Last of the Mohicans* would have to be bathed in silence at the death of Cora. The opposite holds true: after Cora's death, the novel virtually explodes in discourse when Cooper imagines the burial scene, the ambassadorial role that Natty henceforth plays between the white and native characters of the novel, the eloquence of the Native American chief, and of Natty in his final offer of friendship to Chingachgook. The scene of linguistic fantasy has shifted in the course of the novel: proliferating discourse takes the place of race as the site of the novel's cultural negotiations.

After the climactic deaths of Cora and Uncas, the novel's most clearly racialized characters, *The Last of the Mohicans* abandons the register of race for the discourse of sentimentality. Chingachgook mourns his son Uncas' death. He sees himself in complete isolation from his fellow man, and casts himself as the eponymous last of the Mohicans. Faced with his despondent friend, Hawkeye bursts out in sentimental effusion:

> 'No, no,' cried Hawkeye, who had been gazing with a yearning look at the rigid features of his friend, with something like his own self-command, but whose philosophy could endure no longer, 'no, Sagamore, not alone. The gifts of our colors may be different, but God has so placed us as to journey in the same path. I have no kin, and I may also say, like you, no people. He was your son, and a redskin by nature; and it may be that your blood was nearer — but if ever I forget the lad who has so often fou't at my side in war, and slept at my side in peace, may He who made us all, whatever may be our color or our gifts, forget me! The boy has left us for a time; but, Sagamore, you are not alone.' (Cooper 1989: 373)

In a novel that has negotiated racial divisions in the registers of courtship (Magua-Cora-Uncas) and kinship (Alice-Munro-Cora, Chingachgook-Uncas), a third model for negotiating difference wins out. This model of sentimental attachment is based on sympathetic identification. In mourning Uncas, Hawkeye forges a bond with Chingachgook that is based on his "yearning look" and his identification with the other's suffering. Hawkeye finds his "own self-command" reflected in the "rigid features of his friend." Instead of being "alone," Chingachgook and Hawkeye find themselves on a "journey in the same path." Hawkeye recognizes that his pain and Chingachgook's are not the same — their shared grief is not based on a sense of complete identity. Such identity would collapse the differences that must exist for sympathetic identification to occur. It is precisely because of their lack of kinship and their racial difference from each other that they are able to forge their sympathetic bond. For Cooper, that bond is primarily linguistic: sympathetic identification and differentiation are subsets of a broader linguistic enterprise to locate American literature in translation.

The recurrence of race at the site of translation raises the question who can access translation, and in what way. Like English, Native American languages are internally differentiated. In the plural, they are for Cooper corrupted versions of a singular native language that presumably existed before contact among native and non-native peoples occasioned these languages to become blended. To explore the significance of that lost language, Cooper stages moments when, for instance, "the Huron used his native language" (Cooper 1989: 105). In such instances, the native language seems to function much like a mother tongue: it seems to be the language of a tribe of ethnically and culturally related people, who are Huron by virtue of speaking Huron. Native languages are in these passages then also synonymous with national languages: the nation of the Huron speaks Huron. Yet these native languages point to the loss of linguistic origins and ethnic commonality. As Cooper points out,

> the confusion of nations, and even of tribes, to which Hawkeye alluded, existed at that period in the fullest force. The great tie of language, and, of course, of a common origin, was severed in many places; and it was one of its consequences, that the Delaware and the Mingo (as the people of the Six Nations were called) were found fighting in the same ranks, while the latter sought the scalp of the Huron, though believed to be the root of his own stock. (Cooper 1989: 206)

Although Cooper fantasizes about a time when a single native language existed, he argues that the hallmark of modernity is the absence of such linguistic unity.[28] Paradoxically, to speak a "native language" (Cooper 1989: 105) reflects the loss of native language; modernity marks a pluralization of linguistic contexts that define native languages by their differences from one another. Modern national languages mark the loss of linguistic origin and ethnic commonality. It is only in comparison with other languages and through a process of linguistic proliferation that these languages achieve the status of distinct individual languages. They arise from the proliferation of linguistic and national differences; discursive pluralism and national differentiation go hand in hand. Cooper reinforces this point by the fact that the reader only ever encounters this model of linguistic nativism in translation: moments when Cooper tells us that characters speak in their "native language" are in fact moments of translation. The language translated into is itself a complex blend, and not an organic natural language. In Cooper's theoretical construct, English does not homogenize the languages it translates; instead, translation elicits the complexity of both linguistic contexts. Language is first and foremost a mode in Cooper's works: it is always in process, and shifts depending on its contexts.

Yet how readily characters can enter into this non-essentialist model of language differs, and reflects the extent to which they are determined by race. Because of his race-based hatred of Munro, Magua "affects, like most of his people, to be ignorant of the English, and least of all will he condescend to speak it, now that war demands the utmost exercise of his dignity" (Cooper 1989: 12). Only when he sees himself "urged by some motive of more than usual moment" will Magua deign "to use the English tongue" (Cooper 1989: 96). At such moments, his speech is marked by a lack of linguistic sophistication. His English is "broken" (Cooper 1989: 18, 89) and "rude" (Cooper 1989: 131). However, Cooper insists that so long as characters do not let racial prejudices interfere, translation is an egalitarian mode of communication. For instance, when Duncan Heyward and the Munro sisters find themselves in captivity, Duncan speaks French with the Huron chief. The Huron chief then assumes the role of the translator: he "translated the meaning of the stranger's words into the Huron language, a suppressed murmur announced the satisfaction with which the intelligence was received" (Cooper 1989: 278). In theory at least, the role of the translator is not specific to any one race; but in practice, it is reserved most often for Cooper's white characters because they are more fully transculturated than his Native American characters. Race reasserts itself in Cooper's model in the following sense: because Cooper's model of language is foundationally anti-essentialist, it cannot account for essentialist models of linguistic and cultural identity. Moments when Cooper thinks about race create an unevenness, by which white characters are more readily able to express themselves in the blended forms of communication that require acts of translation.

Paradoxically, that unevenness stems in part from Cooper's desire to imagine his national translation as distinct from imperial translation, that is, as different from the *translatio imperii et studii* that appropriates difference and imposes homogeneity.[29] As I mentioned above, Cooper's model of translation not only draws on commonalities but also ensures the existence of alterity. Because translation operates only in the "neutral ground," there are always aspects of languages and cultures that remain outside of translation. Because a realm of difference exists that does not readily participate in a model of negotiable diversity, translation does not become a totalizing discourse. Cooper draws attention to these limits and limitations of translation and develops a particular strategy for resisting cultural uniformity. Through repeated gestures of inadequacy, Cooper prevents his text from simply appropriating what it translates. For example, he prefaces his rendition of a Native American "hymn" with the disclaimer: "if it were possible to translate the comprehensive and melodious language in which he spoke, the ode might read something like the following" (Cooper 1989: 339) — and the translation follows. Cooper imagines Native American language and culture as existing in excess of his translations. His gesture of inadequacy amounts to a strategy of making what is translated irreducible to its translation. Cooper insists that it is not possible to translate the ode adequately because he cannot capture the "comprehensive" language in which it was composed. Limited to a "neutral ground" of shared language, Cooper recognizes that the scope of the translated language eludes and exceeds the translation. As a representation of the original, translation is always a failed enterprise: the elements of a language that are essential and specific to one language exclusively remain outside of a model that relies on an anti-essentialist understanding of language. Cooper acknowledges the existence and importance of cultural alterity. Yet he also makes that alterity the site of a cultural essentialism with which he ultimately cannot come to terms.

That failure becomes particularly apparent at the end of *Last of the Mohicans*. Jane Tompkins has argued about the novel's end that "Cooper turns away finally from the possibility of union, with an elegiac gesture that mourns not so much the passing of the 'wise race of the Mohicans' as the dream of human brotherhood" (Tompkins 1985: 112). That inability to find a "human brotherhood" plays itself out through the failure of translation as the characters confront a situation of racial essentialism. In the funeral scene, Natty refuses to translate the Native American orations for Munro and Heyward:

> The scout, to whom alone, of all the white men, the words were intelligible, suffered himself to be a little aroused from his meditative posture, and bent his face aside, to catch their meaning, as the girls proceeded. But when they spoke of the future prospects of Cora and Uncas, he shook his head, like one who knew the error of their simple creed, and resuming his reclining attitude, he maintained it until the ceremony — if that might be called a ceremony, in which feeling was so deeply imbued — was finished. Happily for the self-command of both Heyward and Munro, they knew not the meaning of the wild sounds they heard. (Cooper 1989: 367)

At the end of the novel, the Lenape conceive of Cora's and Uncas' joint funeral celebration as a marriage when they speak "of the future prospects of Cora and Uncas" (Cooper 1989: 367). This "simple creed" meets with Natty's skepticism: he resists the substitution of an afterlife for the possibilities of national reconciliation. For Cooper, the breakdown of reconciliation and linguistic communication go hand in hand. Not only does Natty fail to translate the scene for Heyward and Munro, the very basis for such translation has vanished: although the ceremony they witness is one in which "feeling was so deeply imbued," the Anglo-American characters can no longer enter into a sympathetic bond with the Native American characters. At that moment of failed sympathetic identification, language itself enters uncertain territory — it is no longer clear what the ceremony "might be called" at a point where sentimental sociability, the very basis for communication, has collapsed under the pressures of violence and warfare. Although Heyward and Munro are poised to lose their "self-command" if they identify (with) "the meaning" of the hymns, the words themselves have become only "wild sounds" to them. The obscurity of those sounds and unintelligibility of the scene mark a significant shift in the novel: throughout, Heyward has demonstrated his ability to interpret "the language of the Mohicans" and their gestures with "little difficulty," and to follow "the thread of their argument" (Cooper 1989: 208). At the end, Heyward is struck with cultural amnesia because the very ground for sympathetic identification and linguistic interpretation has given way under the racist pressures of the war. Cooper imagines this moment as one where translation becomes impossible in the face of overwhelming racial division. In the funeral scene, the "neutral ground" that is necessary for translation and for the very emergence of an American culture collapses.

That failure of communication does not just apply to the Native American side but cuts both ways. Cooper also shows Natty refusing to translate what Munro has to say:

> 'Say to these kind and gentle females, that a heartbroken and failing man returns them his thanks. Tell him, that the Being we all worship, under different names, will be mindful of their charity; and that the time shall not be distant when we may assemble around his throne without distinction of sex, or rank, or color.' The scout listened to the tremulous voice in which the veteran delivered these words, and shook his head slowly when they were ended, as one who doubted their efficacy. 'To tell them this,' he said, 'would be to tell them that the snows come not in the winter, or that the sun shines fiercest when the trees are stripped of their leaves.' Then turning to the women, he made such a communication of the other's gratitude as he deemed most suited to the capacities of his listeners. (Cooper 1989: 371)

Munro wants to imagine that race-blind reconciliation will occur even after his daughter's and Uncas' death. But Natty no longer sees such reconciliation as a possibility. Giving up on the notion of such reconciliation makes it impossible for him to translate: because Natty can no longer imagine a "neutral ground," he sees Munro's speech as a violation of Native Americans' essential beliefs. Those beliefs are no longer ones that can sustain communication — for that matter, Natty reverts here to a metaphoric language that remains obscure in the context of this passage. The ability to imagine an anti-essentialist form of communication has collapsed, and Natty's refusal to translate points out that languages have become incomprehensible to one another.

Cooper's model cannot come to terms with cultural essentialism, whether that essentialism is imperially mandated or indigenously produced.

In a chapter epigraph that for me captures Cooper's project, he quotes Campell's Gertrude of Wyoming: "For here the exile met from every clime, And spoke, in friendship, every distant tongue" (Cooper 1991: 96). It is that double fantasy, of an exilic friendship based on sympathetic identification, and of a translation into "distant tongues" that Cooper sets up in *Last of the Mohicans*, but that seems to collapse for his characters at the end of his novel.

The breakdown of communication threatens Cooper's own project of writing a novel as and in translation. In the silencing that occurs at the novel's end, *The Last of the Mohicans* confronts the failure of its own methodology. However, Cooper imagines the collapse of translation as a historical stage that his novel offsets. Although Natty refuses to translate the scene for Munro and Heyward in the first instance, and for the Native Americans in the second instance, the reader is in the privileged position of understanding what it is that Natty withholds. Whereas Natty refuses to translate the scene for his bystanders, Cooper himself does produce a translation for his readers. Thereby, Cooper offsets the plot's outcome (the failure of translation). Utopian translatability prevails as Cooper imagines his novel to exceed the limitations of a specific moment and to make possible at a later time the act of communication that had historically failed.

III.

Through his use of translation, Cooper casts the reader in Natty's role. Inscribed in neither the Native American nor the Anglo-American community, Natty and the reader come to occupy a "neutral ground" from which they understand both sides but belong to neither. Their position of liminality challenges us to rethink what claims we make about the cultural work that the nineteenth century novel performs.

Benedict Anderson's influential *Imagined Communities* (1991) inaugurated an extended inquiry into the relationship between discourse and nationalism. Following Anderson, critical accounts "have taken the nation-novel connection as axiomatic: the tales of sympathy, seduction, incest, and captivity that typify early American novels have been primarily interpreted as allegories of American nationhood — as narratives that thematize the vicissitudes of citizenship and national identity in the new polity" (Dillon 2005: 235). But Cooper's work refuses to align novel and nation. Cooper situates his discourse and his reader between different communities. By imagining that in-betweenness as a discursive site, Cooper challenges the very premise on which Anderson bases his understanding of nations and novels: for Anderson, the modern nation is first and foremost defined by its linguistic cohesion. He explains that "communities ... developed ... early conceptions of their nation-ness" because "the various Americas shared languages and cultures with their respective metropoles" (Anderson 1991:

50–1). Anderson associates the rise of nationalism with "the development of a standardized language-of-state" (Anderson 1991: 56) and the existence of a culturally unifying language (Anderson 1991: 76). Yet as we have seen, it is precisely the notion of a monolingual nation that Cooper dismisses in his Leatherstocking novels by inventing a language of and in translation. For Cooper, the novel and the nation relate to one another through the intermediary of linguistic translation, which profoundly redefines what we might mean by either term, "novel" and "nation."

Jonathan Culler has described writing that draws on but is not limited to the discourse of nationhood as constituting a "*supra*national genre" (Culler 1999: 25). Useful as that formulation is, thinking of Cooper's writing in relation to *genre* does not yet get at my point. Unlike Anderson who emphasizes the importance of *form* in thinking about the novel, I am arguing that Cooper invents a supranational *methodology* to which formal considerations are at best secondary. Based on two considerations, that discursive methodology is transatlantic: first, Cooper's novels directly engage with the relationship between America and the colonial European powers. But second, and less prosaically, Cooper develops a methodology that makes the "transatlantic" a multilingual discourse of and in translation.

Cooper's explicit engagement with the transatlantic emerges when we juxtapose the canonized Leatherstocking novels with his all-but-forgotten European novels. After the publication of *The Last of the Mohicans*, Cooper fulfilled a long-standing dream: finally free of the debt his father had left him and again financially solvent, Cooper responded to his success as an American author by moving with his family to France. While he lived there, Cooper wrote and published the third Leatherstocking novel, *The Prairie* (1827), alongside a trilogy of novels set in Europe, *The Bravo* (1831), *The Heidenmauer* (1832), and *The Headsman* (1833).

In *The Heidenmauer*, a historical novel set in Germany during the Reformation, Cooper revisited the ending of *Last of the Mohicans* and replayed the scene of translation. Pitting an order of monks with feudal power against an exploited group of townspeople, Cooper tested the power of language to bring a community into existence. In its climactic confrontation, the novel revolves around the conflict between the illiterate townspeople who speak in the vernacular, and the monks, who express themselves in Latin and in writing. After they lay siege to the nearby abbey of Limburg, the townspeople of Duerckheim receive a "missive of the monks [that] was written in Latin" (Cooper 1832: II.121). The illiterate townspeople depend on Ludwig, a man trained for the Church but barred from his clerical office by "some irregularities of life" (Cooper 1832: II.121) to read the Latin text. Cooper describes that Ludwig

> forgot no part of the intonation or emphasis, while he uttered the unintelligible phrases of the monkish missive. His auditors listened the more attentively, because they did not understand a syllable of what

was said; attention seeming usually to be riveted in an inverse ratio to the facilities of comprehension. (Cooper 1832: II.122)

Cooper examines what it means to think of Latin as a universal language. The text that Ludwig reads is written in a sacred language that does not address itself to an audience. The fact that the townspeople cannot comprehend the letter's content without translation reveals Latin as the least universal of languages: it is spoken only by an elite, by the same elite in all countries, and rendered sacred by cabal. The townspeople mistrust their own ability to judge and place faith in Ludwig, who "was known to be instructed" (Cooper 1832: II.122), because "most believed there were means of judging that belonged to the initiated, which did not fall to the lot of those who worshipped in the outer court" (Cooper 1832: II.122). For Cooper, "the initiated" use knowledge to relegate the populace to the affect of worship. Nominally the most transparent and universal of languages, Latin remains utterly opaque to an illiterate, vernacular audience; its use is limited to a sector of society rather than being broadly available to the people. Cooper suggests that consolidated power depends on such monolingual opacity and that a hierarchy of languages develops in a society in which only an elite is multilingual. Cooper explains that at the time of his novel's setting, "every noble or town was obliged to maintain a scholar to perform what are now the commonest duties of intercourse" (Cooper 1832: II.121). His insistence that the "commonest" dialogic exchange depended on mediators who facilitated a community's (self-)understanding indicates that Cooper equates a spread in the ability to translate with a democratization of discourse; for him, multilingual communication and community directly condition one another.

On some level, the townspeople understand the significance of the performance without understanding its content. Despite their ignorance of Latin, the townspeople understand the text *as* a performance: Cooper describes the "higher dignitaries" actively attempting to participate in such textual power: they feign an understanding of the text so that "their inferiors might be duped into the belief of their attainments ... [and] to increase their influence, since there is no better evidence of the innate aspirations of our intellectual being, than the universal deference that is paid to knowledge" (Cooper 1832: II.122). Though intended to perpetuate social hierarchy, this aspiration inadvertently democratizes power. The scene turns the townspeople's seemingly passive consumption of the text into an active participation in that power when the performance of the text engenders a community experience that allows the individual members of the audience to overcome their isolation. Cooper insists that "not an individual was there ... who did not affect to have received more or less pleasure from the communication" and shared in "the pure force of sympathy ... that seemed so strong and so general" (Cooper 1832: II.123). Based on "affect" and "sympathy," the townspeople's response transforms the experience of power into an experience of community. Yet that sense of community is based exclusively on the relationship among the townspeople themselves and is at odds with the punitive missive. In the absence of translation, such sympathetic identification is ultimately misguided.

Cooper reinstates the centrality of linguistic knowledge and multilingualism to this scene when he stages a translation of the Latin into the German vernacular. The townspeople's participation in the power of the Latin text turns out to be deceptive when Ludwig

> commenced translating the letter into the harsh, energetic German of the Rhine. The wonderful capabilities of the language enabled him to convert the generalities and comprehensive terms of the Latin, with a minuteness of signification, which put the loss of any shade of idea utterly out of the question. What the monks had meant, and perhaps even more, was laboriously, and with malignant pleasure, rendered; and so rendered, as to give to each expression the fullest weight and meaning. (Cooper 1832: II.122)

By the logic of Anderson's argument, the shift into the vernacular should establish an imagined community. Based on a shared vernacular and a shared opposition against feudal power structures, Cooper's novel seems to stage the historical conjunction that Anderson wishes to establish between novels and nations. However, the community that arises in this scene does not depend on the shift to the vernacular, but on a double act of translation — the one performed by Ludwig and the one performed by Cooper himself. Cooper imagines the community in this novel to emerge across national boundaries in the discursive space of the transatlantic.

Translation plays a dubious role in this scene. On the one hand, translation enables the townspeople to understand the content of the missive. But the translator himself seems unreliable: his "malignant pleasure" and desire to translate "even more" than the text contained makes the townspeople vulnerable to an unreliable source of linguistic authority (Cooper 1832: II.122). Cooper's novel offsets the effect of this inadequate translation. Although it is not possible for the townspeople to see the excesses of Ludwig's translation, Cooper's readers recognize how he is deploying language to exercise power. Cooper facilitates that recognition by translating the scene of translation for his readers. This act of double translation unhinges the connection between the novel and the nation; it makes translation the central mode of Cooper's writing, a mode that can offset even the bad translation we see Ludwig perform. Although Cooper composed the European Trilogy in English, parenthetical comments such as "(the discourse was in German)" reinvent the novels as (fictive) translations (Cooper 1833: II.58). By creating for his readers the illusion that they themselves are experiencing an act of translation, Cooper creates a sense of sympathetic identification with the townspeople. However, that shared exposure to translation does not simply inscribe the reader in the community Cooper portrays in his novel. If the readers were in fact part of the German community, they would not need this second translation into English. Cooper's translation facilitates yet offsets an identification between his readers and his characters. The locus of Cooper's identification is a discursive community that is open-ended because it is founded on and in transatlantic translation.

Much like the impartial spectator and language itself, Cooper imagines his readerly community to exceed national divisions. As Jonathan Culler has argued, novels "may do much to encourage the imagining of those communities that become nations, but they do not do so, I submit, by addressing readers *as nationals*" (Culler 1999: 30). Despite the fractures within the community of Duerckheim, and despite the temporal distance that separates Cooper's contemporaries from Reformation-era Germans, his novel creates an abstract identification with the community. The community of readers that Cooper creates through his act of double translation is simultaneously national and transnational, cis- and transatlantic. Cooper thinks of nationalism as a displaced discourse that negotiates its relationship with global as well as with local contexts in a "neutral ground." Cooper's fiction imagines a writing in excess — a utopian coming into being that is always both immanent and delayed. For Cooper, the transatlantic is neither a precursor nor a successor to the national tradition he invents; instead, by developing his model of translation he places the transatlantic at the core of a national literature that is always excessive. The American novel Cooper imagines emerges in transatlantic translation.

But the question arises whether and with what justification the literature of and in translation that I have been describing can still be seen as "American literature." In trying to define what we might mean by "American literature," William Spengemann has argued: "If we can locate, somewhere, a literary work whose form can be attributed directly to the impact of America on the written language, then, no matter where we find it or who wrote it, we can say that we have discovered a literature that deserves to be called American" (Spengemann 1984: 387). Cooper's works, whether set in America or in Europe, are about "the impact of America on the written language." For Cooper, the American scene is quintessentially multilingual. That multilingualism requires constant acts of translation. Those acts of translation are the "impact" that Cooper's conception of America has on his "written language." Cooper's novels are American literature in the sense that they constantly display their multilingual negotiation. That multilingual negotiation makes "American" a term that does not fit any strictly national categorization. The nation is not a formal entity, but instead a modality for Cooper.

In that emphasis on modality, Cooper represents a strand of American Romanticism that has been largely obscured because the "Emersonian tradition ... has shaped what several generations of readers have understood to be the distinctive qualities of both of American literature and American experience" (Rowe 1997: x). In the next chapter, I argue that Ralph Waldo Emerson's linguistic transcendence competed with the model of American translation that I am outlining in this book. In response to Margaret Fuller's model of an American literature founded in linguistic acts of translation, Emerson located originality in a linguistically transcendent, naturalized monolingualism. Whereas Emerson imagined literature as a solipsistic enterprise, Fuller drew on the sentimental model of translation that I have discussed in this chapter to theorize a transatlantic American literature that emerged in its intimate linguistic connections to others. Fuller developed a practice by which American literature came into being when acts of translation established a sense of intimacy across national and linguistic borders. *How* Fuller imagined a literature that became national by virtue of its global translation is the problem to which I now turn.

3 American world literature
Margaret Fuller's particular universality

When Margaret Fuller drowned in a shipwreck off the American coast in 1850, her spirit, though finally disembodied, still haunted the imagination of her male peers. She was returning to conservative New England as a figure of both political radicalism and sexual transgression. Fuller had reported first-hand on the revolution in Rome, and there was scandalized speculation that she had conceived her infant son out of wedlock. Haunted by these excesses, Nathaniel Hawthorne resurrected her as the defiant, flagrantly sexual Zenobia in *The Blithedale Romance* (1852) and reenacted her drowning in a paradoxical attempt to "disempower . . . by fully sexualizing her" (Berlant 1989: 35).[1] If Hawthorne's motive was to influence perceptions of Fuller as a woman, his intervention was complemented by Ralph Waldo Emerson's attempt to control her as a writer. After the shipwreck, Emerson sent Henry David Thoreau to comb the beach in search of Fuller's lost manuscript on the history of the Italian Revolution.[2] Like Fuller's body, the manuscript was never recovered.

The literary loss occasioned by Fuller's drowning extends to her publications and surviving manuscripts, which were disemboweled by a group of her friends.[3] Their primary aim seems to have been to repatriate Fuller by erasing the central feature of her theory of a multilingual American literature: translation. Fuller had been known in her lifetime as a translator, but her literary executor, her brother Arthur Fuller, purged her books of the translations they contained, and her book-length translations passed out of print.[4] At a time when increasing numbers of immigrants were coming to the United States in the wake of the European revolutions and U.S. imperial expansion was taking aggressive militaristic form, Fuller's silencing coincided with a xenophobic backlash against the foreign, accompanied by an epistemological shift. Whereas Fuller had been able to define the foreign as an integral part of her American identity, such alterity was sacrificed as the logic of *e pluribus* gave way to an *unum* of national identity. With Fuller's failed physical and literary return from Europe, the United States lost its premier theorist of literary cosmopolitanism, who practiced translation as a social ethics.[5]

Fuller's desire to think of American literature as multilingual is resurging today as scholars increasingly regard the scope of American studies as transnational. Recent multilingual anthologies have extended our understanding of how linguistic and cultural subjectivities effect and refract one another in the complex scenes of American literature.[6] Yet translation, Fuller's chosen methodology, has met with ambivalence. The new anthologies depend on translations to make multilingual texts accessible to (often monolingual) readers, but they also "un-translate" texts by reprinting them in their original languages. Although translations are "helpful tools," Werner Sollors warns us that they "can also be treacherous once they become substitutes for originals" (Shell and Sollors 2000: 10). This anxiety over textual usurpation stems from the fear that translation may function as a tool of imperialism. In *The Poetics of Imperialism* (1997), Eric Cheyfitz defines the "treacherous" (Shell and Sollors 2000: 10) aspects of translation when he interprets the "historic relationship between translation and metaphor" through the "figure of *translatio*" (Cheyfitz 1997: xxiii). Jointly, the *translatio imperii* and the *translatio studii* functioned in classical antiquity to impose imperial domination — and the knowledge systems that enabled it — onto colonial others. Cheyfitz echoes Nietzsche's claim that for the Romans, "to translate meant to conquer" (Schulte and Biguenet 1992: 69) when he speaks of the "monologic politics of translation" (Cheyfitz 1997: xxvi). It is no wonder, then, that in contemporary critical discourse, translation is multilingualism's unloved stepchild: as monolingualism by other means, translation both allows for and annihilates multilingualism.

Yet this understanding of translation fails to account for a set of romantic translation theories that informs the epistemology of American multilingualism and enables its practices. For Fuller, cultural identity was not solipsistically original but intimately relational, and translation was the linguistic equivalent of that contingency. In *Woman in the Nineteenth Century* (1845), Fuller staged multilingual translation to develop her model for gender equity. Fuller developed this alternative vision of translation in response to theoretical challenges from Emerson, whose understanding of universality she wished to question, and as an alternative to a politics of othering. Rather than essentializing or erasing linguistic and cultural complexity, translation enabled Fuller to define cultural identity as a model of personhood that depends on a dialogue with others in a nation whose culture emerges in global context. When in 1843 Fuller experienced the Illinois frontier as a culturally contested space where race, ethnicity, and class threatened to foreclose dialogic relations among native, immigrant, and Anglo-American people, she drew on translation to give multilingualism full play. By insistently giving prominence to the translations she incorporated into her writing, Fuller developed a strategy of fragmentation and suture that brings into being an American literature that is domestically and globally transnational — or, we might say, translational.[7]

I.

For Fuller, figuring out what it meant to write an American literature that would be viably multilingual and global in its appeal, significance, and circulation raised challenging questions about the nation's relation to a collective world culture and the individual's relation to national and international collectives. Goethe's ability to negotiate these relations attracted Fuller to his writing. Praising Goethe in her translator's preface to *Conversations with Goethe* (1839) for a "mind which has known how to reconcile individuality of character with universality of thought," Fuller sought to popularize this capacity of German transcendentalism in the United States (Eckermann and Fuller 1839: xx). Because she believed that Goethe's works were best understood in relation to his life, of which little was known in New England, she planned to write his biography.

Considering the source materials available to Fuller, we can conclude that her research gave her an education in theories of translation. In England, Goethe was coming into vogue through translations of his works by such prominent Romantics as Walter Scott, Samuel Taylor Coleridge, and Thomas Carlyle. Less well-known today are the influential women who made names for themselves as translators in the 1830s and 1840s, including two whose work Fuller respected: British translator Sarah Austin and French novelist Germaine de Staël.

In her introduction to *Characteristics of Goethe* (1833), Austin examines the theories of translation available to her. Distancing herself from John Dryden and Samuel Johnson, who wanted to establish a close correspondence in language and style between source texts and translations, Austin points out that the ability to achieve such correspondence depends in part on how closely the two languages in play are related. In instances in which no close relation exists, Dryden and Johnson believed that the translator must "be content with something equivalent"(Goethe 1833: xxx). Austin claims that eighteenth-century theorists saw the translator's task as creating an illusion that the author's thoughts had originally been expressed in English. This emphasis on similitude and equivalence is "onesided," Austin argues, because "it may be that the very thing I want to know is, what *are* the 'modes of expression' which are, or were, esteemed elegant in another language. Here is an important key to all that constitutes the individual character of the poetry of a nation, and of the nation itself;—a key which, according to Dr. Johnson, the translator is to hide or to falsify" (Goethe 1833: xxxii). Austin understood translation not as the nationalization of a text by appropriation but as a means of drawing attention to linguistic differences and keeping national distinctions in play. She argues that her own work serves as a "plaidoyer in favour of the Germanisms with which I have made bold to affright English readers" (Goethe 1833: xxxvii). Wary of an English nationalism that reproduced the different as the same, Austin viewed translation as a way of representing another text without sacrificing its linguistic and national specificities to her own.

Such an agenda set Austin apart from some of her more prominent male contemporaries. Although "glad to refer unconditionally to the writings of my friend Mr. Carlyle," Austin makes it clear that she disagrees with some of Carlyle's views on Goethe, especially those concerning translation (Goethe 1833: xvi). In a review of William Taylor's *Historic Survey of German Poetry* (1828), Carlyle expressed his hope for the cultural work of translation:

> [D]o not many other indications, traceable in France, in Germany, as well as here, betoken that a new era in the spiritual intercourse of Europe is approaching; that instead of isolated, mutually repulsive National Literatures, a World-Literature may one day be looked for? The better minds of all countries begin to understand each other, and, which follows naturally, to love each other.[8]

If Carlyle advocates abandoning literary particularity, Austin's Germanisms draw attention to the importance of national distinctions for world literature. However, Austin does not simply dismiss Carlyle's position. Because her subject is Goethe, she draws on Goethe's translation practices, which accommodate Carlyle's view as well as her own:

> It appears to me that Goethe alone ... has solved the problem. ... 'There are two maxims of translation;' says he, 'the one requires that the author of a foreign nation be brought to us in such a manner that we may regard him as our own; the other, on the contrary, demands of us that we transport ourselves over to him and adopt his situation, his mode of speaking, his peculiarities.' (Goethe 1833: xxxii–iii)

Instead of viewing so-called familiarizing translations (which obscure the particularities of the foreign text) and foreignizing translations (which reveal the unfamiliar aspects) as opposite methods between which a translator must choose, Goethe understood the merit of each approach in relation to its purpose.[9]

While Austin does not consider how preserving the foreignness of the original text might affect national literature, Fuller found in Madame de Staël's practices and theories of translation a theoretical model for this aspect of translation. In "The Spirit of Translations" (1816), a case study of Italian literature, de Staël begins by criticizing authors of the Italian Renaissance for writing in Latin, a supposedly universal language that was "both dead and artificial" at the time, proving utterly inaccessible to the majority of Italians, who knew only their vernacular. De Staël expresses her sympathy with the ideal of eliminating translations by having all people know all languages, but given the impractical nature of this ideal, she proposes translation as another solution for negotiating the desire to be universal, comprehensible, and culturally specific:

Ultimately, it is the universal to which one must aspire in attempting to do good for the human race. I would go even further: even if one had a good understanding of foreign languages, a successful translation of a work into one's own language would provide a more familiar and intimate pleasure than the original. The imported beauty that a translation brings with it gives the national style new turns of phrase and original expressions. To preserve a country's literature from banality, a sure sign of decadence, there is no more effective means than translating foreign poets.[10]

With her idea that the original is more familiar and more intimately pleasing in translation, de Staël proposes that we should think about translation as a method for negotiating universality through particularity. Translation provides a point of entry by expressing the text in familiar terms, but it also mingles the familiar with "new turns of phrase and original expressions." This claim is quite remarkable. De Staël, in effect, proposes that translation does not just reflect the source language's idiomatic originality, as Austin explains, but also generates expressive originality for the language and culture into which a text is translated. De Staël underscores this principle when she insists on the importance of translating foreign poetry as a way of avoiding banality. By her account, translation is a means of being nationally original and participating in transnational universality. The two choices that Goethe proposes and that Austin discusses coincide here: de Staël thinks of translation as simultaneously familiarizing and defamiliarizing, as establishing intimacy and estrangement, as domesticating and making foreign.[11] In these passages, de Staël is working out the implications of the two central components of romantic translation theory: an intralingual practice on which the very notion of a national language depends and an interlingual method that will realize what Goethe calls *Weltliteratur*, world literature.

As an intralingual practice, translation is foundational to modern vernacular languages. In his "Sendbrief vom Dolmetschen" (1530), Martin Luther justifies his translation of the Bible as a national resistance against imperialism, complaining that "Latin is a great hindrance to speaking good German," but German itself comes into being only through his act of translation.[12] According to Antoine Berman, Luther's translation of the Bible "*determines the relation of the mother tongue to itself*," for it does not reflect an already existing vernacular but establishes that vernacular in the process: "[W]hat is at stake, then, is to translate into a German that in a certain way rises above the multiplicity of *Mundarten* [dialects] without denying or crushing them in the process. Hence, Luther's twofold attempt: to translate into a German that *a priori* can only be local — his German — *Hochdeutsch* ['high' German, which becomes the standard written language] but to raise this local German in the very process of translation to the level of a common German, a *lingua franca*" (Berman 1992: 18, 25).

Such translation inaugurates what Mikhail Bakhtin theorizes as a dialogic process in his exploration of the proposition that "one's own language is never a single language"(Bakhtin 1981b: 66). Although Bakhtin is best known for his understanding of heteroglossia, that concept depends on an understanding of polyglossia, "the simultaneous presence of two or more national languages interacting within a single cultural system" (Bakhtin 1981a: 431). For Bakhtin, polyglossia is "inseparable from . . . the problem of heteroglossia within a language, that is, the problem of internal differentiation, the stratification characteristic of any national language" (Bakhtin 1981b: 67). Speech diversity "achieves its full creative consciousness only under conditions of an active polyglossia" (Bakhtin 1981b: 68). In his work on Rabelais, Bakhtin comments on the "immense importance of translations in the . . . mutual clarification of languages. . . . [W]orks had to be translated into a language that had not been finally developed and formed. Indeed it had to be shaped in the very process of translation" (Bakhtin 1968: 470). Although Bakhtin historicizes the importance of translation when he suggests that "it is possible to place oneself outside one's own language only when an essential historic change of language occurs," his claims posit a relationship with the other, the foreign, the alien as the basis for the formation of cultural identity (Bakhtin 1968: 471).

For de Staël as for Goethe, this relation to the other is not just a historical phase or a precondition for the development of national language and culture; it is, rather, a condition of modernity and a requirement for establishing a world literature. Goethe argues that "in venturing to announce a European, indeed a world literature, we did not mean merely to say that the different nations should inform themselves about one another and about each other's works . . . No! It is rather a matter of living . . . men of letters getting to know each other and, through their own inclination and sense of community, to find occasion to act socially" (in Berman 1992: 56). For Goethe, translation enables such personal, national, and global intimacy: "[I]t is just these connections between original and translation that express most clearly the relationship of nation to nation and that one must above all understand if one wishes to encourage a . . . world literature."[13] Berman argues that for Goethe, world literature is "not the totality of past and present literatures accessible to the encyclopedic gaze, nor the more limited totality of works . . . that have attained universal status," but a mode of writing that explicitly conceives its "existence and . . . unfolding in the framework of an incessantly intensified interaction" (Berman 1992: 55).

One of the most astute readers of romantic language theory, Walter Benjamin, examines this "intensified interaction." Like Goethe, whose translation theory he explicitly admires, Benjamin contends that "translation . . . ultimately serves the purpose of expressing the central reciprocal relationship between languages" (Benjamin 1969: 72). For Benjamin, that relationship is both intra- and interlinguistic: "[F]ar removed from being the sterile equation of two dead languages," translation is "charged with the special mission of watching over the maturing process of the original language and the birth pangs of its own" (Benjamin 1969: 73). Yet for Benjamin, translation ultimately overcomes the linguistic differences that give play to its significations. Defining languages as sharing a "central kinship" and as being "interrelated in what they want to express," Benjamin argues that different words share the same meaning, which does not reside in them as a fixed condition but emerges through a process of linguistic expression (Benjamin 1969: 72). This argument anticipates deconstruction as much as it echoes the linguistic program of Emersonian transcendentalism. As I will discuss presently, Benjamin is close to Emerson when he observes that "meaning is never found in relative independence, as in individual words or sentences; rather, it is in a constant state of flux — until it is able to emerge as pure language from the harmony of all the various modes of intention" (Benjamin 1969: 74). Rather than sustaining differences, translation ultimately aims to establish a "realm of reconciliation and fulfillment of languages." As "pure language," that realm "no longer means or expresses anything but is . . . that which is meant in all languages" (Benjamin 1969: 75, 80). Such a definition sacrifices the multilingualism of empirical translation to a linguistic metaphysics that privileges a unified signified over diverse signifiers.

II.

If translation establishes a global modernity, how can it maintain its constitutive diversity and how can it avoid the pitfall by which "'border crossings' and comparative connections, however attractive, may also contribute to the formation of homogenized ideas" (Rowe 2002: xxii)? Fuller's interest in continental translation theory challenged her to develop a model of empirical translation that protected national diversity and literary globalism from homogenizing universality. The struggle to articulate her own theory of cultural identity set into play evolving, often painful, relationships with both her intellectual mentor, Goethe, and Emerson, her chief interlocutor, whose understanding of language threatened the viability of her theory of translation. Despite her fervent admiration of Goethe, Fuller complained early in her career of his "immense superiority":

> It seems to me as if the mind of Goethe had embraced the universe. . . . He comprehends every feeling I have ever had so perfectly, expresses it so beautifully, but when I shut the book, it seems as if I had lost my personal identity; all my feelings linked with such an immense variety that belong to beings I had thought so different. What can I bring? There is no answer in my mind except 'It is so,' or 'It will be so.'[14]

Fuller expresses a similar esteem for and vexation with Emerson, and a similar sense of personal diminution:

> After the first excitement of intimacy with him . . . I was greatly disappointed in my relation to him. . . . I found no intelligence of my best self—far less was it revealed to me in new modes; . . . He had faith in the Universal, but not in Individual Man; he met man, not as a brother, but as a critic.[15]

Why does Fuller experience Goethe's universal genius and Emerson's "faith in the Universal" as a threat to her "personal identity" and "best self"? Fuller indicates that Goethe's ability to unite what is "different" and of "immense variety" erodes distinctions. Where differences dissolve in a "comprehend[ing]" and comprehensive embrace, Fuller feels a diminution that manifests itself verbally in the breakdown of discourse. Goethe's "beautiful" expressions leave her unable to respond (she cannot "answer" even her own questions); she can make only affirmative, ontological statements: "It is so." This ontology of the self comes at the cost of Fuller's "intelligence" and "best self," which can no longer unfold in the "new modes" of translation. Fuller understands personal identity not as a static category but as a discursive movement between poles of communicable difference: translation and personal identity elicit one another.

Fuller experimented with translation to develop a methodology for relating to others without experiencing or exerting the pressures of universal genius. As in her descriptions of her responses to Goethe and Emerson, Fuller drew on the sentimental register of feeling, intimacy, and relation to develop a model for translation not dependent on such universality. In her "Translator's Preface" to *Günderode* (1842), Fuller explains: "In translating, I throw myself, as entirely as possible, into the mood of the writer. . . . The style thus formed is, at least, a transcript of the feelings excited by the original; and is a likeness, if a caricature" (Arnim and Fuller 1842: vi). Fuller experiments with a mode of self-alienation that allows her to experience the mood of the other, but she also transcribes her own feelings. Although she regrets that she has "not the advantage of consulting any person who could aid me from an intimate knowledge of . . . the two girls," she insists that the "translation retains the delicate lineaments of the original . . . for their beauty has been keenly felt by the interpreter"(Arnim and Fuller 1842: v). For Fuller, translation is not a single, monodirectional act but a mode of reciprocity. She does not just translate others but fantasizes about being translated.[16] Translation apparently became Fuller's mode of choice for the expression of feelings. In 1836, she wrote to Eliza Farrar: "As to my feelings, I take no pleasure in speaking them; but I know not that I could give a truer impression of them, than by these lines which I translate from the German of Uhland. They are entitled 'Justification.'"[17]

Fuller negotiates her relation to emotional and textual authenticity in scenes of translation, yet the stakes of her enterprise are not merely personal. The intimacy that she developed via translation became her ideal model for realizing gender equity by discursive means. In *Woman in the Nineteenth Century* (1845), the work for which she is best known today, Fuller writes:

> Ye cannot believe it, men; but the only reason why women ever assume what is more appropriate to you, is because you prevent them from finding out what is fit for themselves. Were they free, were they wise fully to develop the strength and beauty of woman, they would never wish to be men, or manlike. The well-instructed moon flies not from her orbit to seize on the glories of her partner. No; for she knows that one law rules, one heaven contains, one universe replies to them alike. It is with women as with the slave.
>
> 'Vor dem Sklaven, wenn er die Kette bricht,
> Vor dem freien Menschen erzittert nicht.'
>
> Tremble not before the free man, but before the slave who has chains to break.
>
> In slavery, acknowledged slavery, women are on a par with men. Each is a work-tool, an article of property — no more! In perfect freedom, such as is painted in Olympus, in Swedenborg's angelic state, in the heaven where there is no marrying nor giving in marriage, each is a purified intelligence, an enfranchised soul, — no less! (Fuller 1998: 36–7)

Fuller casts her description of equality in terms of an educational enterprise that her own translation enacts. She argues that women do not wish to emulate men (they do not "wish to be men, or manlike"), but to develop a "purified intelligence" that reflects specifically what is "fit for themselves." To that end, they develop an aesthetic — their own "strength and beauty" — via an educational process that leaves them "well-instructed." The content of their instruction seems quite conservative when Fuller describes woman as sticking to a separate sphere ("her orbit") in recognition of "one law ... one heaven ... one universe" that governs all. But Fuller's "one" is always many, and translation is the ideal realization of that liberating plurality. Governance becomes dialogic in Fuller's imagination — it "replies to them alike" — via her act of translation.

Quoting Schiller, whom she had earlier accused of lacking prophetic vision in his treatment of women (Fuller 1998: 24), Fuller's translation enacts an intellectual liberation that strikes both a gendered and, in its invocation of slavery, a national note. In their letters to each other, Emerson and Fuller invoke society and the nation with an insistence that indicates their attempt to determine, through their own personal relationship, what role translation plays in cultural identity for "those larger individuals, the Nations."[18] In a letter to Fuller in October 1838, Emerson uses translation as a conceit:

> We are armed all over with these subtle antagonisms which as soon as we meet begin to play, and translate all poetry into such stale prose! It seems to me that people *descend* somewhat into society. All association must be a compromise; and what is worst, the very flower and aroma of the flower of each of the beautiful natures disappears as they approach each other. What a perpetual disappointment is society even of the virtuous and gifted.[19]

Fuller apparently had this passage in mind as she was translating *Günderode*, ending her introduction with the claim that von Arnim and Günderode "needed not 'descend to meet'"(Arnim and Fuller 1842: xii). With this assertion, Fuller confronts Emerson. When he imagines that people "*descend* into society," he suggests that only the isolated individual achieves transcendence. He rejects even casual contact (when "we meet"), equating social dialogue with disruptive "antagonisms" that destroy beauty. For Emerson, translation functions as an antisublime: it signifies a process of socialization that corrupts the individual's transcendent nature and originality.

In a curious sense, then, Emerson agrees with Fuller that linguistic translation produces personal and national identity. He resists empirical translation precisely because it detracts from a transcendence that is impersonal (as the flower metaphor indicates) and universal.[20] Emerson avails himself of the rhetoric of national difference when he expresses his frustration with Fuller's different perception of their friendship: "We use a different rhetoric. It seems as if we had been born and bred in different nations. You say you understand me wholly. You cannot communicate yourself to me. I hear the words sometimes but remain a stranger to your state of mind"(Emerson and Rusk 1939: 2.353). In this passage, Emerson skillfully stages his difference with Fuller over issues of translation. Whereas Fuller finds the "different rhetoric" of "different nations" comprehensible, Emerson refuses to understand the content (even when he cannot overlook the appearance) of such difference. Where national distinctions (i.e., implicitly, different nation states) reflect intellectual differences (i.e., different states of mind), Emerson inhabits the role of the stranger with a vengeance: linguistic, personal, and national differences make understanding impossible.

Yet Emerson's taking such a position reflects the extent to which Fuller's theories of translation and of specificity had unsettled his belief in transcendent language and universality. Emerson's comments to her directly echo his statement in "Nature" that "every natural fact is a symbol of some spiritual fact. Every appearance in nature corresponds to some state of the mind, and that state of the mind can only be described by presenting that natural appearance as its picture" (Emerson 1960: 32). Perhaps we can imagine how profoundly troubling it must have been for Emerson that he could not enter Fuller's "state of mind," having to "constantly aver that you and I are not inhabitants of one thought of the Divine Mind, but of two thoughts, that we meet and treat like foreign states, one maritime, one inland, whose trade and laws are essentially unlike."[21] Assessing her as "essentially unlike" himself was Emerson's pained response to his rhetorical question to Fuller: "And are you not struck with a certain subterranean current of identical thought that bubbles up to daylight in very remote and dissimilar circles of thought and culture?"[22] Emerson fantasizes here about a world in which differences are superficial and disparate identities dissolve into identical thought, where empirical differences vanish in the light of metaphysical unity. Even in his invention of Fuller as a different nation, he tries to restore this ideal. When he asserts that he and she are "two thoughts," he still insists that they are both part of "the Divine Mind," and that they participate in a unified intellect that can make sense of them both.

Emerson played out this fantasy by developing a countermodel to Fuller's translation, opposing her emphasis on literal, linguistic, empirical translation with a metaphysical model that ultimately disavowed linguistic difference. Of course, Emerson recognized the empirical existence of different languages and even wrote translations himself. By 1843, Emerson had begun translating Dante's *Vita Nuova*, and his volume of *Poems* (1847) includes a translation entitled "From the Persian of Hafiz." But as he explains in his journal (26 October 1838), Emerson believed that linguistic differences are essentially insignificant:

> *Vocabularies* — in going through Italy I speak Italian, through Arabia, Arabic: I say the same *things*, but have altered my speech. But ignorant people think a foreigner speaking a foreign tongue a formidable, odious nature, alien to the backbone. So is it with our brothers. Our journey, the journey of the soul, is through different regions of thought and to each its own vocabulary. As soon as we hear a new vocabulary from our own, at once we exaggerate the alarming differences . . . [later] we find he was . . . thinking the same *things* as we, under his own vocabulary. (Emerson et al. 1911: 99–100)

As Emerson imagines himself moving freely into other languages, each of which he inhabits comfortably and in the same way, they are all merely incidental because they gesture at the same essence. Through the odd twists of this passage, Emerson collapses the self and other. Imagining himself first as a traveler, he portrays himself as a foreigner. Then he describes the foreigner as other, only to return to the image of himself as the foreigner. This conjunction of the self and the foreigner is effected through his insistence that thought always addresses the "same *things*." This reification of words corresponds to his contention in "Nature" that "[w]ords are signs of natural facts"(Emerson 1960: 31). Barbara Packer has traced this passage in "Nature" to Emerson's graduation from Harvard, when he enthusiastically copied down commencement speaker Sampson Reed's claim that "words make one with things, and language is lost in nature," a formulation Emerson revised in a notebook entry: "[I]n good writing words become one with *things*."[23] Emerson understands this claim to mean that words are only "borrowed from some material appearance," and therefore, it matters little if there are different words for the same things (Emerson 1960: 31). Hence, when Emerson alters his speech during his imagined travels, his meaning does not change, for he still refers to the same things no matter what language he speaks.

As Packer points out, "[A]t the time of *Nature*, Emerson is thinking or hoping that the book of nature is written in a single tongue"(Packer 1982: 190). Emerson argues that because the same symbols constitute all languages, the more one reverts to natural symbolism, the more similar those languages are. For Emerson, language is thus singular in origin and outcome, and the return to a universal language results in the erasure of linguistic and intellectual difference: "Speech is the sign of partiality, difference, ignorance, and the more perfect the understanding between man, the less need of words. . . . The only speech will at last be action"(Emerson et al. 1911: 84). In this passage, Emerson uses "speech" in two ways: as conventional language (in which words always refer to other words) and as "first language" (in which words are one with things and things are one with words) (Emerson 1960: 33).[24] To return to that "first language," which is conceptually similar to Walter Benjamin's "pure language," Emerson develops a model of translation that runs counter to Fuller's concepts.

For Benjamin, as for Emerson, multilingualism is an empirical but not a metaphysical reality: "It is no longer conceivable, as the bourgeois view of language maintains, that the word has an accidental relation to its object, . . . agreed by some convention;" he goes on:

> Language never gives *mere* signs. However, the rejection of bourgeois by mystical linguistic theory equally rests on a misunderstanding. For according to mystical theory the word is simply the essence of the thing. That is incorrect, because the thing in itself has no word, being created from God's word and known in its name by a human word. (Benjamin 1979: 116–7)

This distinction between conventional and pure language, Benjamin insists, makes it "necessary to found the concept of translation at the deepest level of linguistic theory." Translation occurs among the different human languages that resulted from the biblical Fall, through which "man abandoned immediacy in the communication of the concrete, name, and fell into the abyss of the mediateness of all communication, of the word as means, of the empty word, into the abyss of prattle." From this mediateness, which accounts for the empirical multiplicity of languages, "it could be only a step to linguistic confusion" (Benjamin 1979: 118–20). An understanding of pure language, then, of a language that is immediate, depends on a rejection of multilingualism. Emerson's claim that "speech is the sign of partiality" points to a Benjaminian understanding by which, "in stepping outside the purer language of name, man makes language a means ... and therefore also, in one part at any rate, a *mere* sign; and this later results in the plurality of languages" (Benjamin 1979: 120). Benjamin's two meanings for translation clarify the distinction between Fuller's and Emerson's enterprises. Plurality of language as mere sign creates one type of translation, in which "one language is moved into another through a continuum of transformations . . . , not [through] abstract areas of identity and similarity" (Benjamin 1979: 118).

Fuller revels in the possibilities of this continuous translation because of its contributions to a sense of identity and transformation. But Emerson and Benjamin emphasize another type of translation that reinstates the pure language of God:

> In the translation of the language of things into that of man. . . . objectivity . . . is . . . guaranteed by God. For God created things; the creative word in them is the germ of the cognizing name, just as God, too, finally named each thing after it was created. . . . In receiving the unspoken nameless language of things and converting it by name into sounds, man performs th[e] task [God assigned]. (Benjamin 1979: 118)

Emerson's theory of translation is precisely in this vein, although he does not use the word *translation* in his published writings until *Representative Men* (1850) — with one exception.[25] In "Nature," when Emerson imagines texts as collectively authored, he uses the word "translate" to inscribe the practice in his philosophy of similitude: "[T]he axioms of physics translate the laws of ethics. Thus, 'the whole is greater than its part'; 'reaction is equal to action'" . . . and many the like propositions, which have an ethical as well as physical sense" (Emerson 1960: 35). In physics, to translate designates a movement "from one point or place to another" — "sometimes as distinguished from a reciprocating movement as in a wave or vibration" (Simpson, Weiner, and Oxford University Press 1989). When Emerson invokes the word *translate* to inscribe it within his theory of symbolization, his meaning is antithetical to Fuller's understanding of translation as a multidirectional, reciprocal, conversational engagement. Emerson expresses the anxieties that underlie his fantasy of unity in a passage from his journal (26 May 1839) where he worries that "if . . . the world is not a dualism, is not a bipolar unity, but is *two*, is Me and It, then . . . the alien, the unknown, and all we have believed and chanted out of our deep instinctive hope is a pretty dream"(Emerson et al. 1911: 206). What seems threatening to Emerson becomes an exhilarating possibility for Fuller.

III.

We learn from Emerson that acknowledging the empirical existence of multiple languages is insufficient for developing an epistemology of multilingualism; for that, we must turn to Fuller. In the published account of her frontier experience, *Summer on the Lakes in 1843* (1844), Fuller included two translations: in chapter 5, an Indian transformation myth, and in chapter 6, Justinus Kerner's *Die Seherin von Prevorst* (1829), a mystical account of a young woman's bodily ailment and prophetic capacity.[26] By performing a translation at the moment she enters a state of nature, so to speak, on the Western frontier, Fuller rejects Emerson's deterministic understanding of cultural identity. She experiments with allegory and symbol to explore the possibilities of intertextuality and fragmentation for signification. In her essay "American Literature, Its Position in the Present Time, and Prospects for the Future" (1846), Fuller concludes that cultural and racial diversity are the origin and outcome of a literature that relies on a process of translation.

In the allegorical conversation Fuller stages in *Summer on the Lakes*, she casts herself in the role of Free Hope, who, for translating Kerner's mystical work, comes under siege from her friends, Old Church, Good Sense, and Self-Poise, the latter representing Emerson.[27] In a passage that echoes Fuller's disappointment with Emerson for barring her from an "intelligence of my best self," Free Hope justifies her enterprise in an explicit address to Self-Poise, complaining: "[C]ould but a larger intelligence of the vocations of others and a tender sympathy with their individual natures be added, had you more of love, or more of apprehensive genius, (for either would give you the needed expansion and delicacy) you would command my entire reverence. As it is . . . you tend, by your influence, to exclude us from our full, free life" (Fuller 1991: 82). As we have seen, Fuller developed a theory of translation in response to her fear of being overwhelmed by a genius that emphasizes universals and elides particulars. And indeed, a translation follows here. But Fuller uses allegory to question the assumptions that underlie Emerson's failings, reimagining "Nature" as "individual natures" — as singular yet plural, capable of referring to viable others. Through her use of allegory, Fuller pluralizes Emerson's symbolic economy, anticipating Paul de Man's conclusion that "allegory designates primarily a distance in relation to its own wording, and, renouncing the nostalgia and the desire to coincide, . . . it prevents the self from an illusory identification with the non-self, which is now fully, though painfully, recognized as a non-self"(De Man 1983: 207). Through her use of allegory, then, Fuller accomplishes two things: she shifts the debate over the metaphysical origin and telos of language to a debate over its dialogic connections, and she imagines those dialogic positions as systemically connected yet viably differentiated from one another.

These theoretical speculations manifest themselves in Fuller's translation of *Die Seherin von Prevorst*, as in the following passage, which moves through multiple subject positions:

> Now began still greater wonders; the second sight, numerous and various visits from spirits and so forth.
> The following may be mentioned in connection with theories and experiments current among ourselves.
> 'A friend, who was often with her at this time, wrote to me (Kerner): When I, with my finger, touch her *on her forehead between the eyebrows*, she says each time something that bears upon the state of my soul. Some of these sentences I record. . . .' (Fuller 1991: 87)

Translation allows Fuller to produce a different kind of knowledge: instead of communicating a "state of mind" — as Emerson emphasizes — she inquires into the possibilities of addressing a "state of . . . soul," invoking, as in her translation of *Günderode*, a register of sentimental and spiritual knowledge. The voices of this passage constantly shift: we hear Fuller, Kerner, the friend, and the Seeress as Fuller's translation stages its own multivocalism and its mediations. Fuller makes opacity part of her dialogic method but afterwards states paradoxically: "I do confess this is a paraphrase, not a translation, also that in the other extracts, I have taken liberties with the original for the sake of condensation, and clearness. What I have written must be received as a slight and conversational account of the work" (Fuller 1991: 101). What does she mean by this disclaimer?

In the preface to her translation of Goethe's *Tasso Toquato*, Fuller asks to "be allowed to quote Mr. Coleridge in apology for a somewhat paraphrastical translation, not as presuming to compare mine with his Wallenstein, but to show that this accomplished writer deemed the rendering of the spirit, on the whole, more desirable than that of the letter" (Fuller 1994: 271). Fuller is imagining a translation that is, by some measures, incomplete; it renders the spirit "on the whole," not the spirit of the whole. But whose spirit is rendered? And why would paraphrastic translation accomplish this goal?

For an answer to these questions, we must go back to a footnote in Austin's *Characteristics of Goethe,* where she quotes an unidentified English translation of Novalis (most likely her own): "'A translation . . . is either grammatical, or paraphrastic (*verändernd*, altering), or mythic.'" By "mythic" translation, Novalis means a textualization of natural phenomena. Grammatical translations, for Novalis, strive for strict verbal and stylistic equivalence. While they depend on great erudition, they do not require "the highest poetical spirit" required by paraphrastical translations, if they are "to be genuine." Paraphrastic translations easily "degenerate into travesties," like Pope's translation of Homer, so "the true translator in this kind must, indeed, be himself the Artist, and be able to give the Idea of the Whole, thus or thus, at his pleasure. He must be the poet of the poet, and thus be able to make him speak at once after his own original conception, and after that which exists in his (the translator's) mind."[28] Novalis's recommendation shifts the significance of textual accuracy. Rather than thinking of the original as a definitive object, he suggests that the translator's conceptions and artistry are also important. The "Idea of the Whole" is not a static entity but a dynamic interaction, as becomes evident in Fuller's conclusion to her complaint about Goethe:

> But I persevere in reading the great sage [Goethe] some part of every day, hoping the time will come when I shall not feel so overwhelmed, and leave off this habit of wishing to grasp the whole, and be contented to learn a little everyday, as becomes a pupil. But now the one-sidedness, imperfection and glow of a mind like that of Novalis seem refreshingly human to me.[29]

Fuller's preference for Novalis over Goethe represents a pivotal conceptualization of the means for attaining an "Idea of the Whole," whereby a desire to "grasp the whole" gives way to contentment with a more partial understanding of the "spirit, on the whole."

Fuller's theory of translation challenges us to reexamine how we understand textual fragmentation. Paraphrastic translation enabled Fuller to insist on textual incompletion: she translated only parts of Kerner's text, and those parts are, in turn, part of her larger narrative. She experimented with this strategy much earlier, writing in the preface to her translations of *Conversations with Goethe*: "I am aware that there is a just prejudice against paraphrastic or mutilated translation, and that, in this delicate process, I have laid myself open to much blame"(Eckermann and Fuller 1839: xxv–vi). We can imagine why Fuller would be blamed: her method of fragmentation counters the politics of wholeness and of fixed identity; it provides a textual space for multiple, intimate, and incomplete subject positions. Marjorie Levinson argues that for romantic authors, "the fragment, construed as a symbol ... of the imagined order which the original sought to incarnate, enjoys a more intimate, authorized relation to that order than the first and finished work" (Levinson 1986: 31). By using fragmentation without recourse to an overarching symbolic order — as a lack that defines the "human" through her imperfection — Fuller instead explores the possibilities of the romantic fragment to "express the age's consciousness of its epistemological fall into dualism" (Levinson 1986: 9). Fuller establishes a correspondence between stylistic form — fragmentation — and dialogic method. By reminding us that translation is central to the interpretation of fragments, she implicitly reinscribes linguistic diversity in literary fragments and offsets their participation in a reconstituted wholeness.

How do these concerns about textual form relate to a linguistic theory of translation and amount to the notion of cultural identity with which I began? Concluding her discussion of Kerner, Fuller reveals her understanding of translation's centrality to language:

> Do not blame me that I have written so much about Germany and Hades, while you were looking for news of the West. Here, on the pier, I see disembarking the Germans, the Norwegians, the Swedes, the Swiss. Who knows how much legendary lore, of modern wonder, they have already planted amid the Wisconsin forests? Soon, soon their tales of the origin of things, and the providence which rules them, will be so mingled with those of the Indian, that the very oak trees will not know them apart, — will not know whether itself be a Runic, a Druid, or a Winnebago oak. (Fuller 1991: 102)

The news from the West is that European culture is not an entity elsewhere but one intimately entwined with Native American and Anglo-American cultures. Rather than identifying cultural originality as an organic given that obscures its multiple origins, Fuller develops a model of cultural transplantation with translation as its linguistic equivalent. Fuller's imagined oak tree, which cannot name itself because its cultural roots are multiple, suggests that the "origin of things" is already complexly plural. If Emerson thought it possible to return to a historical and utopic nature where word and object are identical, Fuller uses translation in *Summer on the Lakes* to insist that America is linguistically and culturally plural in origin, outcome, and process. While there is truth to the idea that Fuller wanted to disseminate German literature "among her monolingual compatriots" (J. Wesley Thomas cited in Delphendahl 1994: 75), she also wanted to demonstrate that the citizens and inhabitants of the United States are not monolingual and that monolingualism is a construct, not an ontology. Ironically, the belief that the English language has always been hegemonic in the United States has led critics of exceptionalism to renew this cultural logic by excluding works written in English from the domain of American multilingualism. Fuller's oak, confused about its linguistic and national identity, represents her fantasies about the opacity of her own language. As one language among many, her English participates in a scene of linguistic diversity. Fuller reminds us that as an American language, English is as opaque as the languages it translates, and into which it is translated.

In *Woman in the Nineteenth Century*, Fuller makes clear the national stakes of her translation theory when she laments that "the national independence be blurred by the servility of individuals," but insists nevertheless that

> it is not in vain, that the verbal statement has been made, 'All men are born free and equal.' [...] It is inevitable that an external freedom, such as has been achieved for the nation, should be so also for every member

of it. That which has once been clearly conceived in the intelligence, must be acted out. It has become a law, as irrevocable as that of the Medes in their ancient dominion. Men will privately sin against it, but the law so clearly expressed by a leading mind of the age,

'Tutti fatti a semianza d'un Solo;
Figli tutti d'un solo riscatto,
In qual ora, in qual parte del suolo
Trascorriamo quest' aura vital,
Siam fratelli, siam stretti ad un patto:
Maladetoo colui che lo infrange,
Che s'innalza sul fiacco che piange,
Che contrista uno spirito immortal.' [Manzoni]

'All made in the likeness of the One,
All children of one ransom,
In whatever hour, in whatever part of the soil
We draw this vital air,
We are brothers, we must be bound by one compact,
Accursed he who infringes it,
Who raises himself upon the weak who weep,
Who saddens an immortal spirit.'

cannot fail of universal recognition. (Fuller 1998: 14)

In this passage, Fuller is simultaneously at her most national and at her most global. For Fuller, "universal recognition" comes after an act of translation from the Italian nationalist poet Manzoni. She invokes a theory of "likeness" in which national unity ("all children") is enacted across temporal ("whatever hour") and geographic ("whatever part of the soil") differences. That likeness establishes a fraternal union ("we are brothers") that becomes contractual ("bound by one compact"). Yet that contract is fragile: at the very moment of unity, the cited passage includes a concern for "the weak who weep" because the "external freedom" that has been "achieved for the nation" has in fact not yet been accomplished "for every member of it."

We may then wonder if this construction of a diversified national myth of origin simply obscures the violence that establishes its narrative power. In chapter 6 of *Summer on the Lakes*, Fuller examines this possibility in her account of the Indian myth of a hunter who marries a bear, kills a bear who is his sister-in-law, and eventually returns to his tribe. For Fuller, this tale exemplifies "the sorrows of unequal relations"(Fuller 1991: 126–7), which were visible to her as she observed the treatment of Native Americans on the Illinois frontier in the summer of 1843. This knowledge of racism and the seeming impossibility of amalgamation suggested in the Native American tale made it all the more pressing for her to find a way of thinking about diversity without forcefully obscuring difference or categorically eliminating the other. Fuller uses translation to bring multiple subjects into textual coexistence, using paraphrase, conversation, and fragmentation to resist totalizations and to transpose the subject without violating it. While Fuller's attempt to engage without appropriating Native American culture was limited by her inability to speak Indian languages, she used translation to develop a theory and method of cultural pluralism that at least recognizes linguistic limitation as a problem. Despite her pessimism about a peaceful resolution to frontier relations, Fuller uses translation to allow the cultures of immigrants and natives to coexist in a way that refuses any simple definition of Anglo-American literature.

How, then, did Fuller define American literature? The beginning of her essay on the subject seemingly contradicts the reading I've proposed: "Books which imitate or represent the thoughts and life of Europe do not constitute an American literature. Before such can exist, an original idea must animate this nation and fresh currents of life must call into life fresh thoughts along its shores"(Fuller 1846: 2.298). Perry Miller argues that during her career, Fuller underwent a transition: "[A]s her passion for literary nationalism grew, Fuller became friendly with [Evert] Duyckinck and his 'Young America' band"(Miller 1963: 222).[30] Fuller's attraction to the Young Americans explains why the opening of her essay "American Literature" sounds similar to lines from Herman Melville's review of Hawthorne's *Mosses from an Old Manse* for George and Evert Duyckinck's *Literary World*. Writing in the guise of "a Virginian spending time in Vermont," Melville announces: "No American writer should write like an Englishman, or a Frenchman; let him write like a man, for then he will be sure to write like an American" (Melville 1850: 146). Apparently, it was possible to read *Summer on the Lakes* as one realization of this maxim, for it received praise from unlikely literary constituencies. Duyckinck himself was so impressed with the book that he reprinted it and called it "the most 'American' book he had yet published."[31]

What do we make of Fuller's "nationalism"? Nation was an important concept for Fuller. As I have emphasized, it allowed her to conceive of world literature in terms of constituent particulars that resisted wholeness. In "American Literature," Fuller's passages on nationalism underscore my point that even at her most cosmopolitan, her version of world literature included the nation form. But nationalist readings of Fuller's work, like Miller's and Duyckinck's, demonstrate that Fuller is frequently read out of context. Fuller herself was aware of this problem: "Some thinkers may object to this essay ["American Literature"], that we are about to write of that which has, as yet, no existence"(Fuller 1846: 2.122). This statement is to be understood as part of a dialogue, in which Fuller ventriloquizes the Young Americans' position before stating her own agenda: "We have no sympathy with national vanity. . . . Of those who think and write among us in the method and of the thoughts of Europe, we are not impatient. . . . We have been accused of an undue attachment to foreign continental literature" (Fuller 1846: 2.122). Rehearsing the accusation that she had immersed herself so completely in other languages as to forget English, Fuller explains that "what we loved in the literature of continental Europe was the range and force of ideal manifestation in forms of national and individual greatness" (Fuller 1846: 2.122–3). Although she expresses some admiration for English literature, Fuller ultimately distances herself from it because "what suits Great Britain, with her insular position . . . does not suit a mixed race, continually enriched with new blood from other stocks the most unlike that of our first descent" (Fuller 1846: 2.123).

Fuller's journalistic practices in the mid-1840s made her aware of that "other stock." While she was working on "American Literature," Fuller was also translating articles from the most successful German-American newspaper, the *New Yorker Staatszeitung*, for the *New York Tribune*. Those translations feature one of the earliest mentions of Karl Marx and Friedrich Engels in the United States. We may wonder, then, how the new forms of internationalism emerging in the late 1840s would have affected Fuller's thinking had she returned safely from the Italian Revolution to the United States. Perhaps Fuller's liaison with the Italian nobleman and revolutionary Marchese Giovanni Angelo Ossoli and the birth of their child shortly before their fated departure for the United States were manifestations of her fantasy of a "riper time" when "the fusion of races among us is more complete . . . [and] national ideas shall take birth, ideas craving to be clothed in a thousand fresh and original forms" (Fuller 1846: 2.124).

When Fuller drowned with her family off the American coast in 1850, translational American literature lost one of its premier practitioners and proponents. Yet the questions Fuller was asking about the relationship between universalism and particularism are resurfacing today in texts like Judith Butler, Ernesto Laclau, and Slavoj Zizek's *Contingency, Hegemony, Universality* (2000). Fuller enables us to understand universalism and particularism not as distinct poles but as relational terms. Her theory of translation provides an important paradigm for thinking about culture specifically yet globally, and she models how cultural relationships operate within and between nations. Fuller sees cultural relations as iterative and dialogic, not ontological and fixed. As an identity, culture is always multiple: linguistically, as translation; personally, as dialogue; racially, as amalgamation; nationally, as globalism. Inherently, internally multiple, American culture overlaps with global national communities. Perhaps the closest contemporary equivalent to Fuller's translation is to be found in the work of Gloria Anzaldúa, who reinscribes multilingualism in the American scenes of empire when she negotiates between and within languages that are as mixed as the mestiza herself. Yet Anzaldúa runs the risk of repeating an exceptionalist logic when she isolates the frontier as a space for multiplicity. For Fuller, the frontier is not exceptional precisely because it is the scene of her American translation and thereby comparable to the cosmopolitan settings she inhabited in the last years of her life.

4 Literary exemplarity
Walt Whitman's "specimens"

How can a country that does not have a unified and unifying language generate a representative literature? For literature to function as representative, some notion of exemplarity needs to exist. But how can there be exemplarity when language itself constantly shifts its representational contexts — when language and cultural relations are, as Fuller sees them, iterative and dialogic, not ontological and fixed?

Two accounts help us to understand how Anglo-American poetry defines itself in relation to literary representation. The first argues that a unique *vernacular* distinguishes the American Adam's autochthonous literature. Beginning in the 1940s, critics argued that American literature came into existence when authors distanced themselves from English as a print language and began to transcribe the English language spoken indigenously in the United States.[1] The *Oxford English Dictionary* defines the vernacular as "the native speech or language of a particular country or district" (Simpson, Weiner, and Oxford University Press 1989), and the concept establishes a tautology by which language is an attribute of place, and place an attribute of language.

The second account takes issue with the first for serving, in Jonathan Arac's critique, "nationalist myths of purity" and nativism (Arac 1996: 44). Much like the 1940 census definition of a "mother tongue" that I discussed in the introduction, the concept of the vernacular obscures the fact that no single indigenous language existed in the intensely multilingual American environment. To emphasize the linguistic mixture of America's heterogeneous culture, Arac replaces the term "vernacular" with *creole*. In his discussion of Walt Whitman, the former poster child of arguments about the vernacular and about cultural nativism, Arac proposes that we must understand Whitman's poetry as inventing a diverse and deracinated — that is, uprooted — idiom best exemplified by journalistic language.

As Arac demonstrates, Whitman performed what we may think of as the worlding of America by incorporating non-English words into his poems. Yet Arac's argument for linguistic mixture leaves open the question of how such heterogeneity can be maintained under the homogenizing pressures of the global, metropolitan, capitalist culture he describes — how, in short, *creole* avoids becoming as codified as the *vernacular*. Once Whitman's mixed language takes on the status of a language *in itself*, it runs the risk of being as monolingual in outcome as theories of the vernacular make it in origin.

Whitman's poetic practice indicates a keen awareness that mixture is more easily invoked than maintained. To examine how the American idiom could express and sustain the diversity of its global contexts, how it could — in Allen Grossman's words — "preserve the ends of the enterprise from the predation of the means" (Grossman 1984: 189), Whitman developed a practice of literal, linguistic translation.

In *Specimen Days* (1882), Whitman reflects on the nineteenth century's most prominent American poet-translator, the recently deceased Henry Wadsworth Longfellow:

> His translations of many German and Scandinavian pieces are said to be better than the vernaculars. ... To the ungracious complaint-charge of his want of racy nativity and special originality, I shall only say that America and the world may well be reverently thankful — can never be thankful enough — for any such singing-bird vouchsafed out of the centuries, without asking that the notes be different from those of other songsters; adding what I have heard Longfellow himself say, that ere the New World can be worthily original ... she must be well saturated with the originality of others ... . (Whitman 1982: 917–8)

Based on this passage, Kirsten Silva Gruesz has argued that "Whitman dismisses the translative mode" by contrasting it with his own originality (Gruesz 1998: 405). But what if we were to take Whitman's praise of Longfellow and of translation seriously? What if we were to accept at face value his insistence that translation may be a valuable improvement of "the vernaculars" (Whitman 1982: 917–8) — and of American vernacular literature at that?[2]

In this chapter, I explore the contours of the unlikely attachment between translation and the American vernacular to explain how Whitman negotiated his desire to be nationally unique yet globally representative. Echoing The Venerable Bede, Robert Frost opined in the twentieth century that poetry is that which gets lost in translation, but for Whitman, the reverse holds true: American poetry is that which emerges in acts of translation. To examine what Whitman meant by translation, and why he chose translation as the privileged mode of his literary enterprise, I will show how *Leaves of Grass* (1855) and *Specimen Days* (1882) invoke and reconfigure the discourse of a specific kind of literary anthology, the specimen collection.

As Whitman explored and exploded the boundaries of linguistic naturalism, the conceit of the literary "specimen" provided the testing ground for his desire to be aboriginal and universal. Whitman understood the nature specimen to exemplify the biological diversity within a genus. He saw translations as ideal specimens of American literature: because they were both indigenous and foreign, they reflected the variegation he hoped to achieve in his "American" poetry.

I.

In *Specimen Days*, Whitman examines the role of literary specimens in the most overt project of literary nation-formation: anthologizing. Etymologically, anthologies are flower collections in which each individual poem functions as a botanical specimen. American literature came late to the burgeoning scene of anthologizing practices that flourished in the wake of Dr. Samuel Johnson's invention of a poetic pantheon. Much of Longfellow's work was popularized through anthologies, and such collections preoccupied Whitman after Ralph Waldo Emerson published *Parnassus* (1874), a volume of his favorite poets among whom Whitman was not included. Perhaps in deliberate counter-distinction to such hagiography, *Specimen Days* evokes the formulaic title of a particular type of early-nineteenth century anthology, the literary specimen collection that aimed at a broadly inclusive representation of poetry, beyond the pale of poetic genius.

The vogue started in Britain with George Ellis' popular *Specimens of the Early English Poets* (1790) and Robert Southey's sequel, the *Specimens of the Later English Poets* (1807).[3] In their attempt to define national literature, English specimen collections established nature and nativism as paradigms. As Alan Golding and others have demonstrated, anthologies are not value-neutral in their nation-making enterprises but construct cultural taxonomies.[4] By selecting specific literary pieces to exemplify national literature, the specimen collection simultaneously represented and generated its object. In the English context, "specimen" functioned as a synecdoche: as a specimen, the individual work exemplified a category of objects, English Literature, but that category in turn emerged from the anthology's definition of what counted as a specimen. Hence, the collection defined national literature as much as it constituted that literature in its own collectivity.

Collection incorporated individual specimen into new, holistic knowledge-discourse formations, and the stated aim of these early anthologies was to be broadly comprehensive. Southey included what he himself considered bad poetry and explained his decision by naturalizing poetry:

> My business was to collect specimens as for a *hortus siccus* [dry garden; an herbarium]; not to cull flowers as for an anthology. I wished, as Mr. Ellis had done in the earlier ages, to exhibit specimens of every writer, whose verses appear in a substantive form, and find their place upon the shelves of the collector. The taste of the publick may better be estimated from indifferent Poets than from good ones; because the

former write for their contemporaries, the latter for posterity. (Southey 1807: iv)

Anthologies select only the best literature (the "flowers"), but Southey also includes less qualitatively distinguished literary productions in his holistic attempt to create a literary environment. He wishes to include "every writer" who was sufficiently prolific, so as to give a comprehensive overview of the range of literary productions and to recreate a literary environment in its entirety. Literally translated, a *hortus siccus* is a dry garden (I discuss the term's more specialized meaning below). Whereas anthologies disrupt natural growth (they "cull" flowers), Southey's specimens thrive organically in a distinctive (arid) clime and soil of their own. Southey's use of specimens for the construction of a *hortus siccus* imagines culture as a collection of organisms that it naturalizes as representing a distinct literary environment.

Such broad-scale representation raises the question of how to delimit national literary culture, and the answer English authors lighted upon was language. For this aspect of the specimen's significance, editors drew on ethnographic inquiry. John Clarke's introduction to *Specimens of dialects: short vocabularies of languages; and notes of countries and customs in Africa* (1848) summarizes the ways in which language was used to determine nationhood *linguistically* in a colonial context:

> 1. By means of these [linguistic] Specimens, the countries where the language is the same —where it varies little — and where it departs more widely from the tongue chiefly spoken in the district, may be seen.
>
> 2. It may also to some extent be ascertained where the language becomes essentially different in one country from that which is spoken in the country adjacent. [...]
>
> 6. By means then of these Specimens, countries can be classified, and names of towns before unknown take their respective positions ... according to the country to which they truly belong. (Clarke 1848: 3–5)

This definition of nation by language was also applied to auto-ethnographic purposes at home: in the British collections, "specimens" do not just refer to poems (in a sense that includes themes, imagery, stylistic and metrical devices, voice, authorship, etc.), but these "specimens" exemplify the language, English, specifically in which the poems were originally written — which in turn determines their national affiliation.

However, both Ellis and Southey struggled with the issue of translation when they tried to define "*English*" poetry nationally and linguistically. Ellis hoped to delineate "national manners" and to "exhibit, by a regular series of Specimens, the rise and progress of our language" (Ellis 1790:

vii). But invoking the "progress" of the English language necessitated an engagement with its multilingual roots. The very quest for national poetic origins necessitated translation. Ellis worried that, when confronted with Anglo-Saxon poetry, readers would consider "hopeless ...[the] search for ... sources of amusement and information ... amidst the obscurity of a difficult and almost unintelligible language" (Ellis 1790: 2). He confronted this obstacle by presenting a "specimen of Anglo-Saxon poetry" in literal translation, and he also provided a second, metrical translation more "calculated to convey the spirit of a poetical origin" (Ellis 1790: 13). In arguing for the cohesion of English literature, Ellis had to acknowledge its multilingual complexities. But the translations he provides were a means to an end: they transmitted the text to the reader, but did not themselves count as examples of English versification.

Southey emphatically removed translation from a naturalized *"English"* literature: when he talked about the *"industry* of our good old translators" (Southey 1807: xxiv; my emphasis), Southey excluded translation from his naturalizing metaphor by categorizing it as an alienated, inorganic form of labor and reproduction. Although Southey acknowledged that England shared traditions such as the literary Romance with other countries, he associated translation with transplantation and insisted that: "We [in England] have had foreign fashions in literature ... but have at all times preserved ... a character of our own" (Southey 1807: xiv). He designated the Provençal the "first imported fashion," exemplified by *The Romance of the Rose* (1230) which Chaucer "must have translated for its reputation, and not for its merit" (Southey 1807: xiv). Such importation directly detracted from the creation of national literature: Southey complained that "the time bestowed upon this long and wearying rigmarole, had not been employed upon the *Canterbury Tales*" (Southey 1807: xiv). Eager to define and exemplify *"English"* poetry nationally and linguistically, Southey dismissed translation from his literary epistemology.

Perhaps this British resistance against translation explains some of its appeal to Americans. Yet given the anxiety over being derivative that the work of Harold Bloom, Robert Weisbuch, and Richard Brodhead has taught us to associate with American literature, it might still seem surprising that translations (which Southey so emphatically dismisses as mechanistic replications of foreign texts) appeared in the first collections of American literature edited and published in the United States.[5] Unlike their British counter-parts, American anthologies integrated translations into their cultural taxonomies. Samuel Kettell's *Specimens of American Poetry* (1829; 3 vols.) invented a taxonomy of American literature that included translations, such as John Adams' "Translation of an Ode of Horace," among a collection of vernacular writing that aimed to call "into notice what is valuable and characteristic in the writings of our native poets" (Kettell 1829: I.iii). When he drew up a "Catalogue of American Poetry," which comprised "all the poetical works of American origin which have come under notice in the course of this undertaking" (Kettell 1829: III.379), Kettell listed various translations of the psalms and of classical texts (Horace, Ovid, Virgil — in several translations), "Miscellaneous Poems, with several specimens from the author's manuscript version of the poems of Ossian. By J. M. Sewall," and "The Henriade of Voltaire translated into English verse." How could Voltaire be counted among America's "native poets" (Kettell 1829: I.iii) without making a travesty of Kettell's claim that he represented works of "American origin" (Kettell 1829: III.379)? What does it mean for a translation to count as a specimen of the language and culture *into* which the text is translated? To answer these questions, I now turn to the more specialized definition of the *hortus siccus*.

The *New York Review* reconfigured Southey's naturalizing metaphors when it reviewed John Dwight's translations of German poetry, which appeared in the book series *Specimens of Foreign Standard Literature*:

> Poetry fills in the world of thought the same place as flowers in the physical universe. Every clime has its own peculiar plants ... The universal mind has likewise its clime and soil; the spirits of the south and of the north are as unlike as the flowers of the torrid and of the frigid zones; but in the same manner their thoughts, originally molded in different languages, may be made known to each other, though with the loss of much of their own freshness and beauty. Translations are, after all, but pressed flowers; yet they may unfold to us much that is new in the infinite variety of the thoughts of the human mind ... (1839: 393–4)[6]

The botanical conceit of the *hortus siccus* gives translations a particular status. In its specialized meaning, a *hortus siccus* is an herbarium: it is a book in which multiple specimens are preserved to demonstrate the range of variety within each species and genus.[7] The specimen is not simply a stand-in for the categories it represents: the collection emphasizes the individual specimen and its differentiation from other specimens to demonstrate the variety within classificatory categories. As a literary conceit, translation is the consummate specimen: since no two translations of a text will be exactly the same, translations demonstrate literary and linguistic range. In literature, it is precisely translations that function as specimens. The *New York Review*'s article associates translation with the *hortus siccus* that Southey hoped to create, but reconceptualizes the significance of cultural environments. Instead of reserving intellectual distinction for the original, the review places originality and translation on an organic continuum: for both, the "universal mind" functions as a referent that ensures the different environments' openness to importation and exportation.[8] As a specimen of American literature, translation becomes both the *vehicle* and the *object* of our reading, that is, the translation provides access to a text in another language — it is a vehicle for our reading — yet if we read it as a specimen for American literature, the translation is also the opaque object of our reading. This dual function breaks down our understanding of translation as a linear transposition of a text: translation does not operate along cultural teleologies that would map a linear transposition of a text *from* one context *into* another.[9]

II.

Longfellow's pedagogical practices and his vision of American literature depended on this dual understanding of literary specimens. After having served as Bowdoin College's first professor of modern languages (appointed in 1829), Longfellow succeeded George Ticknor to the Harvard chair in Modern Languages and Belles Lettres (which Longfellow held from 1837–54). To prepare himself for these positions, Longfellow set out on a meticulous course of language study by traveling to Europe in 1826 and again in 1836. Longfellow validated the importance of being a native speaker but also imagined that as an American, one could become a native speaker of multiple languages. He boasted of his own linguistic proficiency to his father:

> With the French and Spanish languages I am familiarly conversant, so as to speak them correctly and write them with as much ease and fluency as I do the English. The Portuguese I read without difficulty. And with regard to my proficiency in Italian, I have only to say that all at the hotel where I lodge took me for an Italian until I told them I was an American. (cited in Longfellow 1886: I. 156)

Longfellow's career as a professor was built around the assumptions encapsulated in this passage in that he supervised all languages taught at Harvard and was limited to none specifically. When a French instructor resigned in 1839, the Harvard Corporation validated Longfellow's boast about his linguistic proficiency by asking him to take the place of a native speaker.[10] How then are we to understand Longfellow's refusal, and his argument that "the French should be taught by a Frenchman, as the other modern languages are by natives of the countries where spoken"? (Longfellow to Harvard College, 1839, Dana Papers). First and foremost, I think we have to assume that Longfellow simply did not want to take on the overly heavy burden of conducting recitations in French in addition to his other duties. But in refusing this position, Longfellow also draws an important distinction: whereas Europeans are defined in relation to one language and one country as native speakers, as an American, Longfellow is a native speaker of modern languages in the plural; he is paradoxically a native speaker in all languages and thus in none specifically.

This emphasis on American multilingualism is particularly significant when we take into account how American universities incorporated literary studies into their curricula. The instruction in language and in literature increasingly went hand in hand. Whereas Greek and Latin had been taught by rote memorization in the eighteenth century, the endowment of a professorship in 1814 by Samuel Eliot of Boston marked an important change: it was the first strictly literary professorship ever established in Harvard College. As of 1814, literature was first being taught at Harvard, and the only place on the curriculum where students encountered literature was through the instruction in languages. One did not study literature without studying language, nor did one any longer study language without studying literature. English literature was not taught separately at Harvard until the mid-nineteenth century, but in his invention of the modern language curriculum at Harvard, Longfellow made sure to integrate English among the languages and literatures that he taught. For example, he records in his journal for 28 September 1838: "Fridays, I lecture on the Spanish drama; at present, 'La Estrella de Sevilla,' with comparisons between it and Fanny Kemble's play 'The Star of Seville.'" Literature written in English became part of this juxtaposition, this side-by-side of different literary traditions, and was always in a relationship of translation to them.

The pedagogical context unsettles the association between nation, nature and language. In 1827, Longfellow prepared a *Cours de Langue Française: Course of Study in the French Language*. After emphasizing the importance of systematic study, Longfellow proposed in his introduction (to the second edition, 1831) to publish a total of four volumes: volume one — the first book ever published with Longfellow's name on the title page — was to comprise "*Elements of French Grammar*: by Lhomond. Translation from the French with Notes and Exercises;" volume two was "*Le Ministre de Wakefield*. Traduction Nouvelle précedée d'un Essai sur la Vie et les Ecrits d'Olivier Goldsmith par M. Hennequin, etc." The proposed project for the study of French curiously relied on translations: the grammar Longfellow published was a translation of a French grammar into English, and the second volume a translation of English into French.

The aim of Longfellow's pedagogical practice was not to familiarize what was foreign, but to engage with difference. As Longfellow said of his translation of a German ballad by Bürger,

> This is one of the finest *specimens* of the Ballad poetry of Germany. It is written with great spirit and simplicity; qualities which I have attempted to preserve in the translation even at the expense of smoothness in the verse. (Longfellow 1833: 198)

By attempting to be faithful to the original and to reproduce it exactly, Longfellow was creating poetry in English that was strange, unfamiliar, and innovative. By mobilizing the conceit of the "specimen," Longfellow was able to construct translations that exemplified American literature in global contexts and that in turn exemplified global literature in American contexts.

Longfellow wrote of his most significant translation, the first full American translation of Dante's *Inferno* (1867):

> The only merit my book has is that it is exactly what Dante says and not what the translator imagines he might have said if he had been an Englishman. In other words, while making it rhythmic, I have endeavoured to make it also as literal as a prose translation ... In translating Dante, something must be relinquished ... It must be, in order to retain something more precious than rhyme, namely fidelity, truth ... The business of the translator is to report what the authors says, not to explain what he means; that is the work of the commentator. What an author says, and how he says it, that is the problem of the translator. (cited in Cunningham 1965: 67)

Instead of anglicizing Dante by imagining what the "might have said if he had been an Englishman," Longfellow embraces his foreignness. He tries to give a "literal" translation that retains those aspects of Dante's poetry least familiar to his English readers. Yet Longfellow trusts that the unfamiliar also provides a common ground for his readers to recognize a universal "fidelity, truth" that exceeds linguistic and national particularities.

In 1845, Longfellow published his own massive anthology of national literatures, in the plural, his translations of the *The Poets and Poetry of Europe*. By reproducing texts faithfully, he was able to create a sense of novelty in American poetry. Charles Sumner paid tribute to Longfellow's success in making poetry emerge in translation when he wrote to Sarah Perkins Cleveland, 15 August 1845:

> You have heard of Longfellow's great book on the Poets & Poetry of Europe [sic], which is one of the most important contributions our literature has recently received. It affords a most instructive *coup d'oeil* of the poetical literature of modern Europe. It is the best book that has been published for a long time in America, to give as a present to a European friend. (Sumner and Palmer 1990: I.150)

Why should a European friend receive a volume of European poetry in translation? Translation both pays tribute to the original, and in that very process, produces new, American poetry that maintains different nations as a reference point, but also exceeds them. Translation was not just a means to an end, but had a value in its own right as an important contribution to American literature. As the *North American Review* argued in July 1849: "Mere nationality is no more or less than so much provincialism, and will be found but a treacherous anti-septic for any poem ... Literature survives, not because of its nationality, but in spite of it" (1849: 202).

For Longfellow, translations — especially those visible, in their opacity, as translations — added variety to the American literary scene. In an 1837 letter to Lewis Gaylord Clark, Longfellow praised a translator for trying to preserve the original's "quaintness in his Translation; so that it will not read like a modern polished tale. So much the better as giving some variety in these stereotype days" (Longfellow and Hilen 1966: II.12). Instead of regularizing historical and linguistic difference and reducing them to the homogenized terms of modernity, translation for Longfellow can function as a force of variation within the collective literary everyday. In distinct opposition to "stereotype days," translation allows specimens to retain their representative diversity — to produce, as it were, specimen days.[11]

Practically, the conception of such a variegated culture found its realization in the antebellum press, which published the reciprocal and often collaborative translations of such men-of-letters as Longfellow and the German poet Ferdinand Freiligrath (1810-76).[12] In a letter dated March 19, 1843, Longfellow praised Freiligrath for his

> wife's translation of the 'Rainy Day' in a German newspaper in New York; also in the *Bürger-Freund* at Bremen. Your 'Excelsior' has also been reprinted in the New York paper — 'Die Deutsche Schnell-Post;' and likewise the 'Death of the Flowers.' Others of yours are to follow. (Longfellow and Hilen 1966: II.519)

This passage indicates that Longfellow's poetry circulated in English and in translation within the United States. For a multilingual society, translation was not merely a way of conducting foreign literary relations, but also a means for the national dissemination of texts. The extent to which translations of and by Longfellow entered America's popular imagination becomes evident in the fact that he makes an appearance in *the* best-seller of 1850: Susan Warner's sentimental novel *Wide, Wide World* includes a chapter heading that cites a poetic excerpt as "Longfellow from the German" (Warner 1987: 114). These publishing practices are one manifestation of copyright law (to which I turn in the next chapter) and attest to the complexity of translation's cultural presence — in virtually all print media, in different countries and multiple languages.

Before publishing some of his ten translations (not counting the full version of *Hiawatha*) from Longfellow's work, Freiligrath submitted them to his friend and incorporated Longfellow's critique into the final version. On one such occasion, Freiligrath explained his linguistic and cultural practice:

> I have attempted as much as possible to remain truthful to the original, and you will notice minor discrepancies only in very isolated instances. I will, possibly in the next weeks, Germanize [verdeutschen] still others.[13]

Freiligrath creates what we may see as a contradiction when he wants to remain truthful to the original, yet describes his translation as a "verdeutschen" — making German — of Longfellow's poem (he could use the generic term "übersetzen" for translate). Apparently, Freiligrath uses "verdeutschen" to define a linguistic transposition of the text into German. By the logic of his adherence to the American original and its reproduction in German, this linguistic transposition does not coincide with a national appropriation; translation allows the text to be both originally American and in German.[14]

Longfellow and Freiligrath worked out a theory of the vernacular through their collaborative practices of translation. In response to Freiligrath's rendition of the "Skeleton in Armor," Longfellow wrote :

> Many thanks, my dear Freiligrath, for your letter and the superb translation. It must have been a hard nut to crack; but you have dispatched it in the style of the most successful Nussknacker [nutcracker]. The old Berserk seems now to speak his native tongue. The changes are not important, and sometimes improvements ...(Hatfield 1933: 1229)

Longfellow's comment anticipates Whitman's claim in *Specimen Days* that translations are improvements of the vernacular. Of course, there is an easy explanation for how translation improves the poem in that Longfellow used Germanic material: in his gothic tale of immigration, a skeleton found near the round tower at Newport narrates how he and his beloved escaped from her father's wrath to marital union in America. Given the poem's own conceit of cultural dislocation, Freiligrath's translation restores the poem to its imagined linguistic origins. Yet the notion that the old Berserk speaks his "native" language in Freiligrath's translation remains curious. If Longfellow's old Berserk speaks his "native tongue" in translation, what did he speak in Longfellow's poem — did he speak in translation? Longfellow's comment invents his own original composition as a translation and displaces textual originality to the translation. Curiously, Freiligrath's translation, rather than Longfellow's poem, produces linguistic nativism. If translation produces a "native tongue," then deracination is at the very core of performances of American linguistic nativism and originality — terms which, in turn, we must reconceptualize so as to accommodate their linguistic multivalence.

III.

Even though he never studied at Harvard, Whitman capitalized on the education in translation and language theory that Longfellow and the antebellum specimen collections were offering him. Drawing on the specimen's capacity to represent and sustain differences, Whitman staged a process of translation in his works. The first untitled poem of the 1855 *Leaves of Grass*, a poem which became "Walt Whitman" in 1860 and "Song of

Myself" by 1892 (the version from which I cite here), contains four direct mentions of translation. Included in all editions of Whitman's own *hortus siccus*, the ever-expanding and changing *Leaves of Grass*, they amount to a systematic statement about translation's relevance for Whitman's life-long project. Whitman begins his poem by drawing on the nature specimen in a manner reminiscent of Southey:

> I loafe and invite my soul,
> I lean and loafe at my ease observing a spear of summer grass.
> My tongue, every atom of my blood, form'd from this soil, this air,
> Born here of parents born here from parents
> the same, and their parents
> the same,
> I, now thirty-seven years old in perfect health begin,
> Hoping to cease not till death. (Whitman 1982: 188)

In contemplating the grass, Whitman establishes an emblem of linguistic nativism. Like the spear of summer grass, Whitman's "tongue" —that is, the poet's physical tongue (the tongue with which he speaks) and his language (the tongue he speaks) — is organically determined by its specific natural environment (it grows from "this soil, this air"). Nature, the poet, and his language are metaphorically and literally coextensive by the odd logic of these lines; they express each other as they express themselves. Like the abundance of grass that continually reproduces its own likeness, Whitman's language is an inheritance from a family that is always "the same" through successive generations. As an emblem for Whitman's tongue, the spear of grass functions as a specimen that is coequal and coextensive with the genera it exemplifies.

In his first mention of translation, Whitman reconfigures this relationship between language and nature by drawing (similarly to the *New York Review*'s assessment of John Dwight's *Specimens of Minor Poets*) on the specimen's capacity to represent variety. Although he initially sees the grass as "a uniform hieroglyphic" (Whitman 1982: 193), his attempt to interpret its meaning alerts Whitman to the variegation of the grass and of the languages it represents:

> This grass is very dark to be from the white head of old mothers,
> Darker than the colorless beards of old men,
> Dark to come from under the faint red roofs of mouths.
> O I perceive after all so many uttering tongues,
> And perceive they do not come from the roofs of mouths for nothing.
> I wish I could translate the hints about the
> dead young men and women,
> And the hints about old men and mothers,
> and the offspring taken soon
> out of their laps. (Whitman 1982: 193)

His family — now differentiated as "old mothers," "old men," "young men and women," and their "offspring" — is no longer monotonously "the same." As Whitman contemplates color, he recognizes that the grass is not a uniform emblem: its shades of darkness represent such diverse aspects of the corpses as "colorless beards" and the "red roofs of mouths." This observation changes Whitman's perception of the grass itself: instead of representing "my tongue," the leaves now express a plethora of "so many uttering tongues." For Whitman, the grass has become an emblem of a linguistic diversity that challenges his interpretive skills. As Whitman's desire to translate makes evident, "tongues" refers literally to the body parts of the corpses he imagines, but also to the multiple languages they speak. Whitman now recognizes linguistic diversity as a quality of the natural landscape that necessitates acts of translation.

Whitman begins to examine the effects of translation when he insists:

> I am the poet of the Body and I am the poet of the Soul,/ The pleasures of heaven are with me and the pains of hell are with me,/ The first I graft and increase upon myself, the latter I translate into a new tongue. (Whitman 1982: 207)

Translation here functions as a process of transcendence to a spiritual realm: in the religious register, "translation" designates the "removal from earth to heaven" (Simpson et al. 1989). Whitman recognizes the potential of such sublimating translation to create what Arac considers a "new type of colonial language" (Arac 1996: 49). Yet Whitman quickly counterbalances its homogenizing tendencies when he echoes the biblical references to speaking in tongues and perpetuates the need for translation: his "new tongue" becomes commonly shared where "[i]t is you talking just as much as myself, I act as the tongue of you, // Tied in your mouth, in mine it begins to be loosen'd" (Whitman 1982: 243). In borrowing a foreign tongue, Whitman finds a new form of self-expression. In an instance of reciprocity similar to the one Longfellow shared with Freiligrath, Whitman's vernacular results from giving expression to another tongue in his own — and from giving expression to his own in another tongue. This understanding of his language makes translation the privileged mode of poetic discourse for Whitman's poem. It conceives of the vernacular as a constant act of translation.

Reading the following passage in this way may seem preposterous at first because of Whitman's skillful use of negation: "I swear I will never again mention love or death inside a house,/ And I swear I will never translate myself at all, only to him or her who privately stays with me in the open air" (Whitman 1982: 243). Just as love and death are the two themes that Whitman incessantly mentions throughout his poem, translation is the mode by which he makes himself comprehensible. Translation has no place within domestic confinements — it takes place in a realm of nature. Yet Whitman's entire poem is based on the assumption that he and his reader are in the open air, contemplating the poetic and natural specimens that he has collected in his *Leaves of Grass*. By the logic of these lines, to hear Whitman's "Song of Myself" means to listen as he translates.

Whitman's negation also demonstrates his interest in the limits of translation. He ends his poem with an image that seems to anticipate Walter Benjamin's argument that translation produces a more definitive language:

> The spotted hawk swoops by and accuses me, he complains of my gab and my loitering./ I too am not a bit tamed, I too am untranslatable,/ I sound my barbaric yawp over the roofs of the world. (Whitman 1982: 247)

One way of understanding this passage is to think that in this primitivist imaginary, a universally comprehensible, pre- or extra-cultural expression ("barbaric yawp") transcends (soars "over") the need for translation. The passage naturalizes language above domestic confinement ("tamed," "roofs") as universal (it exceeds even "the world") and eliminates translation from the nature of American literature: where the "roofs of mouths" (Whitman 1982: 32) have become the "roofs of the world" (Whitman 1982: 87) and nature signifies universally, translation has become obsolete. However, two aspects contradict such a reading: first, the passage's relation to the poem at large, and second, Whitman's practices of linguistic translation.

First, the state of untranslatability marks Whitman's physical and poetic death. In the course of his poem, he moves from being "born here of parents born here from parents the same" (Whitman 1982: 188) to a moment where he imagines: "I depart as air, ... / I bequeath myself to the dirt to grow from the grass I love, / If you want me again look for me under your boot-soles" (Whitman 1982: 247). For Whitman, being untranslatable marks the death of the poet.

Second, in the preface to his 1855 edition of *Leaves of Grass*, Whitman stages his practice of translation when he imagines an elaborate relationship between nature and the poet whose

> spirit responds to his country's spirit ... he incarnates its geography and natural life and rivers and lakes. Mississippi with annual freshets and changing chutes, Missouri and Columbia and Ohio and Saint Lawrence with the falls and beautiful masculine Hudson, do not embouchure where they spend themselves more than they embouchure into him. (Whitman 1982: 7)

Within this invocation of an American literary naturalism, how can we account for his emphatic use of the French word "embouchure" —which usually functions as a noun and means the mouth of a river — to describe how the poet ejaculates and absorbs the liquids of the natural landscape?

If we look again at Whitman's claim that the rivers "do not embouchure where they spend themselves more than they embouchure into him" (Whitman 1982: 7), we realize that Whitman is working out the significance of non-English words through a process of translation. In the cited passage, "spend themselves" translates what Whitman means by "embouchure." At the very moment that Whitman is imagining his relation to the American landscape, he is using multiple linguistic frames to stage the diversity of that relation.[15] By translating "embouchure" but then repeating the word after its translation, Whitman in turn translates "spend themselves" as "embouchure" and disrupts a teleological transference: although to an English readership, "embouchure" would be foreign, in the American landscape, "spend themselves" is just as foreign and in need of the French referent for its interpretation.

Translation makes the foreign comprehensible, but by including that which is translated in his text alongside its translation, Whitman has it both ways: he makes linguistic mixture comprehensible without resolving its diversity. "Embouchure" and "spend themselves" both function as specimens that exemplify the diversity of Whitman's deracinated language. For Whitman, translation is a mode of expression: rather than producing a language in itself, translation provides a process of languaging for American poetry. Throughout his work, Whitman does not merely incorporate or appropriate words foreign to English; he stages scenes of translation that draw attention to linguistic diversity and enact the dynamics of interpretation. Through an *ongoing* process of translation that continually invokes the foreign and tests the boundaries of the familiar, Whitman resists the impetus towards sameness. For Whitman, the vernacular is a process of languaging, realized in acts of translation.

CODA

As Joseph Roach has pointed out, we need to recognize that "a fixed and unified culture exists only as a convenient but dangerous fiction" (Roach 1996: 5). To avoid becoming complicit with that fiction, he argues that we need to understand "the process of surrogation as it operated *between* the participating cultures" (Roach 1996: 5). Highlighting this process of inter-cultural negotiation, Whitman invented his poems as transatlantic works when he told the readers of the first full German edition of *Leaves of Grass* in 1889: "I did not only have my own country in mind when composing my work. I wanted to take the first step towards bringing into life a cycle of international poems" (cited in Erkkila and Grossman 1996: 238). As an export, Whitman remains subject to the kinds of interpretive diversity he himself staged through scenes of translation. In 1868, Longfellow's friend Freiligrath became the first translator of Whitman into German when he published a widely circulated introductory article on Whitman followed by ten translations. Emerson once called Whitman's work "more deeply American, democratic, & in the interest of political liberty" than that of any other author (cited in Kaplan 1980: 274). Whitman's "deeply American" work proved particularly amenable to the German debate over the concepts that Emerson attaches to Whitman's poetry — nationhood, democracy, freedom. According to Johannes Schlaf, a later translator of Whitman into German, Freiligrath translated Whitman "too one-sidedly from the democratic perspective, that is, strictly along political lines" (cited in Grünzweig 1991: 31). Whitman's poems allowed Freiligrath to articulate his utopia of a democratic Germany in terms of an already predestined, iconic American history. Yet translating Whitman appealed equally to European authors in pursuit of a different brand of internationalism: the fact that Whitman was one of the few authors whose works were available in Eastern Europe during the Cold War attests to the appeal he carried for socialist writers. Whitman's mutability and use for different political causes ultimately makes translation a form of American transatlanticism that promises an alternative to the programmatic culture of imperialism realized around the time of Whitman's death. This ability of translations to function in multiple, overdetermined registers depended on the free circulation they enjoyed. In the next chapter, I examine how changes in copyright law contributed to the decline of this culture of translation.

5 Intellectual property
Harriett Beecher Stowe's copyright

Writing for *The Nation* in 1868, John William De Forest coined the phrase "The Great American Novel" in reference to *Uncle Tom's Cabin* (1852). De Forest praised Harriet Beecher Stowe's work for its "national breadth" and "natural speaking" (De Forest 1868: 28). He called the book the "single tale which paints American life so broadly, truly, and sympathetically that every American of feeling and culture is forced to acknowledge the picture as a likeness of something which he knows" (De Forest 1868: 28). To engage such broad sympathy and create a sense of "natural speaking" and "American ... culture," the novel had to be translated for the roughly fifty percent of foreign-born American readers, many of whom did not speak English as their first language.[1] Stowe herself recognized the importance of translation for the American literary market: in 1852, she commissioned H. R. Hutton to translate her book into German, and he undertook the project with Calvin Stowe's help. Within a year of the novel's publication in English, Stowe's publisher John P. Jewett was advertising for the American market "an edition for the million" at 37½ cents alongside "an edition in German" at 50 cents (see figure 5.1). *Within* the United States, Stowe's "national breadth" and "natural speaking" depended on her novel's translation into languages other than English.

The importance of multilingualism and translation for Stowe's literary success within the United States challenges us to reassess the claim that national literature resulted from the rise in *monolingual* print dissemination. Picking up on Jürgen Habermas' argument that *The Structural Transformation of the Public Sphere* (1962) occurred when printing changed political life in the West, Benedict Anderson claims that commodity printing generated "monoglot mass reading publics" which "laid the bases for national consciousness" (Anderson 1991: 43–4). Whereas Anderson links print and nationalism, Michael Warner argues that they were at cross-purposes. He explains that the "*reciprocal* determination ... between a medium [print] and its politics" (Warner 1990: xii) that had existed in eighteenth-century America broke down as a "distinctively indigenous culture" of nationalism "developed in the 1820s and 1830s" (Warner 1990: 119). Richard Brodhead disagrees with Warner's periodization and argues for

Figure 5.1

the persistence into the nineteenth century of a vexed relationship between print and nationalism. He demonstrates that, far from generating a unified national literature, the dissemination of print enabled distinct types of literature to coexist in "differently organized (if adjacent) literary-social worlds, in differently structured cultural settings composed around writing and regulating ... social life" (Brodhead 1993: 5). Although Brodhead limits these various "cultures of letters" to the American scene, Meredith McGill has recently internationalized our understanding of their scope. Her work on the widespread practice of reprinting indicates that, "although we have come to think of the classic works of mid-nineteenth-century American authors as national property, these texts emerged from a literary culture that was regional in articulation and transnational in scope" (McGill 2003: 1).

Important as Warner, Brodhead, and McGill's work has been for complicating our understanding of the relationship between print and nationalism, none of these critics questions Anderson's central assumption, that print produces "monoglot mass reading publics," and that such monolingualism lies at the heart of "national consciousness" (Anderson 1991: 43).[2] Multilingual translation not only participated in both the regional and the transnational aspects of printing, but was at the fulcrum of their connection. Monoglot mass readerships came into existence only belatedly in the United States; they emerged at the end of the nineteenth century as new national and international copyright laws were passed that curtailed the free dissemination of print and regulated translation.

Stowe's work lies at the nexus of that change: whereas the history of her novel's circulation illustrates the culture of translation that I have been outlining in this book, Stowe herself tried to restrict the free translation of her work when she sued F. W. Thomas in Circuit Court for copyright infringement. Stowe claimed that the unauthorized German translations of *Uncle Tom's Cabin* that Thomas published in *Die Freie Presse*, a Philadelphia newspaper, violated the legal property she held in her literary work. By insisting that an author's rights were inalienable from the product of her intellectual labor, that the body and spirit of the book should not be separated in the literary market, Stowe's suit extended to her book *qua* print commodity the argument her novel had made on behalf of slaves' intellectual and physical integrity. Stowe's lawsuit never worked out the complexities of this association between books and slaves, but it exposed two competing and increasingly incompatible understandings of American literature.

Stowe's side argued for an American literature that was monolingual, indigenous, and homogenous — that was, in short, much like the national literature Benedict Anderson envisions.[3] Stowe developed a theory of national literature that hinged on iconic translation, a form of translation by which a text maintained its linguistic and national identity even as it passed into other languages. Stowe's theory was fraught with anxieties over the instability of texts and the effect that immigrants — among whom Stowe numbered slaves — would have on American literary identity. Stowe's lawsuit sought to redress those anxieties: she argued that national literature was inalienable, and that consequently Thomas' translation amounted to an unauthorized copy that infringed on her sales.

Stowe's argument won out in the long run: it formed the basis for legislation passed in the postbellum era, and heralded the advent of an anti-immigrant backlash against the culture of translation. But for the moment at least, a different conception of American literature as multilingual, deracinated and heterogeneous won out. Judge Grier ruled in favor of Thomas and limited Stowe's property to the specific language she had used in expressing ideas that had become public domain. Ironically, the culture of free linguistic translation that Phillis Wheatley had inaugurated in protest against chattel slavery now found support from a pro-slavery judge, whereas the premier abolitionist of the day fantasized that the end of slavery and the regulation of translation would go hand in hand.

I.

When Stowe published *Uncle Tom's Cabin* in 1852, she entered an American literary market that was multilingual and driven by translation. Recent demographic developments had increased the nation-wide presence and importance of such multilingual markets. The Stowes were well aware of the sheer size and force especially of the German immigrant community. When Harriet moved to Cincinnati in 1832, it ranked as the nation's sixth largest and fastest growing city, primarily because German immigrants swelled the population from 25,000 to 46,000 in the 1830s (Hedrick 1994: 67) — even before the European Revolutions of 1848 further boosted these numbers. After her marriage to Calvin, Harriet daily experienced the German immigrant presence in her own household: she employed German servants to help her provide for a rapidly growing family.

Harriet was quick to register the importance of multilingualism for the American scene and to think of verbal exchanges in conjunction with economic transactions: she wrote in her first publication, the *Primary Geography for Children* (1833), about the Mississippi that

> you can see on the shore, the merchants full of business, taking out of the steamboats, or putting on board ships, their sugar, or molasses, or tobacco, or other goods. You may hear the sound of all sorts of languages, French, Spanish, English, and German, spoken by negroes, mulattoes, or white people, — for here are people from almost every country. (Stowe 1833: 104)

The connection Stowe establishes between the circulation of goods, people, and languages indicates her nascent understanding of polyglot consumer markets and the importance that language plays for the production and distribution of books as commodities. Stowe acknowledges that the national scene is deeply transatlantic, but she struggles to find the appropriate vocabulary for conceptualizing these relations and describes the American scene in conflicted terms: she portrays multilingualism as a typically *American* phenomenon, yet she simultaneously foreignizes the people she describes when she says that they "are people from almost every country." A similar slippage occurred when Stowe's lawyer Perkins said that, "owing to the extensive *international* changes in population, translations of copyrighted works will pay *in this country*" (Stowe v. Thomas 1853: 2). Curiously, "international" here stands for "national" in that Perkins is addressing the presence of non-English speaking immigrants, natives and slaves in the United States. These slippages demonstrate how Stowe confronted multilingualism: by foreignizing speakers of languages other than English, she developed a theory of monolingual American literature.

That emphasis on monolingualism may come as a surprise when we take into account that the study of languages and the practice of translation ranked among the Stowes' primary literary interests. After graduating from Bowdoin College in 1824, Calvin Stowe had studied French, Spanish, Hebrew, Greek, German, and Arabic at Seminary in Andover, and had translated Johann Jahn's *History of the Hebrew Commonwealth* (Hedrick 1994: 273). Calvin apparently shared his linguistic passion (especially for the German language) with his wife. The couple's friend Harriet Foote claimed that Calvin was downright "in love with Germany and German customs" and that his wife's enthusiasm was a reason why he and Harriet got along so well (cited in Hedrick 1994: 116). Translation even established a form of intimacy between them: Calvin translated passages for Harriet from German books as he was reading them, and according to Harriet, he tried to offset a "fit of the blues" by undertaking a translation of *Faust* (cited in Hedrick 1994: 123). Harriet's experience of translation was not merely through her husband. The Hartford Female Seminary where Harriet was an instructor before her marriage was modeled, under Catherine Beecher's leadership, after Benjamin Franklin's concept of an "English" school, where students learned modern as well as ancient languages (Hedrick 1994: 35). Much of the language instruction drew on translation as a pedagogical tool, and Harriet herself gained proficiency in foreign languages through translation: on her first trip to Europe, she hired a native speaker to instruct her by reading "several pages from *Uncle Tom* in French" (Beecher, Van Why, and French 1986: 199).

Stowe read translations critically, and in the process developed a conflicted theory of translation.[4] From the translations of her work that had been published in French, she selected Madame Louise Belloc's for its excellence, and decided to authorize it by writing a preface to it. Belloc's granddaughter quotes Stowe as writing admiringly that Belloc's "translation of *Uncle Tom* has to me all the interest of an original composition. In perusing it I enjoy the pleasure of reading the story with scarce any consciousness of its ever having been mine" (cited in Loundes 1939). If Stowe made this statement, it contradicts the opinion expressed on her behalf in the lawsuit against Thomas, which held that translation was a wrongful copy rather than a new book. How is it that in assessing Belloc's work, Stowe grants that translation is a new composition, whereas she insists that Thomas' translation is a replica of the original text? Stowe distinguishes between translation as an international and an intranational practice. In international contexts, she thinks of translation as a new composition, yet she wishes for translation within the American context to be an exact copy of the original. These two seemingly contradictory attitudes share an important literary desire: Stowe wants to imagine national literature as monolingual, and wishes to differentiate between national literatures on a linguistic basis. Stowe suggests that monolingualism and nationalism should go hand in hand — that a work should be French when it is in French. But confronted with the possibility that her work could be linguistically alienated within the United States, Stowe imagines that a work can circulate nationally in different languages yet maintain its identity. It is that fantasy of nationalism as uniform signification that underlies the theory of American literature Stowe developed in *Uncle Tom's Cabin*.

In *Uncle Tom's Cabin*, Stowe sets up two plot lines that are propelled by a dynamic of spatial, cultural, and linguistic displacement. Tom is sold ever further South down the Mississippi. He experiences a veritable gamut of slave institutions as he leaves the paternalistic household of the Selbys for the domestic economy of Augustine St. Clare's home in New Orleans, and eventually arrives at Simon Legree's plantation. Tom is culturally and linguistically displaced as he journeys from anglophone Kentucky to the francophone slave market in New Orleans. He assumes different tasks in each of these settings, but his commodity status and his exchange value as a slave remain constant, so that while he is experiencing the linguistic and cultural diversity of American space, he himself remains a figure of monolingualism and monoculturalism. As Stowe conflates her book with her title character — much the way advertisements for her work did (see figure 5.1) — that constancy turns Tom into Stowe's ideal representative of national literature: Tom incessantly circulates yet maintains his identity.

In contrast to Tom, George, and Eliza Harris flee ever further North to Canada and alter their cultural identity as well as their relation to the market economy. By setting in motion their displacement, Stowe brings into focus her novel's concern with two kinds of alienation: George Harris exemplifies and connects labor alienation with cultural alienation. Stowe literalizes George's alienation from American "culture" when she plays with the word's etymological roots in husbandry: George's rejection of agricultural labor — his refusal to be put again "to hoeing and digging" (Stowe 1986: 55) — and his departure from the soil of the United States logically go hand in hand; he literally and metaphorically removes himself from American culture. That removal occurs after George Harris has experienced an alternative form of cultural production. Temporarily hired out to Mr. Wilson, an industrial manufacturer who owns a "bagging factory," George's "adroitness and ingenuity caused him to be considered the first hand in the place. He had invented a machine for the cleaning of the hemp, which, considering the education and circumstances of the inventor, displayed quite as much mechanical genius as Whitney's cotton-gin" (Stowe 1986: 54).[5] At stake in George's relation to the factory is the legal regulation of intellectual labor, and of mass commodities. Stowe defines intellectual "genius" as an act of invention that is originary, but that inaugurates acts of infinite reproduction. (As I will demonstrate more fully, she imagines literature along the same lines that she sets up for George's labor when she argues for the simultaneous uniqueness yet infinite reproducibility of texts.) For Stowe, the "inventor" should have a stake in all subsequent products of his inaugural labor. Stowe criticizes slavery for allowing one person's intellectual genius to become someone else's property. For her, the commodification of slaves and products goes hand in hand: because someone else can profit from a person's intellectual labor, that person finds himself reduced to the status of an object and stripped of his personhood. Stowe makes that association clear by her wording: even in the factory, George's intelligence can only turn him into a metonymic "hand" who does not gain full status as a human being because of his labor's legal regulation. Stowe explains that, since "this young man was in the eye of the law not a man, but a thing, all these superior qualifications were subject to the control of a vulgar, narrow-minded, tyrannical master" (Stowe 1986: 55). Denied the status of "a man," George and his genius become commodities that are at the disposal of his master: his intellect is merely a "thing," subject to someone else's property rights. Mass production thus holds out two possibilities for Stowe: where intellectual labor and mass production remain the property of "genius," they mark personal and cultural identity. But because the slave system separates intellect from product, it causes forms of personal and cultural alienation that are at cross-purposes with Stowe's vision of national literature in an age of mass publication.

For Stowe, the alienation that slavery produces presents a literary problem that she casts in linguistic terms. Anticipating Bakhtin's definition of "alienation" as "language marked by other people's ownership" (Hawthorn 2004a: 9), and fraught with "a sense of struggle"(Hawthorn 2004b: 77), the acts of appropriation and silencing that are integral to chattel slavery raise the specter of violence that haunts Stowe's work. His master's decisions to appropriate George's labor and remove him from the factory affect him linguistically. He finds himself nearly "breaking out into some dangerous ebullition," and works hard to "repress every disrespectful word; but the flashing eye, the gloomy and troubled brow, were part of a natural language that could not be repressed, — indubitable signs, which showed too plainly that a man could not become a thing" (Stowe 1986: 56). George's "natural language" reverses the logic of slavery: if slavery turns a man into "a thing" (Stowe 1986: 55), his linguistic expression demonstrates that "a man could not become a thing" (Stowe 1986: 56). Stowe imagines George repressing a "dangerous ebullition" that nevertheless finds expression in a "flashing," "gloomy," and "troubled" look that threatens violence. But Stowe also thinks of language as a means of containing that violence and overcoming the alienation produced by slavery. When his master attempts to silence him, George finds a mode of expressing himself that remains inalienably his. He develops a "natural language" — or as De Forest might call it, a mode of "natural speaking" (De Forest 1868: 28) — that marks his master's inability to appropriate George's intellect. In response to his master's attempted appropriation of his intellectual labor, George develops "indubitable signs" that Stowe simultaneously particularizes and universalizes. As the black character least marked throughout the novel by linguistic difference from the white characters, George does not speak in an ethnic or a regional dialect, but expresses himself in clear, standardized English. A figure for linguistic standardization, he speaks in a universalized language that the novel's narrator can easily interpret and identify for her readers. At the very moment of his intellectual alienation, George becomes an example for a universalized form of expression that is premised on a notion of inalienable uniqueness and universal accessibility. For Stowe, slavery causes linguistic alienation that leads to the fragmentation of the national idiom. Stowe imagines that the abolition of slavery will inaugurate a specific kind of translation that will offset this fragmentation: she fantasizes about language achieving national universality. Like Tom, George becomes an emblem for literary nationalism in that he inhabits an inalienable relationship to his intellect and his language.

And yet even as she is turning her black characters into iconic national figures, Stowe repeatedly portrays them as foreign, for instance when she writes: "the negro, it must be remembered, is an exotic of the most gorgeous and superb countries of the world, and he has, deep in his heart, a passion for all that is splendid, rich, and fanciful" (Stowe 1986: 253). For Stowe, African-Americans are "exotic" and not part of the indigenous landscape; they represent other "countries of the world." How are we to understand her desire to remove African-Americans from the American scene, and yet her need to idealize them as fulfilling her own agenda for national literature?

Stowe works out a conflicted answer to this question by reinventing racial difference as national difference, and by portraying slaves as immigrants. As immigrants, slaves become ambiguous figures: on the one hand, they participate in national life, and Stowe tries to find a way of imagining their assimilation into the nation. But on the other hand, they are foreign and in Stowe's imagination ideally return to the places they came from. In the descriptions of Eliza's flight, Stowe creates a fantasy of diasporic return. She describes Eliza as "so white as not to be known as of colored lineage, without a critical survey, and as her child was white also, it was much easier for her to pass on unsuspected" (Stowe 1986: 107). When the slave trader Haley catches up with her, Eliza and little Harry become figures for the biblical flight of the enslaved Israelites from Egypt: as Eliza crosses the frozen Ohio, "her first glance was at the river, which lay, like Jordan, between her and the Canaan of liberty on the other side" (Stowe 1986: 107). By turning Eliza into the figure of the biblical refugee, Stowe suggests she is alienated from the land she leaves, and that her homeland is elsewhere. Eliza performs a reverse middle passage that ultimately leads to her repatriation in Africa, and that allows her, in rescuing Harry, to reclaim the idiom of domestic piety from which slave culture threatened to separate her.[6]

Stowe recasts George's ethnicity by turning him alternately into a Spaniard and a Hungarian. Unlike Eliza, George does not pass for white, but instead disguises himself as a traveler who is "very tall, with a dark, Spanish complexion" (Stowe 1986: 180). To perform in blackface as "Spanish," George uses walnut bark to make his "yellow skin a genteel brown," and he dies his hair black so as not to be recognized: a "slight change in the tint of the skin and the color of his hair had metamorphosed him into the Spanish-looking fellow he then appeared" (Stowe 1986: 182). When George enters the tavern in disguise, a bill with his description hangs on the wall. Even though he mirrors the textual image, presenting himself as Spanish makes George unrecognizable. In this scene of uncanny doubling, Stowe indicates that African-Americans are indistinguishable from immigrants in all but their legal standing — it is literally a text (in this case, the bill advertising George's escape that stands in for the fugitive slave bill) that marks their difference. Stowe solidifies this point when she reflects on George's flight in the context of the political displacements that were bringing European immigrants to the United States:

> If it had been only a Hungarian youth, now bravely defending in some mountain fastness the retreat of fugitives escaping from Austria into America, this would have been sublime heroism; but as it was a youth of African descent, defending the retreat of fugitives through America into Canada, of course we are too well instructed and patriotic so see any heroism in it; and if any of our readers do, they must do it on their own private responsibility. When despairing Hungarian fugitives make their way, against all the search warrants and authorities of their lawful government, to America, press and political cabinet ring with applause and welcome. When despairing African fugitives do the same thing, — it is — what *is* it? (Stowe 1986: 299)[7]

Stowe argues that the distinction between a "Hungarian youth" and a "youth of African descent" lies in the social perception of their actions. Both defy the laws of the land, and their actions are identical — they "do the same thing." Yet a set of educational and national practices prevents these acts from achieving the same status in the eyes of the American public: Americans are "too well instructed and patriotic" to recognize acts of "sublime heroism" that occur before their own eyes. By associating slaves with immigrants, Stowe makes African-American acts of heroism recognizable in national terms.

But even more importantly, she imagines in this passage that education — being "instructed" — holds the key to addressing national problems. Education becomes important precisely because the economic system has failed to address the problems caused by cultural and labor alienation. Stowe makes that failure clear when Augustine St. Clare answers Miss Ophelia's question whether the "nation ever will voluntarily emancipate" by responding:

> This is a day of great deeds. Heroism and disinterestedness are rising up, here and there, in the earth. The Hungarian nobles set free millions of serfs, at an immense pecuniary loss, and, perhaps, among us may be

found generous spirits, who do not estimate honor and justice by dollars and cents. (Stowe 1986: 451—2)

St. Clare argues for an extra-economic generosity by which slaveholders would value "heroism" and "disinterestedness" over "dollars and cents." For all her celebration of the factory system, Stowe's novel is skeptical that such an extra-economic heroism will prevail. Yet Stowe fantasizes that a different kind of value from the use and exchange value of the market system could emerge, and her novel explores what that value might be.

Stowe develops a notion of iconic translation by which texts can circulate linguistically without undergoing a process of alienation. Stowe depicts iconic language as both an extension of the idealized nation and alternative to the flawed, slave-holding nation when George Harris addresses the slave catchers who are pursuing him and his family: "We don't own your laws; we don't own your country; we stand here as free, under God's sky, as you are; and, by the great God, that made us, we'll fight for our liberty till we die" (Stowe 1986: 298). George casts his relationship to the United States in terms of ownership: he points out that he does not "own" the laws or the country, and refers to them by the possessive "your" from which he excludes himself. And yet in that moment of exclusion, George is echoing the American Revolution: he paraphrases Patrick Henry when he says that he will fight for his liberty or suffer death. George's exclamation is a speech act: in the act of articulating his freedom he becomes free, and in the act of proclaiming that he will fight for his liberty, he is already engaging in that fight. When George expresses his exclusion from the American system, he turns that exclusion into the locus of his own nationalism. That nationalism becomes a verbal ideal at that moment: George participates in this nationalism only via his speech. Language marks the nation, and embodies an idealized form of nationalism that exceeds current shortcomings.

By reversing the middle passage and the culture of translation it inaugurated, Stowe does not redress but perpetuates the logic of slavery that her novel seeks to undermine. Stowe's brand of nationalism amounts to a form of imperialism: George Harris ultimately realizes his vision of American patriotism in Africa. Yet Stowe would have been shocked at such a reading of her text. For Stowe, curtailing translation provided a solution to the wrongs of slavery. Ironically, Stowe turns Tom — who is barely literate — into the ideal reader. His verbal limitation makes him central to Stowe's view of the way literary texts themselves should function as stable, inalienable objects that transcend the vicissitudes of market relations. Traveling down the Mississippi River, Tom reads his Bible in search of consolation for his separation from his family. Stowe comments:

> Cicero, when he buried his darling and only daughter, had a heart as full of honest grief as poor Tom's, — perhaps no fuller, for both were

only men; — but Cicero could pause over no such sublime words of hope, and look to no such future reunion; and if he *had* seen them, ten to one he would not have believed, — he must fill his head first with a thousand questions of authenticity of manuscript, and correctness of translation. But, to poor Tom, there it lay, just what he needed, so evidently true and divine that the possibility of a question never entered his simple head. It must be true; for, if not true, how could he live? (Stowe 1986: 229)

Stowe argues that grief equalizes Cicero and Tom, but she is quick to point out that a difference emerges between the two of them that is based on their access to scripture. That comparison works in Tom's favor and Cicero's disfavor: not only did Cicero lack access to the bible, but his intellectual training made him unfit to read the Gospels. That unfitness lies in his relationship to texts: Stowe's hypothetical Cicero would have questioned the "authenticity of manuscript, and correctness of translation." He would have tried to understand both the source material and the translation by a standard that escapes Tom. By contrast, Tom accepts the translation itself as the gospel truth — the translation itself is transparent, and provides what Tom perceives of as an unmediated access to scriptural authority. Stowe's relation to authenticity and to translation emerge here as a complicated subtext. She deplores questioning texts that should be accepted, not examined, for their truth value. In relation to a market driven by exchange value and use value, Stowe imagines a third value that exceeds both, and that is literary and linguistic orthodoxy. Borrowing from Gillian Brown, we may say that her "fetishism ... transforms commodities ... [into] objects outside the market [that] can and do speak" (Brown 1990: 50–51). Stowe imagines that by reading the Gospel as truth, Tom removes the text from the kind of circulation that drives the market economy.

Stowe solidifies that point when she imagines multilingualism as a trait of the slave economy. Although large sections of the novel are set in New Orleans, an intensely multilingual city, Stowe never addresses that multilingualism while Tom is with St. Clare. Only after St. Clare's death, when his wife Mary decides to auction off the slaves, does the multilingual dimension of the city come into play. Stowe describes the slave auction as taking place

> beneath a splendid dome ... [where] men of all nations, [were] moving to and fro, over the marble pave. On every side of the circular area were little tribunes, or stations, for the use of speakers and auctioneers. Two of these, on opposite sides of the area, were now occupied by brilliant and talented gentlemen, enthusiastically forcing up, in English and French commingled, the bids of connoisseurs in their various wares. (Stowe 1986: 475)

Stowe portrays slavery and multilingualism as antithetical to the nationalism she imagines. She stages the auction as a verbal act when she refers not only to the auctioneers but also the "speakers" who can declaim from "tribunes." The language they use demonstrates that they are "brilliant" and "talented," but their powers go to commercial ends. In pursuing those commercial ends, they employ both "English and French." That act of linguistic commingling is one that replicates for Stowe the violence inherent in slavery — it is aimed at "forcing up" the price of the slaves. That force also turns those slaves into commodities: they are "wares" that are subject to the scrutiny of "connoisseurs." Knowledge itself has become part of a slave economy that thrives on a linguistic circulation that is complicit with the circulation of slaves:

> the clatter of the salesman crying off his qualifications in French and English, the quick fire of French and English bids; and almost in a moment came the final thump of the hammer, and the clear ring on the last syllable of the word '*Dollars*,' as the auctioneer announced his price, and Tom was made over. — He had a master! [...] Tom hardly realized anything; but still the bidding went on, — ratting, clattering, now French, now English. [...] The auctioneer sees his advantage, and expatiates volubly in mingled French and English, and bids rise in rapid succession. (Stowe 1986: 478–9)

For Stowe, multilingualism is a form of violence that expresses itself in "quick fire." It turns the slaves' "qualifications" into commodities, and it commingles language ("the word") with currency ("'*Dollars*'"). For Stowe, language is at its worst a currency that is complicit with the slave system, and at best a refuge from its circulation. In imagining Tom reading the Bible, she invents a language that is not subject to circulation, but that forms a counterpoint to slave alienation. Stowe fantasizes that iconic, biblical translation is different from the verbal exchange of the slave market: she imagines that iconic translation can itself carry a sense of orthodoxy that reinforces the authority and autonomy of the literary text. It is that kind of iconic translation that she set out to produce and protect in her lawsuit against unauthorized translations that entered the market economy without her direct supervision.

II.

When Stowe brought suit against Thomas in 1852 for the unauthorized translation of her work that he had published in *Die Freie Press*, a German language newspaper, no legal precedent existed for deciding the case. Given the popularity of translation and its role in establishing both the international and the intranational dissemination of American literature, how do we explain that it took so long for this issue of copyright infringement to reach the courts? The answer to this question lies in the fact that copyright was a recent invention, and that nineteenth century laws were ambivalent about authorial property. On the one hand, copyright laws set out to establish and protect intellectual property in an attempt to foster artistic creation. Yet artistic creation was meant to serve the public good, and legislators were therefore loath to allow for the author's restriction of their works' use. Translation posed a particularly complex problem in an already schizoid attitude: on the one hand, translation further complicated the issue of authorial property in that it multiplied authorship (so that one question at issue was whether the writer or the translator had an authorial right to a translated work). Yet that multiplication of authorship made translation the ideal form of a multiply disseminated and culturally composed text.

As Susan Stewart has shown, rudimentary regulations for textual reproduction existed as early as the Middle Ages when monopolies developed among guilds of stationers and booksellers (Stewart 1991). But the idea that one could claim the ownership of words was not expressed until the seventeenth century, when John Locke formulated the liberal understanding of intellectual property, by which an author legally owned the works he had produced by his intellectual labor. Through Locke's efforts, the Licensing Act that kept in place the guild system expired in 1695, making way for the first modern copyright legislation: the "Act for the Encouragement of Learning, by Vesting the Copies of Printed Books in the Authors or Purchasers of Such Copies, during the Times therein mentioned" was passed into law in 1710. Whereas printer's patent protected the tangible quality of copies, this law — commonly referred to as the Statute of Anne — protected the "intangible and abstract matter of expressive originality" (Stewart 1991: 17). The Statute of Anne newly "constituted the author as well as the bookseller as a person of legal standing" (Rose 1993: 49), and protected the work itself, not just "the stationer's right to publish a work" (Rose 1993: 14).[8]

The question became what made up a work, and specifically, what role language played for the identity of a text. Drawing from Johann Gottlieb Fichte's distinction between the content and the form of a book, William Blackstone argued that

> the identity of a literary composition consists entirely in the *sentiment* and the *language*; the same conceptions, clothed in the same words, must necessarily be the same composition: and whatever method be taken of conveying that composition to the ear or the eye of another, by recital, by writing, or by printing, in any number of copies or at any period of time, it is always the identical work of the author which is so conveyed; and no other man can have a right to convey or transfer it without his consent, either tacitly or expressly given. (cited in Rose 1993: 89–90)

Yet in the multilingual American case, the question arose what exactly it meant for a text to be "clothed in the same words" — whether in fact a translation used the same words as the original, even if those words were in another language. The debate over copyright approached this question via a consideration of intellectual labor.

In a legal system based on Lockean notions of labor-based proprietorship, intellectual labor posed a special problem. For Locke, property originated in individual acts of appropriation from the general state of nature. Because a person owned his own labor, that labor formed the basis for private property. That association made its way into the first copyright law passed in Massachusetts, which provided for the "legal security of the *fruits* of their [the authors'] study and *industry* ... as such security is one of the *natural* rights of all men, there being no *property* more peculiarly a man's own than that which is *produced* by the *labour* of his mind" (Congress and Solberg 1900: 12; my emphasis). In language that oddly blends the pastoral and the industrial, the law established a labor-based rationale for intellectual property. That intellectual property became associated with its producer's personality. As Mark Rose has demonstrated, Edward Young's *Conjectures on Original Composition in a Letter to the Author of Sir Charles Grandison* (1759) fused textuality and personality. Young introduced the concept of original genius as both a quality of the author and of the text: "No longer simply a mirror held up to nature, a work was also the objectification of a writer's self, and the commodity that changed hands when a bookseller purchased a manuscript or when a reader purchased a book was as much personality as ink and paper" (Rose 1993: 121). No wonder, then, that Stowe conflated the commodification of slaves with the issue of intellectual property: whereas Lockean notions of property generally speaking were at odds with slavery, intellectual property specifically raised the specter of slavery by conflating the text with the author, and commodifying both.

As an author, Stowe herself was metaphorically commodified by this conflation of text and personhood. The court wrote that, "by the publication of her book the creations of the genius and imagination of the author have become as much public property as those of Homer or Cervantes. Uncle Tom and Topsy are as much *publici juris,* as Don Quixote and Sancho Panza. All her conceptions and inventions may be used and abused by imitators, playrights [sic] and poetasters" (Stowe v. Thomas 1853: 22). Judge Grier granted that Stowe's work reflected her "genius" and expressed her "imagination," but he personified her creativity by reference to her slave characters, Tom and Topsy. As Meredith McGill points out, "Judge Grier's asymmetrical analogy between property in slaves and property in books provides one account of how reprinting's emphasis on the free circulation of texts is drawn into the orbit of the tense political compromise of the early 1850s" (McGill 2003: 273). By making Stowe's novel and her characters public property, Grier links the commodification of texts and slaves, and argues for the relevance of both to the public domain. He makes textual circulation serviceable to the slave economy, and performs a striking reversal of Lockean property law: instead of labor producing individual property rights, he interprets American law to indicate that intellectual labor produces communal rights that take precedence over individual rights.

Yet this ruling was at cross-purposes with itself. Melissa Homestead has argued that Judge Grier, "the legal guardian of the interests of slave owners, ... paradoxically encouraged the wider circulation of Stowe's abolitionist ideas by refusing to grant her an injunction against Thomas" (Homestead 2002: 220). For Homestead, that paradox hinges on the suit's schizoid reading of Blackstone's metaphor that a text must be "clothed in the same words" to be identical to itself:

> On the strictly abstract level of legal analysis, the metaphor reveals a serious flaw in the copyright metaphor of language as clothing. The metaphor both implies and denies a body underneath the linguistic clothing — it implies a body because clothing by definition covers bodies, but the purported logic of the analogy also denies the presence of a body because language is supposed to be material or corporeal, and the ideas, conceptions, and inventions that are 'clothed' by language are supposed to be *incorporeal*. In a visually stunning but wholly illogical metaphor, then, Grier makes the naked circulating *bodies* of Stowe's characters represent Stowe's *incorporeal* creations. (Homestead 2002: 217)

This inconsistency points to the ongoing difficulty that copyright had in deciding whether it protected only the concrete, physical copies of books or also extended to the abstract, intellectual content.

The issue hinged on an understanding of the role language played for literary and national identity. The first copyright legislation was passed against the backdrop of heated debates over the importance of establishing an independent American language. In 1780, John Adams wrote to the Continental Congress: "It is not to be disputed that the form of government has an influence upon language, and language in its turn influences not only the form of government, but the temper, the sentiments, and the manners of the people" (cited in Erkkila 1983: 22). To ensure governmental independence from Britain, he recommended — against the opposition of Benjamin Franklin — that Congress establish a national language academy. Congress did not follow this recommendation. Despite Adams' calls for a unified language, "in the main, English was regarded as a practical instrument rather than a symbolic unifier" (Crawford 1992: 10). The fact that English was not a symbolic unifier became evident by the fact that the law itself was not uniformly "clothed" in a single language: for instance, Benjamin Franklin translated the American Constitution into French (Kellman 2002: 451), and the proceedings of the Continental Congress were published in German and in French as well as English. A proposal even reached Congress in 1795 to print all federal laws in German as well as English — a proposal that lost by one vote (Heath 1992: 40).

Oddly, these multilingual practices arose in part through attempts at literary protectionism. In 1783, the Colonial Congress recommended to the individual states that they should afford copyright to authors or publishers of new books if and only if they were citizens of the United States. Early copyright legislation supported the revolutionary fervor of those attempting to establish an independent American literature yet created a literary market heavily dominated by foreign works. When the first Congress passed the Copyright Act of 1790, it did not protect works "written, composed, or made by any person not being a citizen of the United States" (Congress and Solberg 1900: 38). As an attempt at national protectionism, the act was a horrible failure, and one that backfired. But as a general attempt to stimulate the printing and circulation of books in America, the act proved a tremendous success. Congress imposed "heavy tariffs on imported books" and thereby "gave considerable incentive for American editions" (Warner 1990: 119). Consequently, the market for fiction was heavily dominated by reprints of English works and translations from languages other than English.[9] Even with the declining percentage in overall market share, translations maintained preeminence in the American book trade at mid-century in that, as Frank Luther Mott's study indicates, they regularly numbered among the best sellers in antebellum America (Mott 1947: 7). Michael Warner has demonstrated that "it was not sluggishness or incapacity that kept eighteenth-century Americans from developing a national literature in the modern sense; it was their way of valuing print" (Warner 1990: xiv). American copyright laws defined print as a public good rather than a private possession. As a public good, print fostered an imagined community that crossed national, linguistic, and geographic boundaries. American copyright generated a publishing sphere by which the nation imagined itself in and through its transatlantic relations.

Those relations came under scrutiny when Stowe entered suit against Thomas, and claimed that his translations infringed on her copyright. By 1860, *Uncle Tom's Cabin* had been translated worldwide into roughly twenty languages, with several rival translations competing in German and French, and had become the most widely circulated work of American literature. From the large number of people who had translated *Uncle Tom's Cabin* without paying her royalties, Stowe singled out Thomas for a specific reason: he infringed on the sales of her authorized translation in the United States, the only country where she held a copyright that entitled her to royalty payments. To prove that Thomas' translation violated Stowe's copyright, her attorney Perkins needed to establish two things. First, he had to document that Stowe in fact held legal copyright for *Uncle Tom's Cabin*. Second, Perkins had to persuade the court that "there is no limitation or restriction" on the property that the author held in her work, except as to the copyright's duration. Although this point does not seem directly to address the issue of translation, establishing the legal breadth of copyright was crucial to the case because it engaged the larger question whether copyright privatized the rights to intellectual property or whether they remained *publici juris*. Perkins argued that if translation was not an infringement of copyright but considered *publici juris*, the translation could be retranslated into the original language and compete there with the author's work. In fact, this practice occurred: for example, the first number of the *New York Review* (1837) discussed the *Morals and Legislation. By Jeremy Bentham. Translated into French by M. Dumont, with notes; and from the French, (2nd. Ed. corrected and enlarged) with Notes, and a Biographical Notice of Jeremy Bentham and of M. Dumont, by John Neal*. Perkins expressed his concern that the practice of translating translations would make copyright meaningless and allow duplicates of a book to compete with one another in the literary market. Translations would compete with original texts in the language in which those texts had first been written. But to argue this point, Perkins had to demonstrate that translation was a copy — and that as an unauthorized copy, Thomas' translation infringed on Stowe's copyright.

Perkins began by defining the author's right to her literary property and by considering the labor upon which such property was based. As the creator of a book, an author could exclude "every other person from any participation in the enjoyment, use, or even the mere knowledge of the existence" of his manuscript (Stowe v. Thomas 1853: 3). Going into print and selling mechanically mass-produced copies reshaped the author's relation to the text: by publishing the book, the author "disposes of the free mental use of his intellectual productions to each purchaser of a copy of his book" (Stowe v. Thomas 1853: 4). Ideas were not protected by copyright, but the author maintained absolute dominion over the specific language she had used to express her ideas. Translation replicated that language: Perkins argued that the task of the translator lay in making the translation correspond as closely as possible to the author's original words and style, so that all variation marked the failure of the translation.

Although Perkins acknowledged that translation required labor — upon which the Lockean conception of property was based — he argued that such labor did not give the translator authorial rights. He quoted Webster's Dictionary as saying that to translate meant to render into a different language, which he compared to printing a book in braille: translation reproduced the copyrighted work in another medium. Perkins drew an analogy between the translator's and the printer's labor when he insisted that the printer could not use an author's labor without his consent, and that similarly "a translation is quasi mechanical" and subject to copyright (Stowe v. Thomas 1853: 5). What Martha Woodmansee says of the author in the Renaissance applies to the translator in the antebellum period: two concepts were at play by which the translator was a craftsman or an intellectual genius. Stowe's lawyer tried to portray the translator as a craftsman and to divorce his writing from the author's genius: he insisted that "translation calls for no creation on the part of the translator" and that "translation is the same book" (Stowe v. Thomas 1853: 4).

These claims are worth pausing over. As we have seen, Perkins was not arguing that Stowe's copyright extended to the ideas expressed in her book. Her copyright protected the language she had used to express her thoughts. For a translation to be "the same book" as the original meant that it had to be expressed in the same language. Perplexingly, Stowe's language turns out not to be linguistically bound: by Perkins' logic, Stowe's English book translated into German reproduces the language in which she wrote. In a dual sense, this line of argumentation makes Stowe's language inalienable: in an economic sense, she cannot be divested of the authorial property she holds in her novel, and in a cultural sense, her American book maintains its linguistic and cultural identity in translation. Perkins' legal argument replays the logic of translation that Stowe had explored in her novel — the fantasy that iconic translation could transcend alienation and establish a coherent national identity.

An anxiety and a fantasy underlie Perkins' claim that American works retain their language even in translation. Perkins expresses a concern that runs somewhat contrary to his argument when he claims that translation will hinder the linguistic integration of immigrant groups: he insists that translation injures an author's sales because "the very large class who but imperfectly understand the language in which the original is written will prefer to read the translation and save themselves the labor and difficulty they would have otherwise taken to read the work in the original tongue" (Stowe v. Thomas 1853: 9). Multilingualism and translation are at odds with a politics of linguistic assimilation: Perkins worries that translation will encourage linguistic diversity and hinder the immigrant "class" from laboring to read English. Yet by insisting that translation replicates the original's language, he offsets this fear by fantasizing about the immigrants' inadvertent participation in a uniform national discourse. As a copy, translation is a nation-building tool: for Perkins, the American book is not only national in scope, but written in a national language that ultimately transcends linguistic differences.

In addressing the charges brought against him, Thomas' lawyer Goepp argued that translation was not a copy. For Thomas' work to be an infringement of Stowe's copyright required "damage to the original from the alleged piracy" to have occurred (Stowe v. Thomas 1853: 10). On the contrary, Goepp argued, the translation increased the profits Stowe could gain from her work: translation served as an advertisement that furthered the sales of the original — as Jewett's advertisement of the book would indicate (see figure 5.1). Goepp pointed out that Stowe had commissioned her own translation because she was aware of these beneficial aspects. The aim of her suit was not to protect her original work, but rather to protect her own German translation. Goepp accused the complainants of attacking the free and public dissemination of literature in an attempt to establish "a monopoly of every use of a book, except the simple reading it" (Stowe v. Thomas 1853: 16). He argued that restricting translation stifled invention and vehemently rejected the claim that literary translations were *"servile and mechanical imitations"* (Stowe v. Thomas 1853: 10). Goepp acknowledged that some translations merely required the use of a dictionary, but he limited such mindless linguistic transposition to "recipes, chemical and algebraic formulas, almanacs, nautical tables, etc." (Stowe v. Thomas 1853: 11). The examples he lists are all scientific: Goepp distinguishes literary translation from the science of language.

Literary translations do not conform to a uniform system but require authorial choice — two translations of the same work always differ from each other because "the translator impresses the work with his individual characteristic" (Stowe v. Thomas 1853: 11). Goepp concluded that

> a translation requires genius in its construction ... But where the genius of the translator is called forth, there he is himself an author, and his translation an original work. The labor of a mechanic involves a denial of his individuality. The translator preserves his individuality. It gives the very character to the work. ... (Stowe v. Thomas 1853: 11)

Goepp extended his opponents' definition of the author to the translator. He considered the exactness of the translation a measure of the translator's genius: he believed that the accuracy of a translation constituted a proof of its originality because it demonstrated substantial intellectual labor and made the translation "a work of the mind, — not mechanical merely" (Stowe v. Thomas 1853: 12). Because of this combination of labor and creativity, he regarded translation as a new text — not an appropriation of another text. Goepp insisted that by the very definition of genius, "no original work can be an infringement of any other. But a translation is an original work, and therefore cannot be an infringement of any copyright" (Stowe v. Thomas 1853: 12). In an interesting turn, this meant that — although the copyright that protected an original did not extend to translations — translations themselves could be copyrighted. Like other originals, they could likewise be temporarily removed from public property.

As Judge Grier made clear when he ruled in favor of the defendant, the translation's originality consisted of its language. According to Grier, who was paraphrasing Blackstone, the identity of two books "does not consist merely in the ideas, knowledge or information communicated, but in the same conceptions clothed in the same words, which make it the same composition" (Stowe v. Thomas 1853: 20). Therefore, a transcript must replicate the *language* an author has used to express his thoughts — "the same conceptions clothed in another language cannot constitute the same composition" (Stowe v. Thomas 1853: 20) because

To make a good translation of a work, often requires more learning, talent and judgment than was required to write the original. Many can *transfer* from one language to another, but few can *translate*. To call the translation of an author's ideas and conceptions into another language a *copy* of his *book*, would be an abuse of terms, and arbitrary judicial legislation. (Stowe v. Thomas 1853: 21)

By this ruling, translation is the ultimate American neologism: it does not replicate the original's language but rather expresses its ideas in a new language. Translation serves a public function in that it encourages individual genius but also generates the dialogic dissemination of ideas. Goepp defined a book as a "communication — a fusion of minds" and argued that an author's "property is simply in the book *itself* bodily; not in the communication" (Stowe v. Thomas 1853: 15). As communication, translation is an ideal act of reading and writing: it is the realization of the hope that the American book and the public sphere could be mutually constitutive. At a time when European law defined authorship, original literature and the nation in terms of one another, American laws brought into being an imagined community that crossed national and linguistic boundaries — for better and for worse.[10]

III.

Although Stowe lost her lawsuit, her argument formed the basis for shifts in the legal definition of copyright that occurred at the end of the nineteenth century. Those changes were brought about by a growing movement to tighten the national dissemination of texts via international copyright legislation. In 1879, "Stylus" argued that the absence of an international copyright law was largely the result of American publishers' "rapacity" and the cause of America's "intellectual vassalage" (Stylus 1879: 5). He singled out Longfellow as an example and accused him of being no more than "an imitator of the poets of the olden time ... [who] has devoted himself to translations and editing Books of Beauty and Poems of Places" (Stylus 1879: 7). Like Stowe's lawyer, "Stylus" defined translation as copy, and argued that the practice of printing books for which American authors would not receive royalties was "one of the worst enemies of our country. Instead of educating our people with American ideas and American principles, the circulation of foreign books fills their minds with anti-democratic sentiments and unpatriotic ideas" (Stylus 1879: 9). Such arguments reveal a particular understanding of what constitutes an American book. "Stylus" defines the American book by negatives: it is not foreign, not a translation, not imported, not written abroad, not monarchical; the matching set of positive definitions is that the American book is indigenous, written in English, domestic, local, democratic. The victory of such claims marks the conceptual and the legal end of the culture of translation that I have been outlining in this book.

Twenty years after Stowe's suit, American copyright was extended to include translation when the Revised Statutes of 1873 recorded in section 4952: "authors may reserve the right to dramatize or to translate their own works" (Congress and Solberg 1900: 50). It took almost another two decades for this provision to be extended: the amendment of 1891 stated that "authors or their assigns shall have *exclusive* right to dramatize and translate any of their works for which copyright shall have been obtained under the laws of the United States" (Congress and Solberg 1900: 55; my emphasis). The law of 1891 also for the first time recognized international copyright. It extended its provisions to include subjects "of a foreign state or nation when such foreign state or nation permits to citizens of the United States of America the benefit of copyright on substantially the same basis as its own citizens" (Congress and Solberg 1900: 56). Over the next years, the number of countries to which this provision applied proliferated: the United States signed copyright agreements with Belgium, France, Great Britain, and Switzerland in 1891; the German Empire and Italy in 1892; Denmark and Portugal in 1893, Spain in 1895, Mexico and Chile in 1896, Costa Rica and the Netherlands in 1899. International copyright laws effectively ended the free circulation of texts.

International copyright also revised an understanding of American literature: as Claudia Stokes has recently demonstrated, the copyright movement periodized nineteenth century literature by dividing it into two parts, an effete, European-inspired antebellum tradition, and a labor-based, aboriginal postbellum movement (Stokes 2005). That periodization revised the United States' linguistic history. The importance of multilingualism and of translation in the United States was programmatically written out of historical consciousness in the early twentieth century. Anglo-conformity and state loyalty became linked at the turn of the twentieth century, as James Crawford has demonstrated, in attempts to combat labor organizing (Crawford 1992: 16). Before 1906, "there was no prerequisite in naturalization laws that an alien either speak or be literate in English. However, the Nationality Act of 1906 required that an alien speak English in order to become naturalized," a requirement that was further codified in the Nationality Act of 1940 and the Internal Security Act of 1950 (Heath 1980: 15). A bill to establish an official language was proposed at the federal level in 1923 (Crawford 1992: 10), and the question of an official language gained new force during the bilingual education hysteria of the 1980s: an outspoken critic of bilingual education, Senator S. I. Hayakawa, introduced a constitutional amendment in 1981 to make English the official language of the United States (Crawford 1992: 2).

Hand in hand with the link between citizenship and English-language mastery went the repression of other languages. In 1916, "it became illegal even to teach many foreign languages in American Schools" as isolationist sentiment and the anti-German backlash gained the upper hand in response to World War I (Shell 2002: 8). Germans had been "the most important group in the early history of bilingual education" (Crawford 1992: 16–17), but they were not the only ethnic group targeted by linguistic restrictions: Native Americans were denied the right to speak their languages, especially in the boarding schools established between 1879–1902. In the period from 1917 to 1923, states removed laws tolerating instruction in languages other than English from their codes. Although bilingual education had once been widespread, "all bilingual schools were abolished in the hysteria of 1917–18" (Gilbert 1980: 265). In the 1920s, the Supreme Court ruled that requiring the language instruction to be English in a state or territory of the United States was constitutional, but it also found that it was unconstitutional to ban secondary language instruction by ethnic groups (Heath 1980: 17). Yet by the time of this ruling, "the damage was such that public bilingual schooling was not attempted again until" the 1960s (Gilbert 1980: 265). To this day,

> the public school system actually *discourages* the use of any language other than English. Education consists, then, of *unlearning* languages, not learning them. Before becoming an elite capable of mastering several languages, children must first pass into the elite of people who speak only English. (Johnson 2003: 32)

In the twentieth century, the multilingualism that nineteenth century authors actively embraced as an educational goal became stigmatized when the bilingual education act made monolingualism a right. The bilingual education act of 1968 was "primarily an act for the Anglification of non-English speakers and not an act for bilingualism" (Fishman 1980: 517). It established what Wallace Lambert has called a 'subtractive bilingualism' by which immigrant children lose their native languages (cited in Sommer 2002: 278). This legislation also continued the racial politics of Stowe's suit: the 1974 Supreme Court decision in *Lau v. Nichols* ruled that failure of school districts to provide non-English speaking children with special assistance violated the Civil Rights Act of 1964. Monolingualism became linked with desegregation, and placed in the service of a monoculturalism that defined itself along linguistic lines.

Repressive language politics also fundamentally changed the legal definition of translation. Instead of regarding translation as a vehicle of literary expression, it became an instrument of state power and a tool for repressive ethnic and linguistic politics. In compliance with an act of 1917, all translations had to be filed with the postmaster for approval; section 19 stipulated that

> until the end of the war it shall be unlawful for any person, firm, corporation, or association, to print, publish, or circulate ... in any foreign

language, any news item, editorial, or other printed matter, respecting the Government of the United States, or of any nation engaged in the present war, its policies, international relations, the State or conduct of the war, or any matter relating thereto: Provided, that this section shall not apply ... [if the publisher has first] filed with the postmaster at the place of publication, in the form of an affidavit, a true and complete translation of the entire article ... and has caused to be printed, in plain typed in the English language, at the head of each such time ... the words 'True translation filed with the postmaster.' (cited in Batsaki 2002: 106–7)

The law now assumed that translation was and needed to be an exact copy — and not the site of innovation. Along with this emphasis on monolingualism, the role of translation in American publishing significantly declined. As an article in the *New York Times* recently pointed out, citing the National Endowment for the Arts, "about 3 percent of the books published in the United States ... [are] translations, compared with 40 to 50 percent in Western European countries" (Salamon 2004). That statistic speaks to the way in which American literature has become nationalized as monolingual and self-referential, but it belies the profound relevance of and engagement with translation that historically informed American literature. At the very time when American Literary Studies was emerging as an academic field, translation lost its status as the site of American multilingualism and literary innovation and became a tool for monolingualism. The emerging field canonized that shift in attitudes towards translation; it is time to step outside of American Studies' linguistic paradigm and to reclaim the linguistically complex sites of contemporary and historic American literature. Nationalism and transnationalism are not alternatives to one another: in the contexts I have been outlining, the nation constitutes itself in transnational contexts that thrive on linguistic circulation and acts of translation. For better and for worse, translation is an indigenous form of American literary transnationalism.

Notes

INTRODUCTION

1. The notion of the American melting pot gained prominence after Israel Zangwill coined the term in 1908. Theodore Roosevelt popularized and politicized the concept in 1917 with his "Children of the Crucible" address.
2. In current critical use, "transatlantic" is most often a subset for the broader field of "transnational" inquiry. Scholars invoke the term to "challenge an analytical fixation on the nation-state," and to suggest that "the dialectic between the national and the transnational has shifted significantly in favor of the latter" (Rouse 1995: 357–8). In this sense, "transnational" and "postnational" frequently function as synonyms for one another. For Arjun Appadurai, transnationalism marks an alternative or an afterlife to distinct nations and nation states. The forms transnationalism takes are both the catalysts and casualties of economic globalization: he locates transnationalism in corporations but also in groups of dispersed people who share a sense of diasporic group affinity with each other; see: Appadurai 1996, Appadurai 2001; see also: Tyrell 1991, Balkir 1995, Buell 1998, Hardt and Negri 2000. When I use the term "transnational," I do not use it as a synonym for cultural connections that come after the nation — for me, postnationalism is a useful term for inquiring into the particular shape that transnationalism takes at our own historical moment, but I do not find the term useful for capturing the historic transnational imaginary. In the historical definition that I develop, transnational inquiry does not succeed the nation — both are historically coexistent and interdependent.
3. Attempts to define a field of "transatlantic studies" are enjoying particular vogue in Europe, where the Maastricht Center for Transatlantic Studies was established in 1995, and Edinburgh University launched the STAR (Scottish Trans-Atlantic Relations) Project and began publishing the *Journal for Transatlantic Studies* in 2002. Much of the work in European transatlantic studies has been influenced by Paul Giles; see for instance the volumes of essays published by the Maastricht Center: Kaufman and Macpherson 2000, Kaufman and Macpherson 2001.

    Under the influence of Paul Gilroy's work, the transatlantic context has proved particularly fertile ground for discussions of race, though largely along lines that run the danger of replicating the more insidious strands of frontier masculinity and crowding out feminist perspectives. As Aiwha Ong has pointed out, "women ... are frequently absent in studies of transnationalism" (Ong 1999: 11). For a notable exception, see: Creighton and Norling 1996. Paul Gilroy described the Atlantic as a space for the emergence of mod-

ern black double consciousness, which for him is implicitly yet normatively male. As I have explained more fully elsewhere (Boggs 2005), Gilroy's model has recently come under criticism for homogenizing the processes of Atlantic consciousness, but usually for its geographical blindspots rather than its gender politics: Loren Kruger has argued that the "black Atlantic" looks very different when we examine it from a South African perspective; see: Kruger 2001. Kruger argues that we need to account for different geopolitical contexts that do not privilege — as she says Gilroy does — the Anglo-American connection. Ronald Judy has criticized Gilroy for globalizing his model of the black Atlantic. Judy argues that: "Reggaes, African-American musical expressions, even the expressions of civil rights and Black Power are not translated, as Gilroy's process suggests, into a global cultural identity — i.e. the black Atlantic. Instead they are indicative, or rather their simultaneous engagement in heteronomous systems — global and local — is indicative, of an emergent 'culture'" (Judy 1997: 28). Paul Jay insists that Gilroy's work "needs to be supplemented by the work of Latin American, Caribbean, and U.S. theorists in order to draw out all of its implications for the study of literature and culture in our hemisphere" (Jay 1998: 167). One way to organize the abundance of information that is available on transatlantic culture is by focusing on diasporic communities. Although Gilroy borrows the term very cautiously from Jewish studies, where diaspora always refers back to a national homeland, the term has gained increasing currency among scholars of the transatlantic. Khachig Tölöyan sees diaspora as one term within the "vocabulary of transnationalism," and defines it as "concerned with the ways in which nations, real yet imagined communities (Anderson), are fabulated, brought into being, made and unmade, in culture and politics, both on land people call their own and in exile" (Tölöyan 1991: 5, 3). Herman Bennett sees the concept of diaspora as an obstacle to transnational inquiry, since the "nation continues to inform the very meaning of diaspora despite the intentions of some scholars to challenge the conventional framework" (Bennett 2000: 101). Yet Helen Thomas uses the term in Tölöyan's sense, when she defines diaspora as "the common historical processes of dispersal, fragmentation, displacement, enslavement and transportation experienced by African peoples ... which unified such peoples at the same time as cutting them off from direct access to their past" (Thomas 2000: 6). One question that has gained particular currency is whether the Atlantic functions separately from the spaces that bound it; see: Lemisch 1968, Ritchie 1986a, Ritchie 1986b, Runyan 1987, Rediker 1987, Springer 1995, Roach 1996, Klein and Mackenthun 2003. In terms of recent novelistic output, transatlantic work has also been in vogue; see: Morrison 1988, Cliff 1990, Johnson 1990, Unsworth 1992, Cliff 1993, Wideman 1996, D'Aguiar 1999, Phillips 2000, Griesemer 2003.
4. I read Hawthorne and Forten as opposites in their attitudes and relation to issues of translation. It should also be noted, however, that Forten befriended Hawthorne's sister Elizabeth in Salem in 1853, and that her journals often praise Hawthorne's works; see: Levine 2005: 287–90.
5. See: Wise 1999.
6. Laura Chrisman has pointed out that critical examinations of the Atlantic as a cultural space began with Gilroy's book, and that the book's most important contribution was the anti-nationalist thrust of its cultural investigation; see: Chrisman 2000.
7. Joan Dayan has criticized Gilroy for turning the middle passage into a metaphor that obscures the historical and ongoing reality of slave suffering; see: Dayan 1996.

8. For a recent critique of the separate sphere paradigm, see: Davidson and Hatcher 2002.
9. See: Derrida 1985, Derrida 1997.
10. Derrida's use of biblical allegory is particularly relevant to the field of American literary studies in that generations of scholars have understood American literature primarily through biblical allegory. See especially: Lewis 1955, Bercovitch 1978, Packer 1982.

    In turning here to poststructuralism, I am picking up on John Carlos Rowe's insistence that a "New American Studies" needs to demonstrate "a much greater reliance on semiotic and poststructuralist approaches than has been the case among those doing traditional work in American Studies" (Rowe 2002: xvii).
11. I am inverting Homi Bhabha's model of mimicry here; see: Bhabha 1994b. Whereas Bhabha reads mimicry as the colonized response to imperialism, I am arguing that Hawthorne's example points to the colonizer's mimicry of diversity. That mimicry pays lipservice to difference and in that act eliminates diversity.
12. Richard Chase depoliticized Hawthorne's work and dismissed the "Custom House" sketch by reading *The Scarlet Letter* as part of a Romance tradition that distinguished American literature from its European counterparts. Chase argued that Hawthorne's work was uniquely American by virtue of its genre. He differentiated Romance, which is fantastic and apolitical, from novels, which are realist and political in their representative aims. According to Chase, the novel — in its preoccupation with reality, manners, and social texture — had never gained hold in America. Particularly in the 1980s, such emphasis on the apolitical nature of American literature met with much critical response, even from scholars desirous of defining the formal qualities of Hawthorne's work. For instance, Samuel Coale insisted that "American Romance is far more than a mere disguise for traditional allegory ... it embodies most of the great cultural and moral questions of American society" (Coale 1985: viii). Michael Davitt Bell rejected the depoliticization of American Romance and saw it, on the contrary, as the location of a uniquely American national articulation; see: Bell 1980. Wary of the American exceptionalism resonant in Bell's argument, Edgar Dryden read Romance as "exemplary" for American literature but insisted that the "genealogy of American romance ... is understood to be constructed rather than natural, or, to use Edward Said's formulation, one that emphasizes a relationship of affiliation rather than one of filiation or natural descent" (Dryden 1988: xi–xii). As Jonathan Arac has shown, Hawthorne constructs a decidedly conservative, anti-abolitionist national politics (Arac 1986), whose nativism keeps at bay both the American Revolution and the European revolutions of 1848 (Reynolds 1988). Donald Pease has argued that Hawthorne's novel carefully constructs a pre-Revolutionary past to "get the Revolutionary mythos out of the nation's history" (Pease 1987: 51). Sacvan Bercovitch has suggested that, in response to the European Revolutions of 1848, the novel evokes the "fear of process run amuck, pluralism fragmenting into diversity, disharmony, discontinuity, chaos" (Bercovitch 1991: 355).
13. Whether one can, as I do here, draw on postcolonial theory to discuss American literature, is a hotly contested issue. The idea of reading American literature as postcolonial was first advanced by Bill Ashcroft et. al. (Ashcroft, Griffiths, and Tiffin 1989). It was picked up by Lawrence Buell, who looked at the United States' relationship to Britain, and who also discussed postcoloniality as a strategy of decolonization in Melville's writings (see: Buell 1992a, Buell 1992b). Buell's discussions of postcoloniality garnered him

severe criticism: John Carlos Rowe has accused him of helping to "obscure the simultaneous development of U.S. colonial ventures at home and abroad" (Rowe 2002: xvi). Gesa Mackenthun has criticized Buell for defining American postcoloniality exclusively in relationship to England, and thereby pouring "the wine of Emersonianism into postcolonial bottles" (Mackenthun 2004: 14). Yet Mackenthun herself wishes to read American literature along postcolonial lines that capture the "ideological dilemma of an emerging nation that identified itself as postcolonial, due to its rebellion against colonial rule, while simultaneously having to admit its function as an offshoot of the parent tree and an heir to the policy of British imperialism" (Mackenthun 2004: 6). She usefully distinguishes between "the positive effects of taking a postcolonial perspective on the history of the United States" and "historically unfounded claims that the United States [is] a postcolonial country" (Mackenthun 2000: 37). Peter Hulme has pointed out that the United States has always been "postcolonial and colonizing at the same time" (Hulme 1995: 122), and Helen Carr shares that assessment when she writes that "the United States was a postcolonial country as well as an aggressive Empire [...] Being postcolonial may mean a wrongful oppression has been overthrown, but it is no guarantee of moral rectitude. Postcoloniality is a historical stage, not a virtue" (Carr 1996: 7); see also: Donaldson 2000. For Jenny Sharpe, the term "does not describe the United States ... as a white settler colony or its emergence as a neocolonial power; rather, it designates the presence of racial minorities and Third World [sic] immigrants" (Sharpe 2000: 104). In the context of translation, postcoloniality resonates most for me with Francoise Lionnet's feminist definition: she wants to think of "'postcoloniality' in terms of 'post contact': that is, as a condition that exists within, and thus contests and resists, the colonial moment itself with its ideology of domination;" she thinks of it as "a process whereby all elements involved in the interaction would be changed by that encounter" (Lionnet 1995: 4). Lionnet sees this mutual influence in terms of a "transculturation" that rejects "the binarism of self and other, nationalism and internationalism, Africa and Europe" (Lionnet 1995: 11–12). For further discussions of American postcoloniality, see: Watts 1998, King 2000.
14. I am drawing on Karl Marx here to argue that Hawthorne fetishizes not only his commodity, his book, but also the language in which that book is written. My reading of language as a fetishized object is informed by Marx's claim that value "converts every product into a social hieroglyphic. Later on, we try to decipher the hieroglyphic, to get behind the secret of our own social products; for to stamp an object of utility as value, is just as much a social product as language" (Marx and Engels 1933: 85).
15. In an early review, Evert Duyckinck argued that "the scarlet letter ... is the hero of the volume" (Duyckinck 1850: 1). Charles Feidelson suggests that the characters in the novel all reenact this scene and Hawthorne's desire to read the scarlet letter; see: Feidelson 1953. Duyckinck and Feidelson emphasize the significance the letter takes on "in Hawthorne's hands" (Duyckinck 1850: 1), thus eliding Hester Prynne's role. That elision of female labor in the creation of a fetishistic national literature in effect reprises much of Hawthorne's own relation to women and the construction of American literature, as I discuss below.
16. For a useful discussion of Hawthorne's relationship to nineteenth century secular and religious theories of language (in the singular), see: Roger 1997.
17. The information in this section is drawn from the chronology in: Forten 1988.

18. Other accounts of Salem support Forten's description of an internationally vibrant community rather than a nationally secluded space. As Charles Wendte recalled in 1885, "a considerable trade with the East Indies and other parts of the globe imparted a stir to its [Salem's] streets and unusual mental activity to its citizens. ... intercourse with far distant peoples and large business relations fostered a certain breadth of view, vigor, and love of culture for which Salem has ever been noted" (cited in Brooks 1885: 6–7).
19. For a contemporary account of national fragmentation, see: Chatterjee 1993).
20. See: Friedrich 1992.
21. Since Roland Barthes proclaimed the "Death of the Author" (Barthes 1975), and Michel Foucault responded by conceptualizing the "author function" (Foucault 1984), we have become used to locating the text in its readers. And yet translation both reinscribes and confounds the distinction between authors and readers. The presence of the translator creates the figure of two authors, one the "original" author of the text, and the second the author of the translation. In turn, this second author is also a reader, especially if he disavows his authorial role as a translator and endows the original with Foucault's author function. Thereby, he creates a readerly text, which will be authoritative in Barthes' sense. Instructive in Barthes' and Foucault's exchange is the infinite reciprocity between reader and author function; in this light, translation is not the telos of the original any more than the original is the telos of the translation. What emerges instead is a text that is inherently multivocal — or dialogic, to put it in Bakhtinian terms. For a discussion of the theories of intertextuality and influence that the exchange between Barthes and Foucault enabled, see: Clayton and Rothstein 1991.
22. Ulf Hannerz helpfully points out that process and structure are not exclusive of each other: he finds the "flow metaphor useful" in that a river exists as a river, yet constantly changes so that "even as you perceive structure, it is entirely dependent on ongoing process" (Hannerz 1992: 4). Aihwa Ong has taken Appadurai to task because his model of transnational flows is indebted to a "top-down model whereby the global is macro-political economic and the local is situated, culturally creative and resistant. But a model that analytically defines the global as political economic and the local as cultural does not quite capture the *horizontal* and *relational* nature of the contemporary economic social and cultural processes that stream across spaces" (Ong 1999: 4).
23. In this reading of Benjamin's "The Task of the Translator," Johnson sides with Jacques Derrida against Paul de Man. For de Man, the crucial concept in Benjamin's essay is "task" or "Aufgabe," which is simultaneously a task and a failure (the German word carries both meanings). Although translation tries to reproduce the original, the fracture of the sign makes all such attempts failures. For de Man, translation is the task and failure of language to (re-)produce meaning; as such, translation is a metaphor for language in general. For Derrida, on the other hand, translation is first and foremost productive, not futile. For a useful discussion of the difference between de Man's and Derrida's readings of Benjamin, see: Bannet 1993.
24. This performance paradigm goes back to Gene Wise, who attributed it to: Mechling, Meredith and Wilson 1973. Wise suggested looking at historical ideas "as a sequence of dramatic acts — acts which play on wider cultural scenes, or historical stages"(Wise 1999: 169). Usefully, Wise thinks of theater as giving culture a "*trans*-actional quality. ... an act in the theater is always in interplay with the scene around it," both in terms of the interaction between

actors on stage and in terms of their interaction with the audience (Wise 1999: 169).

Gayatri Chakravorty Spivak has expanded on this idea from a feminist perspective and has argued that: "one of the ways to get around the confines of one's 'identity' as one produces expository prose is to work at someone else's title, as one works with a language that belongs to many others. This, after all, is one of the seductions of translating. It is a simple miming of the responsibility to the trace of the other in the self" (Spivak 1993: 179).

25. Adelaide Anne Procter (1825–64) "contributed to Dickens's Household Words under the pseudonym 'Mary Berwick'. She was the author of much popular sentimental (and often morbid) verse" (Drabble and Stringer 1996).

Whether we can read "queer" in the current use of the term, as confounding gender categories is a vexed question. The context in which Forten uses the term "queer" seems to bear out Ian Hacking's argument that neologisms respond to and enable new identity categories (see: Hacking 1986). Queerness and multilingualism go hand in hand in Ludwig von Reizenstein's *Die Geheimnisse von New Orleans* which was serialized in the *Louisiana Staats-Zeitung* between 1854–5 and was the first work published in America to openly describe a Lesbian love affair, between a German and a Creole woman; see: Sollors 2002: 124. For Forten, translation becomes a way of imagining a feminist subject along the lines described by Teresa de Lauretis: "not unified or simply divided between positions of masculinity and femininity, but multiply organized across positionalities along several axes and across mutually contradictory discourses and practices" (de Lauretis 1988: 136). Homi Bhabha describes such queerness as cultural hybridity when he writes: "The frontiers of cultural difference are always belated or secondary in the sense that their hybridity is never simply a question of the admixture of pre-given identities or essences. Hybridity is the perplexity of living as it interrupts the representation of the fullness of life; it is an instance of iteration, in the minority discourse, of the time of the arbitrary sign ... through which all forms of cultural meaning are open to translation because their enunciation resists totalization. ... Cultural difference emerges from the borderline moment of translation that Benjamin describes as the 'foreignness of languages'" (Bhabha 1990: 314).

26. Forten's play makes her writing bilingual in Hana Wirth-Nesher's sense of bilingualism as not only the literal presence of two languages, but also the "echoes of another language and culture detected in the prose of the one language of which the text is composed" (Wirth-Nesher 1990: 298).

27. Stuart Hall has similarly argued that the formation of modernity was not just "internalist" but "also a 'global' process. It had crucial 'externalist' features — aspects which could not be explained without taking into account the rest of the world, where these processes were not at work and where these kinds of society did not emerge" (Hall 1996: 224).

28. Read in the way I am proposing here, Webster's definition disavows yet supports the claim that "there is, of course, no American culture without African roots" (Appiah 1991: 354); see also: Morrison 1989.

29. In his seminal intervention into the poststructuralist debate, Frederic Jameson conceptualizes the site of spectral supplementarity as the "political unconscious," that is, the site beyond textual representation that nevertheless underlies representation as an "immanent or antitranscendent hermeneutic model" (Jameson 1981: 23). Jameson inverts the deconstructive insight that language marks the loss of the *Ding-an-sich* when he points out that we can also "never really confront a text immediately, in all its freshness as a thing-

in-itself" (Jameson 1981: 9). Jameson argues that "history is *not* a text, not a narrative, master or otherwise, but ... as an absent cause, it is inaccessible to us except in textual form, and ... our approach to it and to the Real itself necessarily passes through its prior textualization, its narrativization in the political unconscious" (Jameson 1981: 35). With his understanding of language as translation, Jameson shifts the emphasis of textual inquiry from similarity to difference. He admonishes his readers to "repudiate a conception of the process of mediation which fails to register its capacity for differentiation and for revealing structural oppositions and contradictions through some overemphasis on its related vocation to establish identities" (Jameson 1981: 42). Instead of focusing on identities and on the objects of production, Jameson understands "the text as *process*" (Jameson 1981: 45).
30. See: Shell and Sollors 2000, Sollors 1998, Shell 2002.
31. Gesa Mackenthun provides a succinct definition of imperial translation when she writes: "referred to as a 'translation of empire' in imperial prose from the sixteenth century onward, the historical event of European westward expansion embraced a series of discursive or ideological processes that served to 'translate' a cognitively and morally ambivalent enterprise into acceptable history" (Mackenthun 1997: 3–4).
32. See: Cheyfitz 1997.
33. For a more extensive discussion of different Romantic translation theories and practices, see: Berman 1992.
34. I draw these figures inversely from Michael Winship, who documents the percentage of new editions published in the United States as follows: 30 percent in 1820, 40 percent in 1830, 55 percent in 1840, 70 percent in 1850 (Winship 1995: 12). The large number of translations and reprints was made lucrative for American publishers by a trade practice commonly referred to as "courtesy of the trade." The term referred to a code of honor: publishers would not compete with one another once one of them had published a book that was not protected by copyright.

For the early Republic, I have calculated another set of statistics: in the year Wheatley published her *Poems* (1773), translations and publications in languages other than English made up 8.35 percent of works printed in the British colonies. The percentages for the following years (calculated in five-year intervals) are 1790: 9.86 percent; 1795: 14.29 percent; 1800: 4 percent; 1805: 6 per cent; 1810: 7 percent. I arrived at these percentages using Evans 1903, Shaw and Shoemaker 1958–66. For each year, I calculated the total number of books published. Then I read through all the titles, and counted the number of entries that were discernibly translations and/or non-English language publications to arrive at these figures. That method is meant to produce rough estimates — the percentages I provide here are deceptively low for the following reasons: it is often difficult to discern from a title whether it is a translation, especially because translations (as I explain in chapter four) counted as original texts. Moreover, titles alone do not indicate what portions of a book might have been in translation — publications often contained translations that would not show up in the title. Moreover, these bibliographies list works published in the United States, but do not account for works published abroad by Americans. Wheatley for instance initially published her poems in London — an American edition of her works did not appear until 1812, and so her work and her translations would not show up in the statistics for 1773, even though the book was written by an American. Not only were American works published abroad, they were also imported from abroad, and so the

actual circulation of books in translation and in languages other than English was much higher than reflected in these statistics.
35. Frank Luther Mott defines best sellers as books with sales numbers over a decade equaling 1 per cent of the population of the continental United States (Mott 1947: 7). For example, Hugo's *Hunchback* sold over 125,000 copies in the 1830s, and Sue's *Mysteries of Paris* over 175,000 in the 1840s (Mott 1947: 306–7). By comparison, one of the most successful books published by an American author in the Antebellum period, Henry Wadsworth Longfellow's *Song of Hiawatha*, sold 45,461 copies between 1855–9 (Winship 1995: 66).
36. See: Anderson 1991, Warner 1990.
37. See: Gardner 1998.

CHAPTER 1

1. Lean'tin Bracks points out that, since slaves were prohibited from speaking African languages, "the dual purpose of communication necessitated the manipulation of words, images, and meanings that would protect slaves from some listeners while revealing their true intentions to others in a dangerous balancing act. The speaker reached two audiences and voiced multiple meanings in a complex system by using a singular arrangement of words ... English for the slave was thus adapted to focus on survival concerns first and public communication of personal perspectives was secondary since the ownership of self seemed such a remote possibility while the audience itself was untrustworthy. As blacks became more aware of the philosophies and the system of oppression that encompassed their life as slaves, language, too, was recognized as a tool for abolishing that system" (Bracks 1998: 13). For an analysis of the audience Wheatley's poems address, see: Balkun 2002.
2. For a discussion of how Wheatley anticipates Morrison and especially the concept of "re-membrance," see: Thomas 2000: 225.
3. We know from John Wheatley that Phillis acquired English from the family, but he does not tell us how she learned Latin. John Shields guesses that "Mather Byles or Samuel Cooper, ministers whose counsel she sought regarding her poems, tutored her in Latin as well. Or perhaps one of the several itinerant foreign-language tutors in the Boston area ... was enlisted to assist her;" see: Wheatley 1988: 275.
4. Henry Louis Gates has identified troping on the trope as a practice of signifyin'; see: Gates 1988.
5. Wheatley used direct citation in: "On the Death of the Rev. Dr. Sewell," "On the Death of the Rev. Mr. George Whitefield," "On the Death of a Young Lady of Five Years of Age," "Goliath of Gath," "Thoughts on the Works of Providence," "To a Clergyman on the Death of His Lady," "Isaiah lxiii. 1–8," "A Funeral Poem on the Death of C.E. an Infant of Twelve Months," "To a Lady on Her Coming to North America with Her Son, for the Recovery of Her Health," "To a Lady on Her Remarkable Preservation in an Hurricane in North-Carolina," "On the Death of J.C. an Infant," "To the Honourable T.H. Esq; On the Death of His Daughter," "Niobe ...," "An Elegy, to Miss Mary Moorhead, On the Death of Her Father, the Rev. Mr. John Moorhead," "On the Capture of General Lee," "On the Death of General Wooster," "To Mr. And Mrs. —, on the Death of Their Infant Son."
6. Phillis Wheatley's examination may well have been about her gender as much as her race. Although a culture of classicism prevailed in the eighteenth cen-

tury, as Caroline Winterer has shown, "a woman of great classical learning risked becoming dangerously unfeminine, what authors variously called *virilis femina, une homasse* (man-woman), a virago. ... authors warned readers to beware of what the minister and classics teacher John Sylvester John Gardiner (1765–1830) called 'women of masculine minds.' ... Even the most erudite women of the late eighteenth century ... were schooled only haphazardly, if at all, in classical learning," but "by the antebellum era the classical languages and history were viewed in women's academies as useful teachers of virtue;" see: Winterer 2002: 22–3.

7. The College of William and Mary appointed the first American professor of a modern language, French, in 1780, at a time when Harvard first permitted the substitution of French for Hebrew (Spengemann 1994: 10). Timothy Dwight had unsuccessfully lobbied at Yale in the 1790s to include English and belles letters in the curriculum, but under the pressure from the faculty in the classical languages, more than half a century had to pass before instruction in English was truly established in the American university curriculum. In 1827, Amherst College (a self-consciously progressive offspin from Williams College) revised its curriculum and added to the traditional Classical Course of study another, designated the Scientific Course. All candidates for admission were still required to demonstrate knowledge of Greek and Latin, acquired in preparatory schools, but the Scientific Course substituted studies in French and Spanish, the history of English literature, the history of philosophy, and technical education for the study of classical languages and literature (Thomas 1962: 13–5). Pragmatic considerations conflicted with other understandings of academia's mission: the Amherst experiment lasted for only three years (Thomas 1962: 15).

8. I arrive at these figures from counting the works listed for that year in: Campbell 1918.

9. Franklin's claim that his book is the "first" classic translation is odd, considering that he ignores his own earlier publication: James Logan's translation *Cato's Moral Distichs Englished in Couplets* (1735).

10. Fittingly, the *Autobiography* was first published in translation, in France by Chez Buisson as: *Mémoires de la vie privée de Benjamin Franklin, écrits par lui-même, et addresses [sic] à son fils, suivis d'un précis historique de sa vie politique, et de plusieurs pièces, relatives à ce père de la liberté* (1791); see Franklin 1964: 28.

11. Benjamin Franklin recalled: "I went to see the black poetess and offered her any services I could do her. Before I left the house I understood her master was there, and had sent her to me, but did not come into the room himself, and I thought was not pleased with the visit. I should perhaps have inquired first of him; but I had heard nothing of him, and I have heard nothing since of her" (in: Robinson 1982: 27).

12. Franklin is playing here with a familiar trope. In an article on the acquisition of languages, entitled "Learning without A Master," *The National Era* of July 1, 1852 explained: "Not a few books have been published to induct the student into the mysteries of various languages and sciences, 'without a master.' . ... Studying 'without a master' is not, of course, to be understood literally. The master is there, but he appears only in the printed page, and not in his bodily presence. ... Dr. John Mason Good composed his long and elaborate poetical translation of Lucretius in the streets of London, while passing from one patient to another. Dr. Burney, the distinguished musician, learned the Italian and French languages on horseback. ... Think of these examples ... whether it would not be better for you to devote those spare hours to intellectual culture and thus enlarge the sphere of your influence in the world" (Anon. 1852: 108).

13. Of the extant variant poems, Wheatley's "To the University of Cambridge" proves particularly instructive in this context.

    Wheatley, "To the University of Cambridge," 1767:

    While an intrinsic ardor bids me write
    The muse doth promise to assist my pen.
    'Twas but e'en now I left my native shore
    The sable Land of error's darkest night.
    There, sacred Nine! For you no place was found.
    Parent of mercy, 'twas thy Powerful hand
    Brought me in safety from the dark abode. (Wheatley 1988: 196)

    Wheatley, "To the University of Cambridge, in New England" (in *Poems on Various Subjects, Religious and Moral*, published in London in 1773):

    While an intrinsic ardor prompts to write,
    The muses promise to assist my pen;
    'Twas not long since I left my native shore
    The land of errors, and *Egyptian* gloom:
    Father of mercy, 'twas thy gracious hand
    Brought me in safety from those dark abodes. (Wheatley 1988: 15)

    The 1767 version of that poem imagines Africa in the first stanza as "the sable Land of error's darkest night" where for the muses of antiquity, "sacred Nine! For you no place was found" (Wheatley 1988: 196). The revised poem published in the volume of 1773 leaves out these lines. The muses are no longer absent from Africa, and Africa itself is profoundly reimagined: instead of being the land of "error's darkest night," it has become the "land of errors, and *Egyptian* gloom" (Wheatley 1988: 15). I read "Egyptian" here in the context of the poem's engagement with scripture, where Egypt is the land of Hebrew enslavement in the books of Moses. The effect of Wheatley's revision is profound: by substituting *Egyptian* for the "darkest night" that presumably functioned as a racial marker, Wheatley reconfigures her position as a slave to correspond with the Jewish diaspora. But of course that reading ironizes Wheatley's position: turning Africa/Egypt into the locus of slavery would presumably mean that she has reached the promised land of her freedom.
14. As Wheatley records in one of her letters, dated 18 October 1773: "The Earl of Dartmouth made me a Compliment of 5 guineas, and desired me to get the whole of Mr. Pope's Works, as the best he could recommend to my perusal, this I did, also got Hudibras, Don Quixot [sic] & Gay's Fables" (Wheatley 1988: 170).
15. Wheatley owned the 1771 edition of Pope's *Iliad*; see: Pope 1771.
16. Translation from an absent original was in the late eighteenth century the site of cultural emergence on the Celtic and transatlantic fringes of the British empire. In 1762, James Macpherson published a volume of Ossian poems that he claimed were translations from original Celtic texts. A new edition appeared in 1773, the same year that Wheatley published her *Poems*, under scandalized speculation that there were, in fact, no Celtic texts on which Macpherson had based his translations. Macpherson inaugurated a movement of bardic nationalism that relied on cross-cultural connections and verbal repetition for the construction of national originality; see: Trumpener

1997. For a discussion of the scandal's effect on questions of cultural translation and novelistic representation, see Buzard 1995.

CHAPTER 2

1. In the most extensive treatment of Cooper's language, David Simpson suggests that we read him "as a linguistic patriot and the founder of a national fiction" (Simpson 1986: 165). I argue that Cooper's work participates in the model of world literature theorized by Johann Wolfgang von Goethe, who thought of translation as "preoccupied with a mysterious 'third'" and "as the principal medium of negotiation and communication between cultures" (Barry 2001: 165–6). I take up Goethe's relationship to American practices and theories of translation more explicitly in the next chapter.
2. Bryant was in fact paraphrasing Cooper himself. Surprised at his own popularity in France, Cooper reflected on Washington Irving's (1783–1859) comparative obscurity:

   > I do firmly believe that nine tenths of the french [sic] reading world are [sic] ignorant that a book was ever made in America, except by Dr. Franklin and M. Cooper, Americain, as they call me. You will be surprised to hear that Irving is nearly unknown here, notwithstanding, he has lived so long in the place. His style can not be translated, any more than his humour, and when you strip him of that, there is not much left, to go through the refining finish of a bad translation — Let me tell you Madam, a book which can hold up its head after a french [sic] translator has had his will of it, must have some bone and sinew. (Cooper and Beard 1960: I.209)

   This passage criticizes Irving's writing for its resistance to translation, and praises Cooper's own fiction for being easily transposed into other languages. Cooper attributes to his own works a quality that emerges in translation: Cooper is "Americain" precisely in his French context. Cooper describes the American quality of his works as that which emerges in translation.
3. Cooper was particularly proud when his works were translated. For instance, he boasted that *The Spy* (1821) "was early translated into most of the languages of Christendom, including those of Russia, Poland, Denmark, Sweden, &c and I got credit, in my own country, for being translated into French and German" (Cooper and Beard 1960: IV. 342). Cooper had already expressed his hopes for such success in the Preface to this novel: "The very singularity of the circumstance, gives the book some small chance of being noticed abroad, and our literature is much like our wine – vastly improved by traveling [sic]" (Cooper 2002: 2).
4. Bryant's emphasis on the geographic and temporal portability of Cooper's works is at odds with the two major strands of Cooper criticism, the one that territorializes Cooper as an author of "frontier" fiction, and the school that temporalizes Cooper as a historical novelist; see: Lawrence 1978, Lewis 1955, Budick 1989, Dekker 1967.
5. See: Douglas 1977, Davidson 1986, Tompkins 1985, Stern 1997, Barnes 1997.
6. Lynn Festa has taken issue with the argument that novels create nations and vice versa. She argues that "sentimental novels construct an 'imaginary community' that cannot possibly be mistaken for an 'imagined community' as nation because they specifically avoid the very features that Andersen and his

intellectual heirs have identified as those by which an imagined community can be recognized as a nation. First ... these novelistic sympathetic communities *decentralize the nation-state geographically* ... Second, these novels of sensibility *decentralize the vernacular language shared with the resisted nation state* ... Third, sympathetic communities are miscagenated, unlike classic nation-forming communities" (Festa 2002: 134).

7. See: Gardner 1998: 102.
8. For a fuller discussion of Cooper's understanding of Native American languages than I provide in this chapter, see: Rosenwald 1998. To understand translation practices from the Native American perspective, see: Pratt 2002.
9. Cooper's work raises some of the same questions that have been at the center of translation studies since the 1990s. Kurt Mueller-Vollmer and Michael Irmscher have pointed out that "the normative conception of translation which privileges the original text as an absolute point of reference" came under pressure when Itamar Even-Zohar and Gideon Toury developed polysystem theory (Mueller-Vollmer and Irmscher 1998: xi). Even-Zohar and Toury argued that "the principal focus of translation research should lie on the rendered text and its place and function within the receiving literary system" (Mueller-Vollmer and Irmscher 1998: xi). The source language text remained relevant only in so far as it could "cast additional light on the translated text" (Mueller-Vollmer and Irmscher 1998: xi). Cooper's model is closer to the 'Göttingen approach" developed since the mid-1980s, which "considers both source language text and target language text in their respective environments" (Mueller-Vollmer and Irmscher 1998: xii). In the interaction between two cultural contexts through translation, "the crux of the matter is that something new has been created in transit from (A) to (B) which is neither exclusively a source nor a target side phenomenon; it cannot be described satisfactorily or defined solely in their respective terms, nor can it be reduced to their respective limited concerns without incurring some loss" (Kittel 1998: 7).
10. See: Rousseau 1966, Herder 1966, Smith 1907.
11. In his earliest novels, Cooper obsessively stages his relationship to *Ivanhoe's* "Dedicatory Epistle." His first Leatherstocking novel, *The Pioneers* (1823) is set in a village called Templeton that borrows its name from the fictional author of the "Dedicatory Epistle," Lawrence Templeton. Cooper's first successful novel, *The Spy* (1821), borrows Scott's concept of a "neutral ground" between two cultures; the novel is set in the "neutral ground," that is, the colonial space that is exempt from the fighting during the Revolutionary War. Yet that "neutral ground" for Cooper is a deeply conflicted and fragile site. As Emily Budick has demonstrated, for Cooper "the neutral ground stands not only between past and present but between two different national audiences, [...] it becomes the scene of intense violence. The novel's very neutrality is a source of violence" (Budick 1989: 4–5).
12. In writing his historical novels, Scott relied on a linguistic methodology he had adapted from the tales of Maria Edgeworth, whose influence he acknowledged when he concluded his first novel, *Waverley* (1814), by writing in the "Postscript, which should have been a Preface": "it has been my object to describe these persons, not by caricatured and exaggerated use of the national dialect, but by their habits, manners, and feelings; so as, in some distant degree, to emulate the admirable Irish portraits drawn by Miss Edgeworth" (Scott 1986: 341). As Robert Crawford has said, *Waverley* is about "the construction of a new, culturally eclectic unity — Great Britain — but it is also about the need to preserve the cultures within that unity" (Crawford 1992:

130). Scott drew from Edgeworth a methodology of translation by which he could make the Scottish borderlands appealing to a broad international readership while maintaining their cultural opacity. The nation emerges as the "neutral ground" between the lacking specificity of empire, and the excessive specificity of locale.
13. Scott imagined the formation of the English nation through the conflict that arose when the conquering Normans dispossessed the indigenous Saxons and exploited the English Jews. This situation destabilizes the Saxon family: angered by his son Ivanhoe's decision to follow the Norman king Richard to the Crusades, Cedric the Saxon disinherits his son, who gradually redeems himself in the guise of the "Disinherited Knight." The novel resolves these conflicts through a series of displacements: Scott thwarts his own Romance plot when Ivanhoe marries the Saxon princess Rowena instead of the far more spirited and appealing "Jewess" Rebecca, who then leaves England. Cooper adapted this plot when he imagined Templeton as a settlement that encroaches upon the life of the area's older inhabitants, Natty Bumppo and Chingachgook. Their adopted son, Oliver Edwards, is a disinherited knight for much of the novel, until his identity as the rightful heir to his British father's lands becomes known and he marries Judge Temple's daughter Elizabeth. Natty and Chingachgook do not share in this resolution: like Rebecca, they are displaced at the end of the novel.
14. In the 1830 edition of his works, Scott validated the "Epistle" as "expressing the Author's purpose and opinions in undertaking this species of composition" (Scott 2001: viii).
15. James Chandler has shown that interest in cultural translation informed the Scottish understanding of historiography; see: Chandler 1998b. Historians such as William Robertson saw themselves faced with the conundrum of maintaining an intelligible Scottish identity after the Act of Union (1707) and of interpreting, to the contemporary British reader, the complexity and multiplicity of the Scottish and English past. Robertson developed — as his contemporary, the philosopher Dugald Stewart explained — the idea of "translating ... the antiquated phraseology of our forefathers into a more modern idiom" and of "translating (if I may use the expression) their antiquated fashions into the corresponding fashions of our time" (Stewart 1835: vii).
16. Similarly, Budick and Iser have argued that even "if we are always defeated by translation, culture as a movement toward shared consciousness may emerge from the defeat. Thus the story of culture does not end with the experience of that which is nothing more than a secondary otherness. In fact, the multiple half-lives of affiliation known as culture may begin to be experienced, as potentialities, only there" (Budick and Iser 1996: 22).
17. Werner Sollors has pointed to the difficult "course that American ideology has steered between descent and consent [...] Descent relations are those defined by anthropologists as relations of 'substance' (by blood or nature); consent relations describe those of 'law' or 'marriage.' Descent language emphasizes our position as heirs, our hereditary qualities, liabilities, and entitlements; consent language stresses our ability as mature free agents and 'architects of our fates' to choose our spouses, our destinies, and our political systems" (Sollors 1986: 6). Cooper stages such a shift in his work: he demonstrates the power that descent relations have over his characters, but he imagines his novels to be written in the language of consent.
18. For a discussion of these travel writings and the cultural conflict played out in them, see: Chandler 1998a.

19. Cooper revised *The Pioneers* for all three reprints in 1823, and again while in Europe in 1831. I borrow my citation of the 1823 version from Eric Cheyfitz; see: Cheyfitz 1985: 65–6.
20. Lawrence Venuti contrasts the "foreignizing method" with the "domesticating method," which he sees as "an ethnocentric reduction of the foreign text to target-language cultural values, bringing the author back home" (Venuti 1995: 17). Venuti rejects translations that attempt to produce transparent texts, that is, translations that are so fluent that the text seems originally to have been written in the "target" language into which it has been translated from the "source" language. Venuti sees such translation as "symptomatic of a complacency in Anglo-American relation with cultural others, a complacency that can be described ... as imperialist abroad and xenophobic at home" (Venuti 1995: 17).
21. Lawrence Rosenwald has argued that Cooper's methodology in fact "anticipates the best anthropological translators of this century" (Rosenwald 1998: 24).
22. As David Simpson has pointed out, "it cannot be claimed that he [Cooper] is ever very sensitive to the rights of Black English, and he prefers to avoid as far as he can the whole argument building through the middle years of the century about the rights and prospects of Black Americans" (Simpson 1986: 185). Gesa Mackenthun has said that in Cooper's fictionalizations of American history "a master narrative of continental expansion [develops] that simultaneously marginalizes the continuing importance of the Atlantic economic system" (Mackenthun 2004: 7). Similarly, Amy Kaplan quotes historian Thomas Hietall as arguing about Manifest Destiny that "expansionist policies took place under the shadow of the unwanted black" in the 1840s (Kaplan 2002: 18).
23. Webster's dictionary was particularly important to Cooper, whose word usage is always very close to "the distinctly American sense defined by Webster 1828" (Simpson 1986: 150).
24. Cooper belatedly emancipates Agamemnon. In a footnote that he added to the 1832 edition of *The Pioneers*, he writes: "The manumission of the slaves in New York has been gradual. When public opinion became strong in their favour, then grew up a custom of buying the service of a slave, for six or eight years, with a condition to liberate him at the end of the period. ... It was quite usual for men more or less connected with the quakers, who never held slaves, to adopt the first expedient" (Cooper 1991: 55).
25. Lora Romero was one of the few critics to recognize and address this aspect of Cora's character. She pointed out in a footnote that her initial "identification of Cora with the middle-class woman is complicated by the fact that, even though she has been raised white, she is in fact mulatta — the product of the British imperialist effort in the West Indies. It might be more accurate to say that Cora represents the Third World woman through whose agency the colonial power exerts its influence" (Romero 1991: 401).
26. See for instance: Carr 1996, Nelson 1992.
27. The successful slave rebellion in Saint-Domingue "resulted in Haiti's independence in 1804, thus creating the first black republic in the Americas. In 1807 Britain abolished the slave trade, and in 1833 slavery itself was abolished in the British West Indies" (Britannica 2005).
28. This belief in a linguistic origin sparked much interest in Native American languages. For instance, Thomas Jefferson commissioned the Lewis and Clark expedition to collect linguistic specimens because he believed Native American languages were the basis for and thereby held the key to modern languages, such as English.

29. Eric Cheyfitz reads Cooper's works as prime examples of imperial translation; see: Cheyfitz 1985, Cheyfitz 1993, Cheyfitz 1997.

CHAPTER 3

1. Henry James disputed the idea that Hawthorne had Fuller "in his eye for the figure of Zenobia" (James 1903: 1.129). Joan von Mehren insists that "most of Hawthorne's readers believed otherwise," that Zenobia was modeled, and modeled unfavorably, on Fuller (Von Mehren 1994: 348). Von Mehren believes that in "Hawthorne's mind Fuller's sin was ... refusing to recognize the force of her sexual nature" (Von Mehren 1994: 348).
2. Ralph Waldo Emerson to Horace Greeley, 23 July 1850; see Emerson and Rusk 1939: 4.219.
3. Emerson, William H. Channing, and John Freeman Clark took manuscript materials, such as letters they had received from Fuller, and literally cut and pasted them together to produce a book; see: Emerson et al. 1852.
4. Fuller's *Conversations with Goethe* (1839) and *Günderode* (1842) went out of print in 1852 and 1861, respectively. Arthur Fuller excised the two translated texts that Fuller included in *Summer on the Lakes in 1843* from his republication of that work in *At Home and Abroad, or Things and Thoughts in America and Europe* (Boston: Crosby, Nichols, 1856). This bowdlerized version remained the standard text for *Summer on the Lakes* until 1972, when Madeleine Stern published a facsimile of the 1844 edition. Marie Urbanski has argued that Arthur Fuller aimed to make his sister's works conform to mid-century gender norms; see: Urbanski 1980.
5. Fuller's cosmopolitanism is often seen as competing with her nationalism. For an emphasis on the former, see: Martineau 1877: I.280-4 and Arthur Schultz, "Margaret Fuller—Transcendentalist Interpreter of German Literature, *Monatshefte für Deutschen Unterricht* 34 (April 1942): 169–82; reprinted in: Myerson 1979: 195-208. In contrast, Susan Rosowski complains that "critics have given short shrift to [Fuller's] ties to the [American] West;" see: Rosowski 1990: 125 ; see also: Zwarg 1993: 617. I argue that we must think of Fuller as both American and cosmopolitan, because translation allowed her to negotiate both positions dialogically without resolving their incompatibilities.
6. See, for example: Shell and Sollors 2000, Castillo and Schweitzer 2001.
7. For a definition of suture as the "paradoxical function" by which the "endless slide of signifiers ... is brought to a halt and allowed to function 'as if' it were a closed set," see: Copjec 1994: 174–5.
8. Thomas Carlyle, "Taylor's *Historic Survey of German Poetry* (1830)," *Edinburgh Review* 53 (1831): 151–80; quoted in: Johnston 1997: 126.
9. This theoretical distinction between familiarizing and foreignizing translation goes back to Friedrich Schleiermacher and has been adopted more recently by Lawrence Venuti; see: Venuti 1995: 19.
10. Germaine De Staël, "The Spirit of Translation," trans. Doris Y. Kadish, in: Kadish and Massardier-Kenney 1994: 163.
11. Fuller's fellow American translator, Sarah Helen Whitman, reviewed Fuller's translation of Johann Peter Eckermann's *Conversations with Goethe* and pronounced it a success along the lines proposed by de Staël. Whitman finds it an "admirably translated volume" and discusses the "increasing interest with which the German is looked upon among us. We are in no way disturbed by the fear, that its subtleties, refinements and abstractions, should have an evil

influence on our national character. . . . [,] the individuality of which seems in no danger of being neutralized by such antagonistic principles, though it may perchance be favorably modified by them" (Whitman 1840: 22, 53).

12. Martin Luther, "On Translating: An Open Letter," in: Bachmann 1960: 35. 289–90.
13. Johann Wolfgang von Goethe, *Conversations with Eckermann*, trans. John Oxenford (San Francisco: North Point, Press, 1984), 20–21; quoted in: Berman 1992: 56. The concept of world literature has recently met with a resurgence of critical interest. Wai Chee Dimock, for example, takes issue with Benedict Anderson's equation of imagined communities with nations, arguing that a literary "continuum extends across space and time, messing up territorial sovereignty and numerical chronology" (Dimock 2001: 174). Dimock insists that literature, "theorized as the consequences of this global readership, . . . handily outlives the finite scope of the nation. It brings into play a different set of temporal and spatial coordinates. It urges on us the entire planet as a unit of analysis"(Dimock 2001: 174–5). Although Goethe and Fuller might be enlisted to support such a view, they remind us that the nation form is useful for understanding how globalism relates to particulars—when those particulars are understood as polyvalent. Fuller's reading of Goethe provides us with a model in which globalism is itself an integral part of a nation understood through its translations.
14. Fuller to James Freeman Clark, 1 August 1832 (Fuller and Hudspeth 1983: 1.177).
15. Fuller to William Channing, 25 August 1842 (Fuller and Hudspeth 1983: 3.91).
16. Fuller combined intimacy and dialogue when she programmatically assumed the role of a conversationalist. Her first book-length publication, *Conversations with Goethe* (1839), was followed by the educational series she established for women in Boston, which she called "Conversations." As Charles Capper puts it, Fuller advocated a "[c]ollective means of conversation over Emerson's individual ones of lectures and writings" (Capper 1987: 523). On Fuller's "intertextual style" of conversation and verbal interaction, see: Bean 1997. For a discussion of Emerson's rhetoric and Fuller's "conversation," see: Berkson 1994.
17. Fuller to Eliza Farrar, 17 April 1836 (Fuller and Hudspeth 1983: 1.247).
18. Fuller, "1st January 1845," *New York Daily Tribune*, January 1, 1845; quoted in introduction to: Steele 1992: xl.
19. Emerson to Fuller, 8 October 1838 (Emerson and Rusk 1939: 2.168). Emerson's complaint that poetry becomes "such stale prose" contradicts Novalis's comment to Schlegel that "all poetry is translation" (Berman 1992: 99). Fuller admired Novalis and shared his sentiment, though not his conclusions. Novalis sets up a metaphorical understanding of translation as any act of interpretation, inaugurating the school of such translation theorists as Georg Steiner. Although Fuller gives translation wide play, she was invested in conceptualizing it specifically as a linguistic enterprise.
20. Sharon Cameron sees ". . . the rhetorical construction of Emerson's 'I'" as "fetishized universality, . . . obsessively constructed anonymity" (Cameron 1998: 18). Richard Poirier characterizes Emerson's universality as writing off the self (Poirier 1987). Julie Ellison argues that Emerson insistently reinscribes himself through intellectual alienation: "[A]wed by another writer's thought, Emerson discovers that it is his own" (Ellison 1984: 151).
21. Emerson to Fuller, 25 September 1840 (Emerson and Rusk 1939: 2.336).
22. Emerson transcription of his letter to Margaret Fuller, 12 October 1838 (Emerson et al. 1911: 85).

23. Sampson Reed, "Oration on Genius"; quoted in Packer 1982: 3; Emerson, journal entry, cited in Packer 1982: 4.
24. Christopher Newfield argues that Emerson's rejection of conventional language amounts to an endorsement of an "authoritarian" language theory that privileges imitation over invention; see: Newfield 1992: 21.
25. In his training as a minister, Emerson had encountered translation theory in the model of "higher criticism" for biblical scholarship, which viewed biblical texts as a cultural matrix "that only the modern comparatist was in a position to comprehend." This model ultimately forecloses an understanding of the other as other: "to quote another is an act of narcissistic mirroring" (Ellison 1984: 6, 152). It is against such narcissism that Fuller struggles, as she tries to develop a model of translation in which the other is a viable position irreducible to the terms of the self.
26. Justinus Kerner was a friend of Anton Mesmer's, the proponent of animal magnetism. For the far-reaching political implications of mesmerism, see: Winter 1998. Fuller's fellow transcendentalist, Charles Timothy Brooks, translated various poems by Kerner; an 1885 collection of Brooks' works includes "The Wanderer in the Sawmill" and "A Poet's Solace." see: Brooks 1885: 219, 223.
27. By introducing her translation through an allegory, Fuller invokes a long history of romantic theory. In Samuel Taylor Coleridge's distinction between symbol and allegory, the latter "boils down to qualitative tautology" (Brown 1997: 34). Nevertheless, the symbol is not an adequate alternative for Fuller: it operates on a slippery-slope that leads her back to Emersonian notions of universality. Fuller examines the capacity of translation to provide a way of rejecting Locke's and Coleridge's "qualitative tautology" as well as Emerson's bipolar universality to imagine a viable position as other. Translation, for Fuller, thus exceeds Emerson's understanding of the symbol in that it does not merely refer to a single whole but multiplies the available systems of knowledge.
28. Novalis, quoted in: Goethe 1833: xxx n.
29. Fuller to James Freeman Clark, 1 August 1832 (Fuller and Hudspeth 1983: 1.177).
30. As Priscilla Wald explains, the term "Young Americans" refers to a group of writers in the late 1830s who argued that the United States should become culturally independent by embracing what John O'Sullivan called "Manifest Destiny." Literature took on a privileged role in this endeavor, promoting "an American cultural identity through a national narrative" (Wald 1995: 107).
31. Evert Duyckinck, quoted in: Miller 1963: 222.

CHAPTER 4

1. See: Kouwenhoven 1941, Spiller, Thorp, Johnson, and Canby 1948, Lewis 1955, Marx 1988.
2. Although Jonathan Arac considers the "vernacular" a modern term that was not "part of the nineteenth-century discussions of ... 'popular language'" (Arac 1996: 44), Whitman himself used the term when he examined the linguistic importance of translation.
3. Ellis' collection apparently gained renewed and increased popularity nearly a decade after its first publication in 1790: a second edition — with a historical sketch for a preface — appeared in 1801. The third edition appeared in 1803, with two more editions following in 1841 and 1845. Harvard library records

indicate that Longfellow checked out this volume several times, as well as Ellis' *Specimens of Early English Metrical Romances* (London: 1805; 1811; 1848).

The earliest English collection of American poetry, the *Specimens of the American Poets* (1822, published in Britain), modeled itself after Ellis' and Southey's projects yet strained their representational logic. Although the specimens in the collection were written by United States citizens after the War of 1812, the volume's introduction argued that the works were not representative of a nationally distinct American literature. The introduction expressed the commonplace that America "has not yet ... acquired a literature of her own" (1822 [1972]: v). Yet the volume violated Southey's logic of geopolitical naturalization when the editor insisted that the specimens exemplified the two countries' shared culture. He claimed to be "marking the literary progress of a nation, which in spite of all jarring interests and unhappy jealousies is still bound to us by the near ties of a common ancestry, a common language, and in general of common feelings" (1822 [1972]: xxi). Although in a sense the claim that England and America shared the same literature points to a deracinated understanding of culture, the editor's argument undercuts such an interpretation. Ultimately, American literature remains firmly rooted in English imperial culture. The emphasis on English as a shared heritage, language and sentiment addresses itself to the conundrum facing the British Empire over how to maintain a cultural identity distinct from the influences of colonial cultures. The answer, it seems, lay in emphasizing commonality and avoiding (an acknowledgment of) cultural differences that would necessitate translation.

In his introduction to the facsimile of this volume, George Harrison Orians counts the volume among the four earliest anthologies of American literature: a volume edited by John Neal and published under Scottish sponsorship was followed by James Lawson's *Literary Coronel* (with editions appearing in 1821, 1823, 1826, 1828), *Specimens of American Poets* (1822), and *The Columbian Lyre* (1828). Helen Carr adds to this genealogy Elihu Hubbard Smith's *American Poems, Selected and Original* (1793) (see: Carr 1996: 69), as the earliest anthology of American literature. In his overview of American anthologizing practices, Alan Golding says of this volume that its primary goal, preservation, is "logically the first step in canon formation" (Golding 1995: 4), and that Smith pursued a Federalist agenda with this collection. The volume included such translations as "The Speech of Proteus to Aristaeus, Containing The Story of Orpheus and Euridice; Translated from the fourth Book of Virgil's Georgics. A Collegiate Exercise. Written Anno 1770" by John Trumbull.

4. See: Golding 1995.
5. See: Bloom 1973, Weisbuch 1986, Brodhead 1986.
6. The passage also resonates with another type of literary anthology, the gift books or annuals that regularly drew on the metaphor of the literary as a nature specimen. For example, *The Hare-Bell; A Token of Friendship* talks of its titular plant as "a simple flower — and our 'Hare-Bell' is a modest book — simple, both in its style and pretensions" (Everst 1844: iv). Other volumes had similarly botanical titles such as *The Evergreen* (Philadelphia, 1847) or *Forget-Me-Not* (New York and St. Louis, 1847). These volumes participate in the sentimental culture that also reveled in the "language of flowers." Many of the editors for the annuals and the contributors of "original" and "translated" poetry (such as L. E. L, Mrs. Hemans, and Lydia Sigourney) were women — a fact which provides one explanation for Whitman's feminization of Longfellow as the "universal poet of women and young people" (Whitman

1982: 918), considering that many of his poems were published in annuals. Some of the secular annuals explicitly situated themselves within an international publishing culture. For example, *The Bijou; or Annual of Literature and the Arts*, a London-based publication, wanted to inhabit an "elevated station among the Annual publications, not of this country only, but of Europe" (1828: v). Annuals did not (always) exhaust themselves in nationalist rivalry, but also engaged questions of transnational culture formation. Translations were also included in publications that insisted on representing an American and (or) an English literature: *The English Annual* (London, 1835) contained "Paris on the Morning of Louis the Sixteenth's Execution —Translated by Mrs. Hemans, From the Basvigliana" as well as "The Sun and Moon – From the German of Ebert." Similarly, *The American Book of Beauty or Token of Friendship* included an excerpt entitled "The Emperor and the Alchymist. Of the Grandnephew of Faust. Translated from the German." Translation and originality were not antonyms in the literature of this period: the London *Amulet; or Christian and Literary Remembrancer* (1828) conflated originality with translation when it listed T. Croker as having made an "original" contribution to a volume that included only his "Saint Brendan's Prophecy, translated from the Irish." Publishing translations as "original poetry" was a recurring practice — for example, in March 1816, the *North American Review* (no. 6) published "Translation Hor: O. III. 13" under the heading "Original Poetry."
7. For pointing me to this specialized meaning of the *hortus siccus*, I thank Martha Bohrer.
8. For instance, Charles Timothy Brooks said in the preface to his translation of Jean Paul Richter's *Titan* that "the Translator (or Transplanter, for he aspires to the title) of this huge production in his solicitude to preserve the true German aroma of its native earth, may have brought away some part of the soil, and even stones, clinging to the roots (*stones of offence* they may prove to many, stones of stumbling to many more). He can only say that if he had made Jean Paul always talk in ordinary, conventional prose, the reader would not have had *Jean Paul the Only*" (Brooks 1863: ix).
9. In the historical development I am tracing, the importance of location and the localization of literary composition came to undermine the transnational culture that antebellum translation enabled. This development occurred with the series of *Poets and Poetry* anthologies that came into vogue in the wake of Rufus Griswold's *Poets and Poetry of America* (1842) and his *Female Poets of America* (1848). The collections that were formulaically entitled *Poets and Poetry of...* modeled themselves on Griswold's volumes, thereby implicitly claiming a continuity between the region and the nation. They miniaturized and localized Griswold's representational scope when they limited themselves to representing a single state or to constructing a region. *The Poets and Poetry of the West* (1860), which opened with a Southey epigraph, quite literally understood itself to stake out a territory when it promised to "present a *survey* of Western Literature — to make known who have been, and who are the poets, orators, and prose writers of the States which comprise what is properly known, in American history and *geography*, as *The West*" (Coggeshall 1860: v, my emphasis). In her introduction to *The Poets and Poetry of Minnesota* (1864), the editor explained her project's proto-nativism when she argued that she

> could not select those only who were born in the state and continue to reside within its limits, as our state is still in its infancy, and can claim but few of its citizens by birthright only. We must, then, take those who have

> become citizens by residence and adoption, and, indeed, some of those selected do not reside within the State at present, yet hail from Minnesota, the home of their adoption. They belong to our literature by residence, and Minnesota may be justly proud of her adopted children. (Arnold 1864: 10–11)

This definition of a Minnesotan author defined culture as locally grounded and reinscribed even those nominally removed from a territory within landed literary production. *The Poets and Poetry of Indiana* (1900) made this point even more explicit when it aimed to be "a representative collection of the poetical writings of the Indiana people, native and resident" (Heiney 1900: v). The *Poets and Poetry* books operated on the same logic of broad-scale inclusion as Southey's specimen collection, and similarly justified the publication of bad poetry. In their attempts to contain a region's literature in its entirety, they rhetorically abandoned the principle of selection. Aiming to be definitive, they often imagined themselves as annuals; for example, the editor of *The Poets and Poetry of Iowa* (1894) promised to publish a new edition every year to correct omissions and to make the volume as comprehensive as possible. Thus, these volumes did not merely define literature by regions but made themselves commensurate with the literature of the region they represented.

These claims to inclusiveness make all the more poignant their omission of American literature written in languages other than English. The editor of *The Poets and Poetry of Vermont* (1858) imagined that Vermonters would "cordially receive and kindly cherish *their own*" (Hemenway 1858: vi) — where it was a foregone conclusion whom that encompassed. These volumes determined how the public they addressed was constituted when they uniformly published English-only poetry. Rarely did the volumes reflect on their omission of literature written in other languages, and when they did, it was with pride at the region's development into an English speaking community. For example, the editor of *The Poets and Poetry of Buffalo* (1904) suggested that "three or four generations ago, the ancestors of two-thirds of our present population did not speak our English tongue"(Johnson 1904: x–xi). Effectively, these anthologies reinvented the American literary specimen as monolingual and untranslated. By the 1850s, they had begun to replace a deracinated understanding of national literature with an intensely localized representation that linked literature to American places defined by a homogenous vernacular.

10. At the time of Longfellow's employment, Harvard's program of modern languages consisted of four instructors and one professor. The languages that were taught were German, French, Italian, and Spanish, and at times Portuguese. Enrollments varied greatly as the Harvard Corporation, under pressure from the faculty in Greek and Latin, kept changing its curricular requirements in the early 1840s, at times prohibiting the study of more than one modern language, at others requiring that every student study French. The instructors heard recitations in the modern languages, and conducted the examinations of the students studying them. The Professor had to instruct and lecture, and at least once a week, he was expected to attend the recitations of one of the Instructors in his Department, and to "be present at the recitation of every individual studying the language taught by that instructor" (Duties outlined by Harvard in 1837 contract with Longfellow; from HWL letter to Pres. Josiah Quincy, 5 August 1837). Listening to the recitations of every individual was labor intensive indeed, considering that in 1851, the German language instructor Bernard Rölker alone taught 110 students.

11. I use "stereotype" here in its generic, figurative sense as "something continued or constantly repeated without change; a stereotyped phrase, formula, etc.; stereotyped diction or usage." In the following chapter, I engage with "stereotype" in its reference to "the method or process of printing" (Simpson, Weiner and Oxford University Press 1989), when I examine copyright and its relation to translation.
12. In addition to translations of Longfellow's and Whitman's work, Freiligrath also translated work by Victor Hugo, Alfons de Lamartine, Robert Herrick, Robert Burns, Robert Southey, William Wordsworth, Alfred Tennyson, Robert Browning, Allan Cunningham, Ebenezer Elliott, Bret Harte, and others.

    The anthologies that legislated an understanding of American literature also communicated that conception transatlantically and participated in the transnational dissemination of American writing. When Longfellow and Freiligrath met in Germany in 1842, they were already familiar with the other poet's work through a complex matrix of print dissemination: "Longfellow assured the German poet that his name was well-known in America, and Freiligrath took from his shelves an English anthology containing verses by Longfellow" (Hatfield 1933: 1224). Freiligrath himself participated in anthology-making, as is clear from his reference in July 1842 to an essay that he wrote on "Amerikanische Anthologie" (American Anthology), published in the *Blätter zur Kunde der Literatur des Auslandes* (literally translated, leaves/ pages to advance the knowledge of the literature of other countries). Freiligrath grouped Longfellow among Bryant, Percival, Brooks, Norton, Mrs. Sigourney, and Woodworth but reflected: "I could have named some more significant names, but I note as my excuse, that I wrote the notice before I had received from your bounty *The Poets and Poetry of America*. I already owe much to that book in the little time I have owned it" (Hatfield 1933: 1231). Longfellow knew Freiligrath's work through its transnational dissemination in reviews — he mentions "a notice of his [Freiligrath's] poems and some *specimens* in one of the last English Reviews" (Longfellow and Hilen 1966: II.415). Longfellow was not merely familiar with Freiligrath through the English-language press but also through German papers he read. His knowledge of the German press, in turn, was not limited to papers printed in Germany: Longfellow was also acquainted with German-language papers published in America.

    John Kulas explains the importance of such papers for the immigrant communities and their overall impact, circulation and status within United States journalism, when he points out that during the 1830s and 40s, "more foreign-language newspapers and periodicals were published in proportion to the foreign-born population in the United States than were produced in the home countries in proportion to their native born. ... In 1872 the *New-Yorker Staats-Zeitung* touted itself as the largest German newspaper in the world" (Kulas 1996: 15). The German-American press was particularly pervasive among U.S. newspapers published in languages other than English: it had a ratio of well over two to one to all other non-English publications (Kulas 1996: 2).
13. My translation; Hatfield 1933: 1228.
14. German immigrant culture — a culture that would soon become a lived reality for Freiligrath in the political diaspora that followed the revolutionary upheavals of the late 1840s — provides a practical example of how that coincidence was culturally viable. When Longfellow first knew him, Freiligrath considered himself an apolitical poet. In 1842, he accepted a pension from Prussia's king Friedrich Wilhelm IV in recognition of the works he had begun to write while he lived in Holland as a merchant's apprentice and became

inspired by the exoticism of the overseas trade. Under the influence of the nationalist "Junge Deutschland" poets (whom he had earlier dismissed), Freiligrath rejected his pension in 1844 and radically changed the content of his poetry. When he expressed his political views in *Ein Glaubensbekenntnis* (1844), Prussian authorities issued a warrant for his arrest as a political agitator. Freiligrath fled to Belgium, Switzerland, and eventually England. Longfellow made arrangements for Freiligrath to immigrate to the United States, but Freiligrath abandoned this plan when revolutionary unrest erupted. He returned to Germany briefly and flirted with a different type of transnationalism when he co-edited the *Neue Rheinische Zeitung* with a new friend and fellow exile, Karl Marx. In 1868, after nearly two decades in exile, Freiligrath was still wanted for arrest in Prussia when he moved to Bavaria with money raised by his supporters at broadly popular and often populist literary festivals. Despite or because of the controversy surrounding him, in the latter part of the nineteenth century, Freiligrath was (excepting Emanuel Geibel) the most widely read German lyric poet. See: Freiligrath 1967, Noltenius 1984, Grünzweig 1995.

15. Larry Reynolds has argued that Whitman's engagement with the European Revolutions of 1848 provided the "foundation for the remarkable first edition of *Leaves of Grass*" (Reynolds 1988: 14). Reynolds points out that Whitman was inspired by the international press when he moved to New Orleans and wrote foreign news stories for the *Eagle* and the *Crescent*.

Yet this practice of nestling translations within his poetry is most prevalent in the third edition of *Leaves of Grass* (1860). As Betsy Erkkila has observed, Whitman used more French terms — often to express democratic ideals — in this edition of his work (which he published in Boston when he was trying to establish himself among such Brahmins as Longfellow and Emerson) than in any other; see Erkkila 1980.

CHAPTER 5

1. Foreign-born residents constituted 11 percent of the U.S. populace in 1825, 35 percent in 1845, and 50 percent in 1855; see: Norton 1986: 64. Between 1750–1850, "native English speakers were not as numerous as has been generally assumed. First, non-English European settlers made up one quarter of the total white population: two-fifths of Pennsylvania's population also spoke German. Second, the Amerindians ... spoke numerous languages. Third, the blacks, mostly slaves who numbered more than one-fifth of the total population, had their own African languages" (Shell 2002: 4).
2. This omission is particularly surprising in Brodhead's work, since he begins his book with an account of Szczesny Zahajkiewicz's staging of the Polish language play "Jadwiza, Krolowa Lechitow" in Chicago in August 1892 (Brodhead 1993: 3–5).
3. Indeed, John William De Forest's essay was part of this effort to ensure the creation of such national literature via copyright regulation: De Forest complained that the composition of national American literature was hindered by the "lack of an international copyright" (De Forest 1868: 28–9).
4. Charles Beecher records that on her trip, Stowe was reading "Michiels' translation of *Uncle Tom's Cabin* and criticizing and asking questions. 'He has dulled all the sharp points and flattened all the prominent ones,'" ran Harriet's verdict; see: Beecher, Van Why, and French 1986: 188.

5. For further discussion of Stowe's relation to industrial labor, see: Thomas 1987: 133, Brown 1990: 50–51.
6. Whereas Elizabeth Ammons suggests that Stowe sees motherhood as an alternative to capitalism, Lori Merish argues that Stowe's notions of motherhood remain deeply implicated in commodity capitalism. See: Ammons 1977, Merish 1996.
7. Stowe's brother Henry Ward Beecher wrote an article on the Hungarian Revolution, which the *Independent* published in 1851. Parts of that article were reprinted in the *National Era* alongside chapter 19 of *Uncle Tom's Cabin*; see: Ammons 2000: 70.
8. The first case tried under the statute, *Burnet v. Chetwood* (1720), involved an unauthorized translation; see: Rose 1993: 133.
9. Publishing translations and reprints was made lucrative for American publishers by a trade practice commonly referred to as "courtesy of the trade." American publishers agreed that they would not compete with one another once one of them had published a book that was not copyright protected — and therefore available to other publishers.
10. For a discussion of the response to Stowe's lawsuit in the English and German language press, see: Homestead 2002: 210.

Works Cited

(1822 [1972]). *Specimens of the American Poets*, London: T. and J. Allman [facsimile reproduction: Delmar, New York: Scholars' Facsimiles and Reprints].
(1828) *The Bijou; or Annual of Literature and the Arts*, London: William Pickering.
(1839) "Review of Select Minor Poems, translated from the German of Goethe and Schiller, with notes, by John S. Dwight," *New York Review*, 4(8): 393–9.
(1849) "Longfellow's Kavanagh: Nationality in Literature," *North American Review*, 69 (114): 196–216.
Stowe v. Thomas (1853) PA Circuit Court for the Eastern District. In equity.
Ammons, E. (1977) "Heroines in Uncle Tom's Cabin," *American Literature*, 49: 161–79.
——. (2000) "*Uncle Tom's Cabin*, Empire, and Africa," in E. Ammons and S. Belasco (Eds.) *Approaches to Teaching Stowe's Uncle Tom's Cabin*, New York: The Modern Language Association of America, 68–76.
Anderson, B. (1991) *Imagined Communities: reflections on the origin and spread of nationalism*, Rev. and extended edn, London and New York: Verso.
Anon. (1852) "Learning without A Master," *The National Era* 6(287): 108.
Appadurai, A. (1996) *Modernity at large: cultural dimensions of globalization*, Minneapolis: University of Minnesota Press.
——. (Ed.) (2001) *Globalization*, Durham, NC: Duke University Press.
Appiah, K. A. (1991) "Is the Post- in Postmodernism the Post- in Postcolonial?," *Critical Inquiry*, 17: 336–57.
Apter, E. (1991) *Feminizing the Fetish: psychoanalysis and narrative obsession in turn-of-the-century France*, Ithaca and London: Cornell University Press.
Arac, J. (1986) "The Politics of The Scarlet Letter," in M. Jehlen and S. Bercovitch (Eds.) *Ideology and Classic American Literature*, Cambridge: Harvard University Press: 247–66.
——. (1996) "Whitman and the Problems of the Vernacular," in B. Erkkila and J. Grossman (Eds.) *Breaking Bounds: Whitman and American cultural studies*, New York: Oxford University Press: 44–62.
Aravamudan, S. (1999) *Tropicopolitans: colonialism and agency, 1688–1804*, Durham, NC: Duke University Press.
Arnim, B. V. and Fuller, M. (1842) *Günderode*, trans. M. Fuller, Boston: E.P. Peabody.
Arnold, M. W. J. (Ed.) (1864) *The Poets and Poetry of Minnesota*, Chicago: Rounds, Book and Job Printer.
Ashcroft, B., Griffiths, G. and Tiffin, H. (Eds.) (1989) *The Empire Writes Back: theory and practice in post-colonial literature*, London: Routledge.
Assing, O. (1999) *Radical Passion: Ottilie Assing's reports from America and letters to Frederick Douglass*, trans. C. Lohmann, New York: Peter Lang.

Bachmann, T. (Ed.) (1960) *Luther's Works*, Philadelphia: Muhlenberg Press.
Bakhtin, M. (1968) *Rabelais and his World*, trans. H. Iswolsky, Cambridge: M.I.T. Press.
——. (1981a) "Glossary," *The Dialogic Imagination: four essays*, trans. C. Emerson and M. Holquist, Austin: University of Texas Press: 423–34.
——. (1981b) "The Prehistory of Novelistic Discourse," in M. Holquist (Ed.) *The Dialogic Imagination: four essays*, trans. C. Emerson and M. Holquist, Austin: University of Texas Press: 41–83.
Balkir, I. (1995) "The Discourse on 'Post-Nationalism': A Reflection on the Contradictions of the 1990s," *Journal of American Studies of Turkey*, 1: 25–31.
Balkun, M. M. (2002) "Phillis Wheatley's Construction of Otherness and the Rhetoric of Performed Ideology," *African American Review*, 36(1): 121–35.
Bannet, E. T. (1993) "The Scene of Translation: After Jakobson, Benjamin, de Man, and Derrida," *New Literary History*, 24: 577–95.
Barnes, E. (1997) *States of Sympathy: seduction and democracy in the American novel*, New York: Columbia University Press.
Barry, D. (2001) "Faustian Pursuits: the political-cultural dimension of Goethe's Weltliteratur and the tragedy of translation," *The German Quarterly*, 74: 164–85.
Barthes, R. (1975) *The Pleasure of the Text*, 1st American edn., trans. R. Miller, New York: Hill and Wang.
Batsaki, Y. (2002) "Unfaithful Translation: Bilingual versions as Greek-American Strategies of Concealment," in M. Shell (Ed.) *American Babel: literatures of the United States from Abnaki to Zuni*, Cambridge: Harvard University Press: 55–73.
Bean, J. (1997) "Conversation as Rhetoric in Margaret Fuller's Woman in the Nineteenth Century," in S. L. Linkon (Ed.) *In her own Voice: nineteenth-century American women essayists*, New York: Garland Publishing: 27–41.
Beecher, C., Van Why, J. S., and French, E. A. (Eds.) (1986) *Harriet Beecher Stowe in Europe: the journal of Charles Beecher*, Hartford, CT: Stowe-Day Foundation.
Bell, M. D. (1980) *The Development of American Romance: the sacrifice of relation*, Chicago: University of Chicago Press.
Benjamin, W. (1969) "The Task of the Translator," in H. Arendt (Ed.) *Illuminations*, trans. H. Zohn, New York: Schocken Books: 69–82.
——. (1979) "On Language as Such and on the Language of Man," *One-way street, and other writings*, trans. E. Jephcott and K. Shorter, London: NLB: 107–23.
Bennett, H. L. (2000) "The Subject in the Plot: National Boundaries and the 'History' of the Black Atlantic," *African Studies Review, Special Issue on the Diaspora*, 43: 101–24.
Bercovitch, S. (1978) *The American Jeremiad*, Madison: University of Wisconsin Press.
——. (1991) "Hawthorne's A-Morality of Compromise," in R. C. Murfin (Ed.) *The Scarlet Letter*, Boston and New York: Bedford St. Martin's Press: 344–58.
Berkson, D. (1994) "'Born and Bred in Different Nations': Margaret Fuller and Ralph Waldo Emerson," in S. Marchalonis (Ed.) *Patrons and Protégées: gender, friendship, and writing in nineteenth-century America*, New Brunswick, NJ: Rutgers University Press: 3–30.
Berlant, L. (1989) "Fantasies of Utopia in The Blithedale Romance," *American Literary History*, 1: 30–62.
——. (1991) *The Anatomy of National Fantasy: Hawthorne, utopia, and everyday life*, Chicago: University of Chicago Press.

Berman, A. (1992) *The Experience of the Foreign: culture and translation in romantic Germany*, trans. S. Heyvaert, Albany: State University of New York Press.
Bhabha, H. K. (1990) "DissemiNation: Time, Narrative, and the Margins of the Modern Nation," in H. K. Bhabha (Ed.) *Nation and Narration*, London and New York: Routledge: 291–322.
———. (1994a) *The Location of Culture*, London and New York: Routledge.
———. (1994b) "Of Mimicry and Man: the ambivalence of colonial discourse," in H. K. Bhabha *The Location of Culture*, London and New York: Routledge: 85–92.
Bloom, H. (1973) *The Anxiety of Influence: a theory of poetry*, New York: Oxford University Press.
Boggs, C. G. (2005) "Black Atlantic," in H. Ostrom and J. D. Macey (Eds.) *The Greewood Encyclopedia of African American Literature*, Westport, CT: Greenwood Publishing.
——— (2006) "Translation in the United States," in P. France and K. Hayes (Eds.) *Oxford History of Literary Translation in English*, Oxford: Oxford University Press, 20–33.
Bourne, R. (1916) "Trans-National America," *Atlantic Monthly*.
Bracks, L. T. (1998) *Writings on Black Women of the Diaspora: history, language, and identity*, New York and London: Garland Publishing.
Britannica (2005) "History of the West Indies," Available HTTP: <http://www.search.eb.com/eb/article?tocId=54386> (accessed 25 April 2005).
Brodhead, R. H. (1986) *The School of Hawthorne*, New York: Oxford University Press.
———. (1993) *Cultures of Letters: scenes of reading and writing in nineteenth-century America*, Chicago: University of Chicago Press.
Brooks, C. T. (1863) *Titan: A Romance. From the German of Jean Paul Richter*, trans. C. T. Brooks, Boston: Ticknor and Fields.
———. (1885) *Poems, original and translated*, Boston: Roberts Brothers.
Brown, G. (1990) *Domestic Individualism: imagining self in nineteenth-century America*, Berkeley, Los Angeles and Oxford: University of California Press.
———. (2001) *The Consent of the Governed: the Lockean legacy in early American culture*, Cambridge: Harvard University Press.
Brown, L. R. (1997) *The Emerson Museum: practical Romanticism and the pursuit of the whole*, Cambridge: Harvard University Press.
Bryant, W. C. (1873) *Orations and Addresses*, New York: G.P. Putnam's Sons.
Budick, E. M. (1989) *Fiction and Historical Consciousness: the American romance tradition*, New Haven and London: Yale University Press.
Budick, S. and Iser, W. (Eds.) (1996) *The Translatability of Cultures: figurations of the space between*, Stanford, CA: Stanford University Press.
Buell, F. (1998) "Nationalist Postnationalism: Globalist Discourse in Contemporary American Culture," *American Quarterly*, 50: 548–91.
Buell, L. (1992a) "American Literary Emergence as a Postcolonial Phenomenon," *American Literary History*, 4: 411–42.
———. (1992b) "Melville and the Question of American Decolonization," *American Literature*, 64: 215–37.
Buzard, J. (1995) "Translation and Tourism: Scott's *Waverley* and the Reading of Culture," *Yale Journal of Criticism*, 8: 31–59.
Cameron, S. (1998) "The Way of Life by Abandonment: Emerson's impersonal," *Critical Inquiry*, 25: 1–31.
Campbell, W. (1918) *The Curtis Collection of Franklin Imprints*, Philadelphia: Curtis Publishing.

Capper, C. (1987) "Margaret Fuller as Cultural Reformer: the conversations in Boston," *American Quarterly*, 39: 509–28.

Carr, H. (1996) *Inventing the American Primitive: politics, gender, and the representation of Native American literary traditions, 1789–1936*, New York: New York University Press.

Castillo, S. P. and Schweitzer, I. (Eds.) (2001) *The Literatures of Colonial America: an anthology*, Malden Mass.: Blackwell Publishers.

———. (2005) *A Companion to the Literatures Colonial America*, Malden, MA: Blackwell Publishers.

Chandler, J. K. (1998a) "Concerning the Influence of America on the Mind: Western settlements, 'English Writers,' and the case of US culture," *American Literary History*, 10: 84–123.

———. (1998b) *England in 1819: the politics of literary culture and the case of Romantic historicism*, Chicago: University of Chicago Press.

Chatterjee, P. (1993) *The Nation and its Fragments: colonial and postcolonial histories*, Princeton, NJ: Princeton University Press.

Cheyfitz, E. (1985) "Literally White, Figuratively Red: the frontier of translation in *The Pioneers*," in R. Clark (Ed.) *James Fenimore Cooper: new critical essays*, London: Vision Press Limited: 55–95.

———. (1993) "Savage Law: The Plot Against American Indians in Johnson and Graham's Lessee v. M'Intosh and The Pioneers," in A. Kaplan and D. E. Pease (Eds.) *Cultures of United States Imperialism*, Durham, NC, and London: Duke University Press: 109–28.

———. (1997) *The Poetics of Imperialism: translation and colonization from 'The Tempest' to 'Tarzan'*, Expanded edn., Philadelphia: University of Pennsylvania Press.

Chrisman, L. (2000) "Rethinking Black Atlanticism," *Black Scholar*, 30: 3–4.

Clarke, J. (1724) *Corderii Colloquiorum centuria selecta; or, A select century of Cordery's Colloquies: with an English translation as literal as possible, design'd for the use of beginners in the Latin tongue. By John Clarke, master of the publick grammar school in Hull, and author of the Introduction to the making of Latin.*, 3rd edn., Boston: Printed for Benjamin Eliot at the lower end of the town-house, and Daniel Henchman over-against the Brick Meeting-House in Cornhill.

Clarke, J. (1848) *Specimens of Dialects: short vocabularies of languages; and notes of countries and customs in Africa*, Berwick-upon-Tweed: Daniel Cameron.

Clayton, J. and Rothstein, E. (Eds.) (1991) *Influence and Intertextuality in Literary History*, Madison: University of Wisconsin Press.

Cliff, M. (1990) *Bodies of Water: stories*, London: Methuen.

———. (1993) *Free Enterprise*, New York: Dutton.

Coale, S. (1985) *In Hawthorne's Shadow: American romance from Melville to Mailer*, Lexington: University Press of Kentucky.

Coggeshall, W. T. (Ed.) (1860) *The Poets and Poetry of the West*, Columbus: Follett, Foster and Co.

Cohen, M. and Dever, C. (Eds.) (2002) *The Literary Channel: the inter-national invention of the novel*, Princeton, NJ: Princeton University Press.

Congress, U. S. and Solberg, T. (1900) *Copyright Enactments, 1783–1900*, Washington: Government Printing Office.

Cooper, J. F. (1828) *Notions of the Americans*, Philadelphia: Carey & Lea.

———. (1832) *The Heidenmauer; or, the Benedictines. A legend of the Rhine*, Philadelphia: Carey & Lea.

———. (1833) *The Headsman; or, the abbaye des vignerons. A tale*, London: R. Bentley.

——. (1986) "Introduction," in R. Slotkin (Ed.) *The Last of the Mohicans: A Narrative of 1757*, New York: Penguin Books: 5–8.

——. (1989) *The Last of the Mohicans: A Narrative of 1757*, New York: Bantam Books.

——. (1991) *The Pioneers; or the sources of the Susquehanna*, James D. Wallace edn., Oxford and New York: Oxford University Press.

——. (2002) "Preface," *The Spy: A Tale of the Neutral Ground*, Brooklyn: AMS Press.

Cooper, J. F. and Beard, J. F. (Eds.) (1960) *Letters and Journals*, Cambridge: Belknap Press of Harvard University Press.

Copjec, J. (1994) *Read my desire: Lacan against the historicists*, Cambridge: MIT Press.

Crawford, J. (1992a) "Introduction," in J. Crawford (Ed.) *Language Loyalties: a source book on the official English controversy*, Chicago: University of Chicago Press: 1–19.

Crawford, R. (1992b) *Devolving English Literature*, Oxford and New York: Clarendon Press of Oxford University Press.

Creighton, M. S. and Norling, L. (Eds.) (1996) *Iron Men, Wooden Women: gender and seafaring in the Atlantic world, 1700–1920*, Baltimore: Johns Hopkins University Press.

Culler, J. (1999) "Anderson and the Novel," *Diacritics*, 29: 20–39.

Cunningham, G. F. (1965) *The Divine Comedy in English; a critical bibliography*, New York: Barnes & Noble.

D'aguiar, F. (1999) *Feeding the Ghosts*, 1st edn., Hopewell, NJ: The Ecco Press.

Davidson, C. N. (1986) *Revolution and the Word: the rise of the novel in America*, New York and Oxford: Oxford University Press.

Davidson, C. N. and Hatcher, J. (Eds.) (2002) *No More Separate Spheres! A next wave American Studies reader*, Durham, NC: Duke University Press.

Dayan, J. (1996) "Paul Gilroy's Slaves, Ships, and Routes: the middle passage as metaphor," *Research in African Literatures*, 27: 7–14.

De Lauretis, T. (1988) "Displacing Hegemonic Discourses: reflections on feminist theory in the 1980s," *Inscriptions*, 3–4.

De Man, P. (1983) *Blindness and Insight: essays in the rhetoric of contemporary criticism*, 2nd edn., Minneapolis: University of Minnesota Press.

De Forest, J. W. (1868) "The Great American Novel," *The Nation*: 27–9.

Dekker, G. (1967) *James Fenimore Cooper: the novelist*, London: Routledge & K. Paul.

Delphendahl, R. (1994) "Margaret Fuller: Interpreter and Translator of German Literature," in M. O. Urbanski (Ed.) *Margaret Fuller: Visionary of the New Age*, Orono, ME: Northern Lights: 52–100.

Derrida, J. (1985) "Des Tours de Babel," in J. F. Graham (Ed.) *Difference in Translation*, Ithaca: Cornell University Press: 165–248.

——. (1997) *Of Grammatology*, corrected edn., trans. G. C. Spivak, Baltimore and London: Johns Hopkins University Press.

Desmond, J. and Dominguez, V. (1996) "Resituating American Studies in a Critical Internationalism," *American Quarterly*, 48: 475–90.

Dillon, E. (2005) "The Original American Novel, or The American Origin of the Novel," in P.R. Backscheider and C. Ingrassia (Eds.) *Companion to the Eighteenth-Century*, Oxford: Blackwell Publishing: 235–60.

Dimock, W. C. (2001) "Literature for the Planet," *PMLA: Publications of the Modern Language Association of America*, 116(1): 173–88.

——. (2006) *Through Other Continents: American Literature Across Deep Time*, Princeton, NJ: Princeton University Press.

Donaldson, L. (2000) "Son of the Forest, Child of God: William Apes and the scene of postcolonial nativity," in R. King (Ed.) *Post-Colonial America*, Champaign: University of Illinois Press: 201–22.

Douglas, A. (1977) *The Feminization of American Culture*, 1st edn., New York: Knopf.

Drabble, M. and Stringer, J. (Eds.) (1996) *The Concise Oxford Companion to English Literature*, Oxford: Oxford University Press.

Dryden, E. A. (1988) *The Form of American Romance*, Baltimore: Johns Hopkins University Press.

Dryden, J. (1992) "On Translation," in R. Schulte and J. Biguenet (Eds.) *Theories of Translation: an anthology of essays from Dryden to Derrida*, Chicago: University of Chicago Press: 17–31.

Duyckinck, E. A. (1850) "Nathaniel Hawthorne," *The Literary World* (30 March 1850): 323–25.

Eckermann, J. P. and Fuller, M. (1839) "Translator's Preface," *Conversations with Goethe in the last years of his life*, trans. M. Fuller, Boston: Hilliard Gray and Company: vii–xxvi.

Ellis, G. (1790) *Specimens of the Early English Poets*, London: G. & W. Nichol.

Ellison, J. K. (1984) *Emerson's Romantic Style*, Princeton, NJ: Princeton University Press.

Emerson, R. W. (1851) "Poems," *Liberty Bell*. Boston: National Anti-Slavery Bazaar.

——. (1960) "Nature," in S. E. Whicher (Ed.) *Selections from Ralph Waldo Emerson: an organic anthology*, Boston: Houghton Mifflin: 21–56.

Emerson, R.W., Channing, W. L., and Clark, J. F (Eds.) (1852) *Memoirs of Margaret Fuller Ossoli*, Boston: Philips Sampson and Company.

Emerson, R. W., Emerson, E. W. and Forbes, W. E. (Eds.) (1911) *Journals of Ralph Waldo Emerson, 1820–72*, Volume 5: 1838–41, Boston: Houghton Mifflin.

Emerson, R. W., and Rusk, R. L. (Eds.) (1939) *The Letters of Ralph Waldo Emerson*, New York: Columbia University Press.

Erkkila, B. (1983) "Walt Whitman: the politics of language," *American Studies*, 24: 21–34.

Erkkila, B. and Grossman, J. (Eds.) (1996) *Breaking Bounds: Whitman and American cultural studies*, New York: Oxford University Press.

Evans, C. (1903) *American Bibliography: a chronological dictionary of all books, pamphlets, and periodical publications printed in the United States of America from the genesis of printing in 1639 down to and including the year 1820. With bibliographical and biographical notes*, Chicago: Blakely Press.

Everst, R. C. W. (Ed.) (1844) *The Hare-Bell; a token of friendship*, Hartford, CT: Gurdon [sic] Robins, Jr.

Feidelson, C. (1953) *Symbolism and American Literature*, Chicago: University of Chicago Press.

Festa, L. (2002) "Sentimental Bonds and Revolutionary Characters: Richardson's *Pamela* in England and France," in M. Cohen and C. Dever (Eds.) *The Literary Channel: the inter-national invention of the novel*, Princeton, NJ: Princeton University Press: 73–105.

Fishman, J. (1980) "Language Policy: past, present, and future," in C. A. Ferguson, S. B. Heath, and D. Hwang (Eds.) *Language in the USA*, Cambridge and New York: Cambridge University Press: 516–26.

Forten, C. (1988) *The Journals of Charlotte Forten Grimké*, Brenda Stevenson edn., New York: Oxford University Press.

Foucault, M. (1984) "What is an Author?," in P. Rabinov (Ed.) *Foucault Reader*, New York: Pantheon Books: 101–20.

Franklin, B. (1936) *Representative Selections*, New York: American Book Company.

——. (1964) *The Autobiography of Benjamin Franklin*, L. W. Labaree, edn., New Haven, CT: Yale University Press.
Freiligrath, F. (1967) *Freiligrath's Werke*, Berlin und Weimar: Aufbau-Verlag.
Friedman, S. S. (1998) *Mappings: feminism and the cultural geographies of encounter*, Princeton, NJ: Princeton University Press.
Friedrich, H. (1992) "On the Art of Translation," in R. Schulte and J. Biguenet (Eds.) *Theories of Translation: an anthology of essays from Dryden to Derrida*, trans. R. Schulte and J. Biguenet, Chicago: University of Chicago Press: 11–16.
Fuller, M. (1846) "American Literature, Its Position in the Present Time, and Prospects for the Future," *Papers on Literature and Art*, New York: Wiley & Putnam: 2122–57.
——. (1991) *Summer on the Lakes in 1843*, Urbana and Chicago: University of Illinois Press.
——. (1994) "Tasso Toquato," in M. M. O. Urbanski (Ed.) *Margaret Fuller: visionary of the new age*, Orono Maine: Northern Lights.
——. (1998) *Woman in the Nineteenth Century*, Larry Reynolds edn., New York and London: W.W. Norton.
Fuller, M. and Hudspeth, R. N. (Eds.) (1983) *The Letters of Margaret Fuller*, Ithaca, NY: Cornell University Press.
Gardner, J. (1998) *Master Plots: race and the founding of an American literature, 1787–1845*, Baltimore: Johns Hopkins University Press.
Gates, H. L. (1988) *The Signifying Monkey: a theory of African-American literary criticism*, New York and Oxford: Oxford University Press.
Gilbert, G. (1980) "French and German: a comparative study," in C. A. Ferguson, S. B. Heath and D. Hwang (Eds.) *Language in the USA*, Cambridge and New York: Cambridge University Press: 257–73.
Giles, P. (2001) *Transatlantic Insurrections: British culture and the formation of American literature, 1730–1860*, Philadelphia: University of Pennsylvania Press.
——. (2002) *Virtual Americas: transnational fictions and the transatlantic imaginary*, Durham, NC: Duke University Press.
Goethe, J. W. V. (1833) *Characteristics of Goethe; From the German of Falk, von Müller, &c., with notes, original and translated, illustrative of German literature*, trans. S. Austin, London: E. Wilson.
Golding, A. (1995) *From Outlaw to Classic: Canons of American Poetry*, Madison: University of Wisconsin Press.
Griesemer, J. (2003) *Signal & Noise*, 1st edn, New York: Picador.
Gross, R. (2000) "The Transnational Turn: rediscovering American Studies in a wider world," *Journal of American Studies*, 34(3): 373–93.
Grossman, A. (1984) "The Poetics of Union in Whitman and Lincoln," in W. B. Michaels and D. E. Pease (Eds.) *The American Renaissance Reconsidered*, Baltimore: Johns Hopkins University Press:183–208.
Gruesz, K. S. (1998) "El Gran Poeta Longfellow and a Psalm of Exile," *American Literary History*, 10: 395–427.
Grünzweig, W. (1991) *Walt Whitman: Die deutschsprachige Rezeption als interkulturelles Phänomen*, München: Wilhelm Fink Verlag.
——. (1995) *Constructing the German Walt Whitman*, Iowa City: University of Iowa Press.
Hacking, I. (1986) "Making Up People," in T. C. Heller, M. Sorna and D. Wellberry (Eds.) *Reconstructing Individualism*, Stanford, CA: Stanford University Press: 222–36.
Hall, S. (1996) "The West and the Rest: discourse and power," *Modernity: an introduction to modern societies*, Cambridge: Blackwell.

Hannerz, U. (1992) *Cultural Complexity: studies in the social organization of meaning*, New York: Columbia University Press.
Hardt, M. and Negri, A. (2000) *Empire*, Cambridge, MA: Harvard University Press.
Hatfield, J. T. (1933) "The Longfellow-Freiligrath Correspondence," *PMLA: Publications of the Modern Language Association of America*, XLVIII: 1223–76.
Hawthorn, J. (2004a) "Alienation," in J. Hawthorn (Ed.) *A Glossary of Contemporary Literary Theory*, London: Arnold: 9.
———. (2004b) "Dialogic," in J. Hawthorn (Ed.) *A Glossary of Contemporary Literary Theory*, London: Arnold: 76–8.
Hawthorne, N. (1980) *The Scarlet Letter*, Leo Marx edn, New York: Penguin.
Heath, S. B. (1980) "English in our Language Heritage," in C. A. Ferguson, S. B. Heath and D. Hwang (Eds.) *Language in the USA*, Cambridge and New York: Cambridge University Press: 6–20.
———. (1992) "Why No Official Tongue," in J. Crawford (Ed.) *Language Loyalties: a source book on the official English controversy*, Chicago: University of Chicago Press: 20–31.
Hedrick, J. D. (1994) *Harriet Beecher Stowe: a life*, New York: Oxford University Press.
Heiney, B. (Ed.) (1900) *The Poets and Poetry of Indiana: a representative collection of the poetry of Indiana during the first hundred years of its history as territory and state, 1800–1900*, New York, Boston and Chicago: Silver, Burdett, and Co.
Hemenway, A. M. (Ed.) (1858) *The Poets and Poetry of Vermont*, Rutland, VT: George A. Tuttler and Co.
Herder, J. G. (1966) "On the Origin of Language," *On the Origin of Language*, trans. J. Moran and A. Gode, Chicago and London: University of Chicago Press: 87–166.
Homel, D. and Simon, S. (Eds.) (1988) *Mapping Literature: the art and politics of translation*, Montreal and Cheektowaga: Vehicule Press.
Homestead, M. J. (2002) "'When I Can Read My Title Clear': Harriet Beecher Stowe and the Stowe v. Thomas Copyright Infringement Case," *Prospects: An Annual Journal of American Cultural Studies*, 27: 201–45.
Horace (1988) *Odes and Epodes*, trans. C. E. Bennett, Cambridge and London: Harvard University Press.
Hulme, P. (1995) "Including America," *Ariel*, 26: 117–123.
James, H. (1903) *William Wetmore Story and his Friends; from letters, diaries, and recollections*, Boston: Houghton Mifflin & Co.
Jameson, F. (1981) *The Political Unconscious: narrative as a socially symbolic act*, Ithaca, NY: Cornell University Press.
———. (1987) "The State of the Subject (III)," *Critical Quarterly*, 29: 16–25.
Jay, P. (1998) "The Myth of 'America' and the Politics of Location: modernity, border studies, and the literature of the Americas," *Arizona Quarterly*, 54: 165–93.
Jefferson, T. (1982) *Notes on the State of Virginia*, William Peden edn., New York and London: W.W. Norton & Co.
Johnson, B. (2003) *Mother Tongues: sexuality, trials, motherhood, translation*, Cambridge, MA: Harvard University Press.
Johnson, C. R. (1990) *Middle Passage*, New York: Atheneum.
Johnston, J. N. (Ed.) (1904) *The Poets and Poetry of Buffalo*, Buffalo, NY.
Johnston, J. (1997) *Anna Jameson: Victorian, feminist, woman of letters*, Aldershot Hants England; Brookfield VT: Scolar Press.

Judy, R. (1997) "Paul Gilroy's Black Atlantic and the Place(s) of English in the Global," *Critical Quarterly*, 39: 22–30.
Kadish, D. Y. and Massardier-Kenney, F. (Eds.) (1994) *Translating Slavery : gender and race in French women's writing, 1783–1823*, Kent, OH: Kent State University Press.
Kaplan, A. (2002) *The Anarchy of Empire in the Making of U.S. Culture*, Cambridge, MA: Harvard University Press.
Kaplan, J. (1980) *Walt Whitman: A Life*, New York: Simon & Schuster.
Kaufman, W. and Macpherson, H. S. (Eds.) (2000) *Transatlantic Studies*, Lanham, MD: University Press of America.
——. (Eds.) (2001) *New Perspectives in Transatlantic Studies*, Lanham, MD: University Press of America.
Kazanjian, D. (2003) *The Colonizing Trick: national culture and imperial citizenship in early America*, Minneapolis and London: University of Minnesota Press.
Kellman, S. (2002) "Translingualism and the American Literary Imagination," in M. Shell (Ed.) *American Babel: literatures of the United States from Abnaki to Zuni*, Cambridge, MA: Harvard University Press: 450–64.
Kettell, S. (Ed.) (1829) *Specimens of American Poetry with Critical and Biographical Notes*, Boston: S.G. Goodrich and Company.
King, R. (Ed.) (2000) *Post-Colonial America*, Champaign: University of Illinois Press.
Kittel, H. (1998) "Inclusions and Exclusions: the 'Göttingen Approach' to translation studies and inter-literary history," in K. Mueller-Vollmer and M. Irmscher (Eds.) *Translating Literatures, Translating Cultures: new vistas and approaches in literary studies*, Stanford, CA: Stanford University Press: 3–13.
Klein, B. and Mackenthun, G. (Eds.) (2003) *Sea Changes: historicizing the ocean*, New York: Routledge.
Kouwenhoven, J. A. (1941) "Arts in America," *Atlantic Monthly*, 168: 175–80
Kruger, L. (2001) "Black Atlantics, White Indians, and Jews: locations, locutions, and syncretic identities in the fiction of Achmat Dangor and others," *The South Atlantic Quarterly*, 100: 111–43.
Kulas, J. (1996) *Der Wanderer of St. Paul*, New York: Peter Lang Publishing.
Lawrence, D. H. (1978) *Studies in Classic American Literature*, New York: Penguin Books.
Lee, B. (1995) "Critical Internationalism," *Public Culture*, 7: 559–92.
Lefevere, A. (1992) *Translating Literature: practice and theory in a comparative literature context*, New York: Modern Language Association of America.
Lemisch, J. (1968) "Jack Tar in the Streets: merchant seamen in the politics of revolutionary America," *William and Mary Quarterly*, 25: 371–407.
Lenz, G. (1999) "Toward a Dialogics of International American Culture Studies: transnationality, border discourse, and public culture(s)," *Amerikastudien*, 44: 5–23.
Levernier, J. (1981) "Wheatley's 'On Being Brought from Africa to America'," *Explicator*, 40: 25–6.
Levine, R. (2005) "Antebellum Feminists on Hawthorne: reconsidering the reception of The Scarlet Letter," in L. S. Person (Ed.) *The Scarlet Letter and Other Writings*, New York and London: W.W. Norton & Company: 274–90.
Levinson, M. (1986) *The Romantic Fragment Poem: a critique of a form*, Chapel Hill: University of North Carolina Press.
Lewis, R. W. B. (1955) *The American Adam: innocence, tragedy, and tradition in the nineteenth century*, Chicago and London: University of Chicago Press.

Lionnet, F. (1995) *Postcolonial Representations: women, literature, identity*, Ithaca, NY: Cornell University Press.

Locke, J. (1968) *The Educational Writings of John Locke*, James Axtell edn., Cambridge: Cambridge University Press.

Logan, J. (1744) *M.T. Cicero's Cato Major, or his discourse of old-age*, Philadelphia: Benjamin Franklin.

Longfellow, H. W. (1833) "The Brave Man. A Ballad, by Bürger," *New England Magazine*, 5(3): 198–200.

—— (17 August 1839) Private correspondence to President and Corporation of Harvard College, Dana Papers, Longfellow House, Cambridge, MA.

Longfellow, H. W. and Hilen, A. R. (Eds.) (1966) *The Letters of Henry Wadsworth Longfellow*, Cambridge, MA: Belknap Press of Harvard University Press.

Longfellow, S. (1886) *Life of Henry Wadsworth Longfellow, with extracts from his journals and correspondence*, Boston: Ticknor and Company.

Looby, C. (1986) "'The Affairs of the Revolution Occasion'd the Interruption': writing, revolution, deferral, and conciliation in Franklin's Autobiography," *American Quarterly*, 38: 72–96.

Loundes, M. B. (1939) unpublished manuscript. Stowe-Day Center Library.

Lynch, D. S. (2002) "The (Dis)locations of Romantic Nationalism: Shelley, Staël, and the home-schooling of monsters," in M. Cohen and C. Dever (Eds.) *The Literary Channel: the inter-national invention of the novel*, Princeton, NJ: Princeton University Press: 194–224.

Mackenthun, G. (1997) *Metaphors of Dispossession: American beginnings and the translation of empire, 1492–1637*, Norman: University of Oklahoma Press.

——. (2000) "America's Troubled Postcoloniality: some reflections from abroad," *Discourse*, 22: 34–45.

——. (2004) *Fictions of the Black Atlantic in American Foundational Literature*, London and New York: Routledge.

Martineau, H. (1877) *Harriet Martineau's Autobiography*, Boston: J. R. Osgood and Company.

Marx, K. and Engels, F. (1933) *Capital: a critique of political economy*, trans. S. Moore and E. Abeling, New York: Modern Library.

Marx, L. (1988) *The Pilot and the Passenger: essays on literature, technology, and culture in the United States*, New York: Random House.

Matthiessen, F. O. (1931) *Translation, an Elizabethan art*, Cambridge, MA: Harvard University Press.

——. (1941) *American Renaissance: art and expression in the age of Emerson and Whitman*, London and New York: Oxford University Press.

McGill, M. (2003) *American Literature and the Culture of Reprinting, 1834–53*, Philadelphia: University of Pennsylvania Press.

Mechling, J., Meredith, R. and Wilson, D. (1973) "American Culture Studies: the discipline and the curriculum," *American Quarterly*, 25: 363–89.

Melville, H. (1850) "Hawthorne and His Mosses. By a Virginian Spending July in Vermont," *Literary World*.

Merish, L. (1996) "Sentimental Consumption: Harriet Beecher Stowe and the aesthetics of middle-class ownership," *American Literary History*, 8: 1–33.

Miller, P. (1963) *Margaret Fuller: American Romantic*, Ithaca: Cornell University Press.

Morrison, T. (1988) *Beloved*, New York: Plume.

——. (1989) "Unspeakable Things Spoken: the Afro-American presence in American literature," *Michigan Quarterly Review*, 28.

Mott, F. L. (1947) *Golden Multitudes: the story of best sellers in the United States*, New York: Bowker.

Mueller-Vollmer, K. and Irmscher, M. (1998) "Introduction," in K. Mueller-Vollmer and M. Irmscher (Eds.) *Translating Literatures, Translating Cultures: new vistas and approaches in literary studies*, Stanford, CA: Stanford University Press: ix–xviii.
Myerson, J. (Ed.) (1979) *Critical Essays on Margaret Fuller*, Boston: G. K. Hall.
Nelson, D. (1992) *The Word in Black and White: reading 'race' in American literature, 1638–1867*, New York and Oxford: Oxford University Press.
Newfield, C. (1992) "Controlling the Voice: Emerson's Early Theory Language," *ESQ: A Journal of the American Renaissance*, 38: 1–29.
Noltenius, R. (1984) *Dichterfeiern in Deutschland: Rezeptionsgeschichte als Sozialgeschichte am Beispiel der Schiller- und Freiligrath-Feiern*, München: Wilhelm Fink Verlag.
Norton, A. (1986) *Alternative Americas: a reading of antebellum political culture*, Chicago: University of Chicago Press.
Odell, M. M. (1838) *Memoirs and Poems of Phillis Wheatley, A Native of African and A Slave. Also, Poems By A Slave*, Boston: Isaac Knaap.
Ong, A. (1999) *Flexible Citizenship: the cultural logics of transnationality*, Durham, NC, and London: Duke University Press.
Packer, B. (1982) *Emerson's Fall: a new interpretation of the major essays*, New York: Continuum.
Pease, D. E. (1987) *Visionary Compacts: American Renaissance writings in cultural contexts*, Madison: University of Wisconsin Press.
Phillips, C. (2000) *The Atlantic Sound*, 1st edn, New York: Alfred Knopf.
Poirier, R. (1987) *The Renewal of Literature: Emersonian reflections*, 1st edn., New York: Random House.
Pope, A. (1771) *The Iliad of Homer*, London: J. Whiston.
———. (1969) *Poetry and Prose of Alexander Pope*, Aubrey Williams edn., Boston: Houghton Mifflin Company.
Pratt, M. L. (1992) *Imperial Eyes: travel writing and transculturation*, London and New York: Routledge.
Pratt, S. L. (2002) *Native Pragmatism: rethinking the roots of American philosophy*, Bloomington and Indianapolis: Indiana University Press.
Ragussis, M. (1991) "Silence, Family Discourse, and Fiction in *The Scarlet Letter*," in R. C. Murfin (Ed.) *The Scarlet Letter*, Ross C. Murfin ed. Boston and New York: Bedford St. Martin's Press: 316–29.
Readings, B. (1996) *The University in Ruins*, Cambridge, MA: Harvard University Press.
Rediker, M. B. (1987) *Between the Devil and the Deep Blue Sea: merchant seamen, pirates, and the Anglo-American maritime world, 1700–1750*, Cambridge and New York: Cambridge University Press.
Reynolds, L. J. (1988) *European Revolutions and the American Literary Renaissance*, New Haven, CT: Yale University Press.
Ritchie, R. C. (1986a) *Captain Kidd and the War against the Pirates*, Cambridge, MA: Harvard University Press.
———. (1986b) *Pirates: myths and realities*, Minneapolis: Associates of the James Ford Bell Library University of Minnesota.
Roach, J. R. (1996) *Cities of the Dead: circum-Atlantic performance*, New York: Columbia University Press.
Robinson, W. H. (Ed.) (1982) *Critical Essays on Phillis Wheatley*, Boston: G.K. Hall & Co.
Roger, P. M. (1997) "Taking a Perspective: Hawthorne's concept of language and nineteenth-century language theory," *Nineteenth-Century Literature*, 51: 433–54.

Romero, L. (1991) "Vanishing Americans: gender, empire, and new historicism," *American Literature*, 63: 385–404.

Rose, M. (1993) *Authors and Owners: the invention of copyright*, Cambridge, MA and London, England: Harvard University Press.

Rosenwald, L. (1998) "The Last of the Mohicans and the Languages of America," *College English*, 60: 9–30.

Rosowski, S. J. (1990) "Margaret Fuller, an Engendered West, and *Summer on the Lakes*," *Western American Literature*, 25: 125–44.

Rouse, R. (1995) "Thinking through Transnationalism: notes on the cultural politics of class relations in the contemporary United States," *Public Culture*, 7: 353–402.

Rousseau, J.-J. (1966) "On the Origin of Language," *On the Origin of Languages*, trans. J. H. Moran and A. Gode, Chicago and London: University of Chicago Press: 5–74.

Rowe, J. C. (1997) *At Emerson's Tomb: the politics of classic American literature*, New York: Columbia University Press.

———. (2002) *The New American Studies*, Minneapolis and London: University of Minnesota Press.

Runyan, T. J. (Ed.) (1987) *Ships, Seafaring, and Society: essays in maritime history*, Detroit: Published for the Great Lakes Historical Society by Wayne State University Press.

Salamon, J. (2004) "Online Magazine Removes Cultural Blinders," *New York Times*, Wednesday, February 18.

Sassen, S. (2001) "Spatialities and Temporalities of the Global: elements for a theorization," in A. Appadurai (Ed.) *Globalization*, Durham: Duke University Press: 260–78.

Saussure, F. D. (1959) *Course in General Linguistics*, Charles Bally, Albert Sechehaye, Albert Reidlinger edn., trans. W. Baskin, New York: Philosophical Library.

Schulte, R. and Biguenet, J. (Eds.) (1992) *Theories of Translation: an anthology of essays from Dryden to Derrida*, Chicago: University of Chicago Press.

Scott, S. W. (1986) *Waverley; or, 'Tis Sixty Years Since*, Oxford: Oxford University Press.

———. (2001) *Ivanhoe*, Sharon Kay Penman edn, New York: Penguin Books.

Sharpe, J. (2000) "Is the United States Postcolonial? Transnationalism, immigration, and race," in R. King (Ed.) *Post-Colonial America*, Champaign: University of Illinois Press: 103–21.

Shaw, R. and Shoemaker, R. (1958-66) *American Bibliography; a preliminary checklist for 1801–1819*, New York: Scarecrow Press.

Shell, M. (Ed.) (2002a) *American Babel: literatures of the United States from Abnaki to Zuni*, Cambridge, MA: Harvard University Press.

———. (2002b) "Introduction," in M. Shell (Ed.) *American Babel: literatures of the United States from Abnaki to Zuni*, Cambridge, MA: Harvard University Press: 3–33.

Shell, M. and Sollors, W. (Eds.) (2000) *The Multilingual Anthology of American Literature: a reader of original texts with English translations*, New York: New York University Press.

Shulenberger, A. (1972) *Cooper's Theory of Fiction: his prefaces and their relation to his novels*, New York: Octagon Books.

Simpson, D. (1986) *The Politics of American English, 1776–1850*, New York: Oxford University Press.

Simpson, J. A., Weiner, E. S. C. and Oxford University Press. (1989) *The Oxford English dictionary*, 2nd edn., Oxford and New York: Oxford University Press.

Smith, A. (1817) *The Theory of Moral Sentiments: or, An essay towards an analysis of the principles by which men naturally judge concerning the conduct and character, first of their neighbours, and afterwards of themselves: to which is added, A dissertation on the origin of languages*, 1st American from the 12th Edinburgh edn., Philadelphia: A. Finley.

———. (1907) *The Theory of Moral Sentiments To Which Is Added, A Dissertation On The Origin of Languages*, London: George Bell & Sons.

———. (1982) *The Theory of Moral Sentiments*, D. D. Raphael and A. L. Macsie edn., Indianapolis, IN: Liberty Fund.

Sollors, W. (1986) *Beyond Ethnicity: consent and descent in American culture*, New York: Oxford University Press.

———. (Ed.) (1998) *Multilingual America: transnationalism, ethnicity, and the languages of American literature*, New York: New York University Press.

———. (2002) "Ferdinand Kürnberger's *Der Amerika-Müde* (1855): German-Language literature about the United States, and German American writing," in M. Shell (Ed.) *American Babel: literatures of the United States from Abnaki to Zuni*, Cambridge, MA: Harvard University Press: 117–29.

Sommer, D. (2002) "Contrapuntal Languages: the games they play in Spanish," in M. Shell (Ed.) *American Babel: literatures of the United States from Abnaki to Zuni*, Cambridge, MA: Harvard University Press: 263–82.

Southey, R. (Ed.) (1807) *Specimens of the Later English Poets*, London: Longman, Hurst, Ress and Orne, Pater-Noster Rowe.

Souvestre, M. (1851) "Influence de L'esclavage sur les Maîtres," *Liberty Bell*. Boston: National Anti-Slavery Bazaar.

Spengemann, W. C. (1984) "The Earliest American Novel: Aphra Behn's *Oroonoko*," *Nineteenth-Century Fiction*, 38: 384–414.

———. (1994) *A New World of Words: redefining early American literature*, New Haven, CT: Yale University Press.

Spiller, R. E., Thorp, W., Johnson, T. and Canby, H. S. (Eds.) (1948) *Literary History of the United States*, New York: Macmillan.

Spillers, H. J. (2003) "Mama's Baby, Papa's Maybe: an American grammar book," in H. J. Spillers (Ed.) *Black, White and in Color: Essays on American literature and culture*, Chicago and London: University of Chicago Press: 203–29.

Spivak, G. C. (1993) *Outside in the Teaching Machine*, New York: Routledge.

Springer, H. S. (Ed.) (1995) *America and the Sea: a literary history*, Athens, GA: University of Georgia Press.

Steele, J. (Ed.) (1992) *The Essential Margaret Fuller*, New Brunswick, NJ: Rutgers University Press.

Stern, J. A. (1997) *The Plight of Feeling: sympathy and dissent in the early American novel*, Chicago: University of Chicago Press.

Stewart, D. (1835) "Account of the Life and Writings of William Robertson, D.D.," *The Works of William Robertson*, London: F. Westley and A.H. Davis.

Stewart, S. (1991) *Crimes of Writing: problems in the containment of representation*, New York: Oxford University Press.

Stokes, C. (2005) "Copyrighting American History: international copyright and the periodization of the nineteenth century," *American Literature*, 77: 291–317.

Stowe, H. B. (1833) *Primary Geography for Children, on an improved plan with eleven maps and numerous engravings*, Cincinnati: Corey & Fairbank.

———. (1986) *Uncle Tom's Cabin or Life among the Lowly*, Ann Douglas edn., New York: Penguin.

Stylus (1879) *American Publishers and English Authors*, Baltimore: Eugene L. Didier.

Sumner, C. and Palmer, B. W. (Eds.) (1990) *The Selected Letters of Charles Sumner,* Boston: Northeastern University Press.
Thomas, B. (1987) *Cross-examinations of Law and Literature,* Cambridge: Cambridge University Press.
Thomas, H. (2000) *Romanticism and Slave Narratives: transatlantic testimonies,* Cambridge: Cambridge University Press.
Thomas, R. (1962) *The Search for a Common Learning: general education, 1800–1960,* New York: McGraw-Hill.
Todorov, T. (1984) *The Conquest of America,* New York: Harper & Row.
Tölöyan, K. (1991) "The Nation-State and Its Others: in lieu of a preface," *Diaspora,* 1: 3–7.
Tompkins, J. P. (1985) *Sensational Designs: the cultural work of American fiction, 1790–1860,* New York: Oxford University Press.
Trumpener, K. (1997) *Bardic Nationalism: the Romantic novel and the British Empire,* Princeton, NJ: Princeton University Press.
Tyrell, I. (1991) "American Exceptionalism in an Age of International History," *The American Historical Review,* 96: 1031–55.
Unsworth, B. (1992) *Sacred Hunger,* 1st edn., New York: Doubleday.
Urbanski, M. M. O. (1980) *Margaret Fuller's Woman in the Nineteenth Century,* Westport, CT, and London: Greenwood
Venuti, L. (1995) *The Translator's Invisibility: a history of translation,* London and New York: Routledge.
Von Mehren, J. (1994) *Minerva and the Muse: a life of Margaret Fuller,* Amherst: University of Massachusetts Press.
Waggoner, D. (1980) "Statistics on Language Use," in C. A. Ferguson, S. B. Heath and D. Hwang (Eds.) *Language in the USA,* Cambridge and New York: Cambridge University Press: 257–73.
Wald, P. (1995) *Constituting Americans: cultural anxiety and narrative form,* Durham, NC: Duke University Press.
——. (1998) "Minefields and Meeting Grounds: transnational analyses and American Studies," *American Literary History,* 10: 199–218.
Walker, G. (1840) *The Chess Player, illustrated with engravings and diagrams, containing, Franklin's 'Essay on the Morals of Chess',* Boston: Nathl. Dearborn.
Warner, M. (1990) *Letters of the Republic: publication and public sphere in eighteenth-century America,* Cambridge, MA and London: Harvard University Press.
——. (1993) "Savage Franklin," in G. Balestra and L. Sampietro (Eds.) *Biblioteca di Anglistica,* Rome: Bulzoni: 75–87.
Warner, S. (1987) *Wide, Wide World,* New York: The Feminist Press at CUNY.
Watts, E. (1998) *Writing and Postcolonialism in the Early Republic,* Charlottesville: University Press of Virginia.
Webster, N. (1828) *American dictionary of the English language,* converse.
Weisbuch, R. (1986) *Atlantic Double-Cross: American literature and British influence in the age of Emerson,* Chicago: University of Chicago Press.
Wheatley, P. (1988) *The Collected Works of Phillis Wheatley,* New York: Oxford University Press.
Whitman, S. H. (1840) Review of *Conversations with Goethe, in the last year of his life, Boston Quarterly Review* 3(1): 20–57
Whitman, W. (1860) *Leaves of Grass,* Boston: Thayer and Eldridge.
——. (1982) *Poetry and Prose,* New York: The Library of America.
Wideman, J. E. (1996) *The Cattle Killing,* Boston: Houghton Mifflin.

Winship, M. (1995) *American Literary Publishing in the Mid-nineteenth Century: the business of Ticknor and Fields*, Cambridge and New York: Cambridge University Press.

Winter, A. (1998) *Mesmerized: powers of mind in Victorian Britain*, Chicago: University of Chicago Press.

Winterich, J. T. (1935) *Early American Books and Printing*, Boston and New York: Houghton Mifflin Company.

Winterer, C. (2002) *The Culture of Classicism*, Baltimore: Johns Hopkins University Press.

Wirth-Nesher, H. (1990) "Between Mother Tongue and Native Language: multilingualism in Henry Roth's *Call it Sleep*," *Prooftexts*, 10: 297–312.

Wise, G. (1999) "'Paradigm Dramas' in American Studies: a cultural and institutional history of the movement," in L. Maddox (Ed.) *Locating American Studies: the evolution of a discipline*, Baltimore: Johns Hopkins University Press: 166–214.

Zwarg, C. (1993) "Footnoting the Sublime: Margaret Fuller on Black Hawk's trail," *American Literary History*, 5: 616–42.

Index

A
Abolition, Grimké, Charlotte Forten, 18–19
Abolitionist press, 21, 129, 134, 141
Acquired secondary language, Wheatley, Phillis, 37
African-Americans, 3–4, 10, 27, 37, 54, 76–77, 134–135
  Wheatley, Phillis, 37–60
African-American translation, 37
African languages, 37
  loss of, 37
Alienation, 17, 38, 51, 53, 59, 74, 132–135, 144
  Bakhtin, Mikhail, 133
  cultural, 132–133
  intellectual, 134
  labor, 132
  linguistic, 133
  self-alienation, 62, 98
Allegory, 6, 47, 104
  de Man, Paul, 104
Alterity, 8–11, 17, 21, 23, 28–29, 38, 60, 62–63, 67–68, 75, 81–82, 91
  Grimké, Charlotte Forten, 17
  The Scarlet Letter, 8–9
American
  redefined, 1, 5–6
  transatlantic relationship, 54
American education, 16, 25, 35, 38–39, 43–45, 68–69, 93, 99, 121, 132, 135, 117–118, 147–149
American exceptionalism, process, 3–4, 10–11, 22–23, 28, 35, 107
American frontier, 4, 30, 33, 62, 76, 92, 104, 108–110
American literary studies, 2–3, 5, 8, 32, 92, 149

relationship to external cultures, 3
transnational era, 2
American literature
  as American translation, 32–33, 89, 91–93
  self-referential, 10, 14–15, 31, 40–41, 149
American poetry, translation, 112–126
American Romanticism, Cooper, James Fenimore, 88–89
American vernacular, translation, 23, 34, 72, 111–126
Anderson, Benedict, 34, 84–85, 87, 127–129
Anglo-American poetry, literary representation, 111
Antebellum press, 120
Anthologizing, 28, 34, 39, 92
  botanical conceit, 113–116
  history, 113
  literary specimens, 113
  Longfellow, Henry Wadsworth, 119
Aporia, *see* Linguistic aporia
Atlantic Ocean, 3–5, 20, 24, 26–27, 37, 54
Austin, Sarah, 93–95
  Goethe, Johann Wolfgang von, 93–95, 105–106
Autobiography of Benjamin Franklin, 46–48
  impact, 47

B
Babel
  Derrida, Jacques, 7
  languages, 6–7, 8, 15
Bakhtin, Mikhail, 2, 7, 8, 76, 96
  alienation, 133
  double-voiced discourse, 76

Bakhtin, Mikhail (*continued*)
  heteroglossia, 7, 76, 96
  polyglossia, 7, 96
Beloved (Toni Morrison), 37
Benjamin, Walter, 14, 23, 96–97, 102–103, 124, 155 n. 23
Bhabha, Homi
  hybridity, 50–51, 156 n. 25
  mimicry, 153 n. 11
Bilingual education, 23, 25, 35, 147–149
  monolingualism, 7, 127–129, 148
Black Atlantic, 3–4, 20, 151–152 n. 3
  as gendered space, 20, 55
Black sailors, 3–4
Blanched Atlantic, 4, 32, 63, 77
Blended language, Cooper, James Fenimore, 63–69, 80–81

C
Captivity narrative, 40, 84
Carlyle, Thomas, 21–22, 93–94
Chess, 49–50
Circum-Atlantic, 24
Clarke, John, 25, 44–45, 69
Classics, 44, 45
  purposes, 44
Collection, *see* Anthologizing
Communal rights, intellectual labor, 140–142
Communication breakdown, 78, 83–84
Connection, difference, 50–51
Contact zones, transculturation, 30–31
Continental translation theory, Fuller, Margaret, 97
Conversion narrative, 40
Cooper, James Fenimore, 33–34, 61–89
  American Romanticism, 88–89
  being translatable, 62. 161 n.2
  blended language, 63–69, 80–81
  composite order, 68
  conceptualizing language, 65
  European novels, 85
  gender, 71
    gender binary, 78–79
  influence of Walter Scott, 66–68
  language formation, 64–65
  language instruction, 68–69
  modality, 88–89
  model of language, 71
  mother tongue, 71
  neutral ground, 33, 62, 70, 74, 81–84, 88

race, 76–83
  separating language from race, 76–77
slavery, 62
translation, 63, 75
  America's linguistic originality, 72
  captivated by practices of translation, 61–62
  cultural and linguistic blend, 75–76
  defining national literature, 74
  division between familiar and foreign, 75
  triangulation, 63
  understanding of Smith's linguistic philosophy, 66
Copyright, 129, 138–149
  authorial choice in translations, 145
  conflation of text and personhood, 140–141
  distinction between book's content and form, 139–140
  establishing legal breadth of, 142–144
  extended definition of author to translator, 145
  first copyright legislation, 141–142
  history of regulations for textual reproduction, 139
  international copyright, 147
  language's role in literary and national identity, 141–142
  literary protectionism, 142
  Lockean notions of labor-based proprietorship, 140
  neologism, 146
  as recent invention, 139
  Revised Statutes of 1873, 147
  shifts in legal definition of, 146–147
  translation, 34–35
Creole, 111
Cultural diversity, 33–34
  Grimké, Charlotte Forten, strategies, 17
Cultural identity, 34
  model, 24
  surrogates, 24–25
Cultural legitimacy, *The Scarlet Letter*, 8–9
Custom
  defined, 11–12
  meaning, 11–12
"The Custom House" (Nathaniel Hawthorne)

economic exchange, 11–12
national identity, closed economy of linguistic signs, 12
strategy of twice-telling, 9

D

Derrida, Jacques, 6–7, 8, 29, 50
  Babel, 7
  différance, 50–51
  supplement, 7–8, 20, 28
  trace, 2, 7, 8, 11, 55, 66
de Man, Paul, 104, 155 n. 23
  allegory, 104
de Staël, Germaine, 93, 94–96
Diaspora, 25, 134, 152 n. 3
Différance, Derrida, Jacques, 50–51
Difference
  connection, 50–51
  sentimentality, 62
  linguistic model for negotiating, 62
Distance, intimacy, 26
Double translation, Wheatley, Phillis, 38, 51–52
Dryden, John, 29, 48, 57, 93
Duyckinck, Evert, 56–57, 109, 154 n. 15

E

Economic exchange, "The Custom House," 11–12
Eden, languages, 6–7
Educational reform, Franklin, Benjamin, 45, 131
  purposes, 45–46
Emerson, Ralph Waldo
  Fuller, Margaret, 98, 100
  translation
    metaphysical model, 101–104
    personal and national identity, 100
    transcendent language, 100–101
    universality, 100–101
Empirical translation, 34, 97, 100–104
English paupers, 19
Equality, Fuller, Margaret, 99–100
Ethnographic inquiry, language, 114–115
Exile, 12

F

Familiarizing translations, Goethe, Johann Wolfgang von, 94
Fetishization
  of monolingual originality, 6, 11, 23, 28, 60, 137

of patriotism, 19–20
of reading, 13, 16–17
The Scarlet Letter, 13–14
Foreignizing translations, Goethe, Johann Wolfgang von, 94
Forten, Charlotte, *see* Grimké, Charlotte Forten
Fractures, 6–7
  globalism, 1, 38, 97, 110
  methodologies, 2, 5, 51
Fragmentation, 34, 106–107
Franklin, Benjamin, 44, 45–51
  educational reform, 45, 131
    purposes, 45–46
  languages, concept of, 47–48
  multilingualism, 45–46
  translation
    concept of literal translation, 46–48
    emancipatory, intellectual mastery, 49
    paraphrase, 48
    references to play, 49
    translations published, 46
Freiligrath, Ferdinand, 120–121, 125–6
Fuller, Margaret, 20–21, 34, 91–110
  continental translation theory, 97
  defined American literature, 109
  drowning, 91
  Emerson, Ralph Waldo, 98, 100
  equality, 99–100
  gender, 99–100
  Goethe, Johann Wolfgang von, 98, 100
  as Hester, 20–21
  individual's relation to national and international collectives, 93
  monolingualism, 20–21
  nation, 109–110
    relation to collective world culture, 93
  Native Americans, 108–109
  silencing, 91
  slavery, 99–100
  theory of multilingual American literature, 91
  translation
    centrality to language, 107
    cultural identity, 107
    emotional and textual authenticity, 99
    model of empirical translation, 97–99

Fuller, Margaret (*continued*)
   sentimental and spiritual knowledge, 105
   textual fragmentation, 106–107

G

Gender
   Cooper, James Fenimore, 71
   gender binary, 78–79
   Fuller, Margaret, 99–100
   power relationships, 20
Gender politics, Grimké, Charlotte Forten, 18–19
Geotemporal relationship, 26–27
German language, 21, 92–110, 119–121, 125–126, 127–149
Globalism, fractures, 1, 38, 97, 110
Global media, 26
Goethe, Johann Wolfgang von
   Austin, Sarah, 93–94, 105–106
   familiarizing translations, 94
   foreignizing translations, 94
   Fuller, Margaret, 98, 100
Göttingen approach, 162 n. 9
Grass, emblem of linguistic nativism, 122
Grimké, Charlotte Forten
   abolition, 18–19
   alterity, 17
   approach, 2
   background, 18
   cultural diversity, strategies, 17
   gender politics, 18–19
   Hawthorne, Nathaniel, working within same literary frame, 28–29
   journals, 18
   literary accomplishments, 18–19
   literary canons, 20
      as object marked by traits *vs.* as process, 22–23
   reading, 20
   Salem, 18
   as teacher, 18
   translation, 21
   views, 22

H

Hawthorne, Nathaniel
   invention of American literature as monolingual, 10
   monolingual ontology, 7
   national signs, 11
   organic monolingualism, 8
   transitive trope surplus, 11
The Heidenmauer (James Fenimore Cooper), 85–88
Herder, Johann Gottfried, 1, 63
Heteroglossia, Bakhtin, Mikhail, 7, 76, 96
Hortus siccus, translations, 113–116, 122
Hybridity, 31
   Bhabha, Homi, 50–51, 156 n. 25

I

Iconic translation, 34–35, 129, 136–138, 144
Iliad (Homer), 56, 59
Imitation, 29–30, 48, 57, 70, 145
Imperialism
   nationalism critical of, 20, 95, 126
   translation, 29, 54, 68, 81, 91–92, 136
Impartial Spectator, 33, 62–64, 70, 88
Intellectual labor
   communal rights, 140–142
   individual rights, 140–142
Intellectual property, 129, 138–149
   authorial choice in translations, 145
   conflation of text and personhood, 140–141
   copyright recent invention, 139
   distinction between book's content and form, 139–140
   establishing legal breadth of copyright, 142–144
   extended definition of author to translator, 145
   first copyright legislation, 141–142
   history of regulations for textual reproduction, 139
   international copyright, 147
   language's role in literary and national identity, 141–142
   literary protectionism, 142
   Lockean notions of labor-based proprietorship, 140
   neologism, 146
   Revised Statutes of 1873, 147
   shifts in legal definition of copyright, 146–147
"Intellectual Property," 34
Interior other, *The Scarlet Letter*, 11, 29
International, national, incessant interpenetration, 20
Intimacy, distance, 26

Ivanhoe (Walter Scott), 66–69, 163 n. 13

L

Language
  definition of nation by language, 114–115
  diachronic, 49–51
  ethnographic inquiry, 114–115
  first language, 102
  mastery, 21
  nation, assuming link, 1
  process of abstraction, 62–63
  pure language, 102
  Scott, Walter, origin not in past, 70
  synchronic, 49–50
  states, 50, 64–66
Language formation, Cooper, James Fenimore, 64–65
Languages
  Babel, 6–7, 8, 15
  diversification, 6
  Eden, 6–7
  Franklin, Benjamin, concept of, 47–48
  linguistic commonalities, 75
  literature, nexus, 35
  Native Americans, 65, 71, 75–77, 78, 79–84
  pedagogy, 35, 148
  repression of other, 147–149
  varieties, 1
Language theory, history of, 63
The Last of the Mohicans (James Fenimore Cooper), 65, 71, 77, 78, 79–84
  race, 77–78
  sentimentality, 79
  slavery, 77–78
Latin, Wheatley, Phillis, 38, 43–44
Leaves of Grass (Walt Whitman), 121–125
  grass, emblem of linguistic nativism, 122
Letter A, *The Scarlet Letter* (Nathaniel Hawthorne), 15–16
Lingua franca, 6, 95
Linguistic alienation, Wheatley, Phillis, 53–54
Linguistic aporia, 8, 15, 17–18, 52
Linguistic exceptionalism, unsettling, 28
Linguistic mobility, 3, 21–22
Linguistic naturalism, Whitman, Walt, 112–113
Linguistic representation, 34
Literary canons
  Grimké, Charlotte Forten, 20
  multiculturalism, 5
Literary exemplarity, 34, 111–126
  Longfellow, Henry Wadsworth, 117–121
Literary representation, Anglo-American poetry, 111
Literary specimens, anthologizing, 113
Literature
  languages, nexus, 35
  nature, structural homology, 12–13
Locke, John, 25, 43–45, 48, 51, 139–141, 143
Longfellow, Henry Wadsworth, 34
  anthologizing, 119
  career as professor, 117
  emphasis on American multilingualism, 117–118
  language study of, 117
  literary exemplarity, 117–121
  pedagogical practice, 117–119
  translation, 117–121
Luther, Martin, 95

M

Mastery, 49–50
  language, 21
Matthiessen, F.O., 7–8, 29
Mediation
  nationalism, 20
  translation, 26
Melville, Herman, 109
Mestiza, 110
Metaphor, 17, 63–65, 83, 92
Metaphrase, 29–30
Middle passage, 37
  naturalized mother tongue, 17
Miller, Perry, 109
Mimicry, Bhabha, Homi, 153 n. 11
Modality, Cooper, James Fenimore, 88–89
Modern vernacular languages, translation, 43, 85–87, 94–96, 121–125
Monolingualism, 7, 127–129, 148
  bilingual education, 23, 25, 35, 147–149
  Fuller, Margaret, 20–21
  Stowe, Harriet Beecher, 130–131
Monolingual national identity, fiction of, 1–2
Monolingual nationalism, self-adequation, 21–22

196 Index

Monolingual ontology, Hawthorne, Nathaniel, 7
Mother/mother tongue, 1–2, 8–10, 15–25, 19, 33, 37, 43–44, 51–55, 60, 62, 71, 77–78, 80
Mother tongue
 change in definition, 1–2
 Cooper, James Fenimore, 71
 defined, 1–2, 111
 vs. mother's tongue, 1–2, 15–25, 37
Multicultural difference, 3
Multiculturalism
 literary canons, 5
 transatlantic studies, 5
Multilingualism, 1, 7
 epistemology, 103–104
 Franklin, Benjamin, 45–46, 131
 historical relevance, 32
 as relational methodology, 22
 slavery, 137–138
 Stowe, Harriet Beecher
  demographic developments, 130
  importance, 127–128
Multilingual translation, 35
Multilingual unframing, 17

N
Naipaul fallacy, 54
Nation
 definition of nation by language, 114–115
 Fuller, Margaret, 109–110
 language, assuming link, 1
National
 international, incessant interpenetration, 20
 supranational, 85
 transnational, relationship, 4–5
National consciousness, 127–129
National identity, "The Custom House," 12
Nationalism
 mediation, 20
 patriotism, 20
 transnationalism
  false dichotomy, 3
  in negotiating linguistic plurality, 3
  related discursive strategies, 3
National myth
 of origin, 108–109
 of purity, 111
National signs, Hawthorne, Nathaniel, 11

Native Americans
 Fuller, Margaret, 108–109
 languages, 65, 71, 75–77, 78, 79–84
Nativism, 111
Naturalized mother tongue, middle passage, 17
Nature, literature, structural homology, 12–13
Nature (Ralph Waldo Emerson), 102
Neoclassical translation, Wheatley, Phillis, 38
Neutral ground, Cooper, James Fenimore, 33, 62, 70, 74, 81–84, 88
New England, 8, 10, 72, 91, 93
"Niobe in Distress for her Children Slain by Apollo, from Ovid's Metamorphoses, Book VI. and from a view of the Painting of Mr. Richard Wilson" (Phillis Wheatley), 51, 54–55, 57
Nietzsche, Friedrich, 92
Notions of the Americans (James Fenimore Cooper), 71
Novalis, 105–106, 166 n. 19

O
"On Being Brought from Africa to America" (Phillis Wheatley), 37, 39–42
 captivity narrative, 40
 conversion narrative, 40
 direct citation, 41
 English as self-referential episteme, 40–41
 linguistic self-referentiality, 41
 middle passage, 39
 opening lines, 40
 reconfigured transatlantic voyage, 40
 redemption, 40
 title, 39–40
 tropological construction of American episteme, 40
Organic monolingualism, Hawthorne, Nathaniel, 8
Original, text, 22–23
Originality, translation, 29

P
Paraphrase, 29–30, 48, 55, 57, 59, 105–106, 109
Particular universality, 91–110
Patriotism

nationalism, 20
race, 19
Pedagogy, languages, 35, 148
Performance, 24, 43, 86–87, 104, 121, 134, 155 n. 24
The Pioneers (James Fenimore Cooper), 73–74, 77
slavery, 77
Poems on Various Subjects, Religious and Moral (Phillis Wheatley), 38, 55
Political power, Scott, Walter, 68
Polyglossia, Bakhtin, Mikhail, 7, 96
Polyglot consumer markets, 130
Polysystem theory, 162 n. 9
Pope, Alexander, 56–57, 105
view of translation, 59
Postnational, 5, 151 n. 2
Postcolonial, 153–154 n. 13
Power relationships, gender, 20
Pratt, Mary Louise, 30–31
Process
American exceptionalism, 3–4, 10–11, 22–23, 28, 35, 107
translation, 22–23

R
Race, 33–34
Cooper, James Fenimore, 76–83
separating language from race, 76–77
The Last of the Mohicans (James Fenimore Cooper), 77–78
patriotism, 19
transatlantic studies, 3–4
Reciprocity, 26, 30–31, 34, 42, 58, 64, 98, 123
Redemption, 40
Reification, 13, 22, 102
Wheatley, Phillis, 40–42, 55
Repressive language politics, 35, 147–149
Rousseau, Jean-Jacques, 63

S
Sancho, Ignatius, 57
Saussure, Ferdinand de, 49–50
The Scarlet Letter (Nathaniel Hawthorne), 8–17
alterity, 8–9
cultural legitimacy, 8–9
difference to occlude diversity, 10–11
fetishization, 13–14

geographical differences, 9–10
Hester, 15–16
interior other, 11, 29
Letter A, 15–16
Pearl, 15–17
preface, 9, 13
Schleiermacher, Friedrich, 22, 165 n. 9
Scott, Walter, 66–68
language
origin not in past, 70
political power, 68
translation, communication and, 70
Self-adequation
monolingual nationalism, 21–22
surplus value, 13
Sentimentality, 46–47, 58, 89, 98, 105, 161 n. 6
difference, 62
linguistic model for negotiating, 62, 70, 83, 139, 141, 146
The Last of the Mohicans (James Fenimore Cooper), 79
Theory of Moral Sentiments (Adam Smith), 62, 64, 66
Sign
exclusion of differences, 13–14
signified, signifier
division of, 6–7
unit of, 14
Signifier
purposes, 45–46
repetition, 13–14
Simulacra, 52
Slavery, 37–60
Cooper, James Fenimore, 62
Fuller, Margaret, 99–100
The Last of the Mohicans (James Fenimore Cooper), 77–78
multilingualism, 137–138
The Pioneers (James Fenimore Cooper), 77
slave trade, 3–4
Uncle Tom's Cabin (Harriet Beecher Stowe), 127–138
Smith, Adam, 64, 65–66
translation, 66
"Song of Myself," *see Leaves of Grass*
Specimen Days (Walt Whitman), 112
Specimens of the Early English Poets (George Ellis), 113
Specimens of the Later English Poets (Robert Southey), 113–116

Index

Stowe, Harriet Beecher, 34, 127–149
  monolingualism, 130–131
  multilingualism
    demographic developments, 130
    importance, 127–128
  translation
    conflicted theory of, 131–132
    demographic developments, 130
    importance, 127–128
Subjects, subjectivity, 4, 20, 30, 105, 106, 109
  cultural, 43–44, 52, 92
  formation, 38, 42, 44, 48, 50–51, 52–53, 60
  normative male subjectivity, 4, 79
Summer on the Lakes (Margaret Fuller), 104, 107, 108–109
Supplement, Derrida, Jacques, 7–8, 20, 28
Surplus value, self-adequation, 13
Surrogates, cultural identities, 24–25
Symbol-myth-image scholarship, 3
Sympathetic identification, 58, 62, 79–80, 82–84, 86–87, 104, 127, 161–162 n. 6

T

Tertium quid, 51, 63
Text
  in the original, 22–23
  original, 22–23
Theory of Moral Sentiments (Adam Smith), sentimentality, 62, 64, 66
Thoreau, Henry David, 91
"To Maecenas" (Phillis Wheatley), 55, 57–58
  Trace, Derrida, Jacques, 2, 7, 8, 11, 55, 66
Transatlantic
  American, relationship, 54
  Americanists' special provenance, 5
  characterized, 5–6
  locus, 6
  meaning, 25–28, 54
  as multilingual discourse, 27–28
  term, 5–6
  term development, 26–27
  Wheatley, Phillis, 54
Transatlanticism, 2–3
  foreign humanities scholarship on U.S., 3
Transatlantic studies
  multiculturalism, 5

  normative male subjectivity, 4, 79
  race, 3–4
Transculturation, contact zones, 30–31
Translation
  African, 27, 37
  alphabetized print culture, 33
  American poetry, 112–126
  American vernacular, 23, 34, 72, 111–126
  anti-immigrant backlash, 129
  British resistance against, 113–115
  characterized, 28
  Cooper, James Fenimore, 63, 75
    America's linguistic originality, 72
    captivated by practices of translation, 61–62
    cultural and linguistic blend, 75–76
    defining national literature, 74
    division between familiar and foreign, 75
  copyright, 34–35
  cultural logic, 25–26
  definitions, 39
  Emerson, Ralph Waldo
    metaphysical model, 101–104
    personal and national identity, 100
    transcendent language, 100–101
    universality, 100–101
  as form of conquest, 29
  Franklin, Benjamin
    concept of literal translation, 46–48
    emancipatory, intellectual mastery, 49
    paraphrase, 48
    references to play, 49
  Fuller, Margaret
    centrality to language, 107
    cultural identity, 107
    emotional and textual authenticity, 99
    model of empirical translation, 97–99
    sentimental and spiritual knowledge, 105
    textual fragmentation, 106–107
  Grimké, Charlotte Forten, 21
  views, 22
  historical relevance, 32
  historical statistics, 32
  hortus siccus, 113–116, 122
  iconic, 34–35, 129, 136–138, 144
  imperialism, 29, 54, 68, 81, 91–92, 136

Index 199

internalization of alterity, 29
interlingual, 95
intralingual, 95
Longfellow, Henry Wadsworth, 117–121
mediation, 26
modern characterization, 92
modern vernacular languages, 43, 85–87, 94–96, 121–125
mythic, 105
"On Being Brought from Africa to America" (Phillis Wheatley), 39–42
originality, 29
practices of, 6
process, 22–23
Renaissance, 8, 29, 94, 143
Romans, 29
Romantic, 30
romantic translation theories, 92
Scott, Walter, communication and, 70
Smith, Adam, 66
Stowe, Harriet Beecher
  conflicted theory of translation, 131–132
  demographic developments, 130
  importance, 127–128
  theoretical model, 28–29
translatio imperii et studii, 29, 81, 92
  United States *vs.* European countries, 31–32, 149
  vernacular, translation as improvements of, 121
Western translation theory, 29–31
Wheatley, Phillis, public *vs.* private persona, 58
Whitman, Walt
  effects, 123
  limits of, 124
  negation, 123–124
  process of transcendence, 123
  state of untranslatability, 124
Transnational
era, 2
national, relationship, 4–5
term, 4–5
Transnationalism, nationalism
  false dichotomy, 3, 34, 88, 95, 128–129, 149
  in negotiating linguistic plurality, 3
  related discursive strategies, 3, 31
Transnational studies, 3, 20, 92

Triangulation
  Cooper, James Fenimore, 63
  Wheatley, Phillis, 51–52
Twice-telling, secondary rendering, 14–15, 23, 45

U
Uncle Tom's Cabin (Harriet Beecher Stowe), 34, 127–138, *128*, 142–143
  access to scripture, 136–137
  black characters, 132–137
    as iconic national figures, 132–134
    portraying slaves as immigrants, 134–135
  education (of characters), 135–136
  kinds of alienation, 132
  mass production, 133
  multilingualism, 137–138
  plot lines, 132
  reversing middle passage, 136–137
  slavery, 127–138
United States, as multilingual country, 1, 111, 117, 149
University education, 43, 117–118
Untranslatability, 14, 30, 124

V
Vernacular, translation as improvements of, 121

W
Wheatley, Phillis, 27, 33, 37–60
  acquired secondary language, 37
  African mother tongue, 33, 37–38, 52–54
  alienation from both African and American context, 52–53
  background, 38–39
  double examination in Latin and in English, 43–44
  double translation, 38, 51–52
  engagement with Pope, 56–57
  examination by Boston's elite, 42–43
  Latin, 38, 43–44
  linguistic alienation, 53–54
  neoclassical translation, 38
  "On Being Brought from Africa to America," 37, 39–42
    captivity narrative, 40
    conversion narrative, 40
    direct citation, 41
    English as self-referential episteme, 40–41

Wheatley, Phillis (*continued*)
   linguistic self-referentiality, 41
   middle passage, 39
   opening lines, 40
   reconfigured transatlantic voyage, 40
   redemption, 40
   title, 39–40
   tropological construction of American episteme, 40
  paraphrasing, 56–58
  pedagogical examination, 43
  reification, 40–42, 55
  transatlantic, 54
  translation, public *vs.* private persona, 58
  triangulation, 51–52
  young slave's education, 38
Whitman, Walt, 34, 111–126
  conceit of literary specimen, 112–113
  incorporating non-English words, 111–112
  linguistic naturalism, 112–113
  translation
   effects, 123
   limits of, 124
   negation, 123–124
   process of transcendence, 123
   state of untranslatability, 124
Woman in the Nineteenth Century (Margaret Fuller), 92, 107–108
World literature, 31, 34, 61, 93–96, 109, 111–112, 134, 142
www.ethnologue.com, 1

Y
Yankee, 72–73
Young America, 109, 167 n. 30